Tried-and-True Recipes
Make For Memorable Moments

Comfort and joy...that's what folks experience as they head home for the holidays to celebrate with family and friends. A tempting spread of home-cooked food is the only thing that can create an even merrier occasion!

Taste of Home Holiday & Celebrations Cookbook 2009 is packed with 245 recipes to make Christmas, Thanksgiving, Easter and other celebrations throughout the year memorable as well as mouth-watering. The timeless treasury provides menu options, helpful timetables and family-tested recipes...so entertaining is easy!

'TIS THE SEASON. From formal sit-down dinners with relatives to casual gatherings with friends, the Christmas season is a flurry of activity. Holiday happenings are even happier when guests are presented with any of this chapter's 110 Yuletide dishes, including Peppercorn Beef Top Loin Roast, Prosciutto Egg Panini, Jarlsberg Popovers, Golden Au Gratin Potatoes, Tortellini Meatball Stew and Irish Creme Drink. Two sections devoted to cookies, candies and desserts showcase such delectable sweets as Toffee Crunch Cheesecake, Cinnamon Crescent Cookies, Peanut Caramel Delights and Coconut Cake Supreme.

GIVING THANKS. A golden, roasted turkey is the highlight of Thanksgiving dinner, and we give you three succulent recipes to choose from: Herbed Turkey, Beer-Brined Turkey with Giblet Gravy and Chai Turkey. Your family will also fall for the bounty of home-baked breads and pleasing pumpkin desserts as well.

EASTER GATHERINGS. Spring has sprung! So focus on fresh flavors at your Easter meal by featuring Glazed Pork Crown Roast and Lemony Fennel Olives. Turn away from heavy winter fare—serve lighter chicken entrees (such as Lemony Chicken Asparagus with Bow Ties) and lively desserts (including Lemon Mousse Cornucopias).

SPECIAL CELEBRATIONS. From March Madness and Independence Day to summer pool parties and spooky Halloween events, there are countless reasons to get together with friends all year long. And check out the outstanding cakes beginning on page 182...they'll make an everlasting impression on guests at any party!

CAN-DO DECORATING IDEAS. There are dozens of ideas for attractive table toppers (like the Dainty Daffodil Centerpiece on page 151), festive party favors (see page 245 for enchanting witch's broom gift bags) and pretty place cards (such as the birch place card on page 23).

Perfect party menus, unforgettable fare, simple decorating ideas...*Taste of Home Holiday & Celebrations Cookbook 2009* has everything to make entertaining easy for you—and memorable for your family!

Would you like to see one of your family-favorite recipes featured in a future edition of this timeless treasury? See page 256 for details!

taste of home
HOLIDAY & Celebrations 2009

SENIOR VICE PRESIDENT, EDITOR IN CHIEF:
Catherine Cassidy

VICE PRESIDENT, EXECUTIVE EDITOR/BOOKS:
Heidi Reuter Lloyd

CREATIVE DIRECTOR: Ardyth Cope

FOOD DIRECTOR: Diane Werner RD

SENIOR EDITOR/BOOKS: Mark Hagen

PROJECT EDITOR: Julie Schnittka

ASSOCIATE EDITOR: Sara Lancaster

CRAFT EDITOR: Jane Craig

ASSOCIATE FOOD EDITORS: Annie Rundle, Karen Scales

ART DIRECTOR: Gretchen Trautman

GRAPHIC DESIGN ASSOCIATE: Heather Miller

CONTENT PRODUCTION SUPERVISOR: Julie Wagner

PROOFREADER: Linne Bruskewitz

RECIPE ASSET SYSTEMS: Coleen Martin, Sue A. Jurack

PREMEDIA SUPERVISOR: Scott Berger

RECIPE TESTING & EDITING: Taste of Home Test Kitchen

FOOD PHOTOGRAPHY: Taste of Home Photo Studio

EDITORIAL ASSISTANT: Barb Czysz

CHIEF MARKETING OFFICER: Lisa Karpinski

VICE PRESIDENT/BOOK MARKETING: Dan Fink

CREATIVE DIRECTOR/CREATIVE MARKETING: James Palmen

The Reader's Digest Association, Inc.

PRESIDENT AND CHIEF EXECUTIVE OFFICER:
Mary G. Berner

PRESIDENT, FOOD & ENTERTAINING:
Suzanne M. Grimes

SVP PRESIDENT, CHIEF MARKETING OFFICER:
Amy J. Radin

PRESIDENT, GLOBAL CONSUMER MARKETING:
Dawn Zier

Taste of Home Books
©2009 Reiman Media Group, Inc.
5400 S. 60th Street., Greendale WI 53129

International Standard Book Number (10):
0-89821-628-1
International Standard Book Number (13):
978-0-89821-628-8
International Standard Serial Number:
1535-2781
All rights reserved. Printed in U.S.A.

"Timeless Recipes from Trusted Home Cooks" is a
registered trademark of Reiman Media Group.

Taste of Home is a registered trademark of
Reader's Digest Association, Inc.

Special thanks to Boston Store Furniture Gallery,
Brookfield, Wisconsin

Cover photo of Chocolate Turtle
Cake (p. 192) by Jim Wieland.
Food styled by Suzanne Breckenridge.
Set styled by Stephanie Marchese.

Back cover photos: Jumpin' Espresso
Bean Chili (p. 197), Caramelized
Onion Torte (p. 145), Pear Place Card
(p. 119) and Chai Turkey (p. 113).

For other Taste of Home books and products, visit:
ShopTasteofHome.com

table of
CONTENTS

'TIS THE *season*

Festive feasts aren't far away with this chapter's assortment of five complete meals—a Merry Meat and Potatoes Menu, a Casual Christmas Dinner, a Bright-Eyed Christmas Brunch, a Progressive Dinner Party and a Let It Snow Celebration. We also offer an appealing array of appetizers, entrees, sides and desserts that bring a merry mood to every Yuletide gathering.

$\mathcal{I}$f you're hosting a sit-down holiday dinner, you don't have to spend hours preparing gourmet foods. Instead, give everyday ingredients an elegant spin.

With a sweet-and-savory rub and a rich wine sauce, Peppercorn Beef Top Loin Roast is an appealing entree that takes mere minutes to prepare before being baked.

Tried-and-true recipes like Garlic Baby Potatoes and Jarlsberg Popovers are natural complements to the meaty main course.

For an innovative vegetable, try Zesty Broccolini.

DOWN-HOME DINNER
(PICTURED AT RIGHT)

Peppercorn Beef Top Loin Roast (p. 10)
Garlic Baby Potatoes (p. 12)
Zesty Broccolini (p. 12)
Jarlsberg Popovers (p. 10)

a merry
MEAT & POTATOES MENU

Countdown to
Christmas Dinner

A Few Weeks Before:
- Prepare two grocery lists—one for nonperishable items to purchase now and one for perishable items to purchase a few days before Christmas.
- Order a 4-pound boneless beef top loin roast.
- Bake the Jarlsberg Popovers. Cool; place in a resealable plastic bag and freeze.

Two to Three Days Before:
- Buy remaining grocery items, including the top loin roast.

The Day Before:
- Set the table.
- Make the filling for Honey-Nut Endive Appetizers; cover and chill.
- Combine the first seven ingredients for the Garlic Baby Potatoes; place in a covered container and keep at room temperature.
- For Coconut Cranberry Shortcakes, bake the cakes; let cool. Store in an airtight container at room temperature. Make the cranberry sauce; cover and chill.
- Coarsely chop the onions for Onion-Topped Cheese Spread. Refrigerate in an airtight container.

- Prepare the wine sauce for Peppercorn Beef Top Loin Roast; cover and chill.

Christmas Day:
- An hour before guests arrive, assemble Honey-Nut Endive Appetizers. Cover with plastic wrap and refrigerate.
- Reheat the caramelized onions for Onion-Topped Cheese Spread. Pour over cream cheese and serve with crackers.
- For the Peppercorn Beef Top Loin Roast, trim fat and season roast with rub; bake as directed. Let stand for 15 minutes before slicing; reheat the wine sauce.
- Halve potatoes and toss with olive oil mixture; bake.
- Prepare the Zesty Broccolini and Creamed Mushrooms.
- While the roast is standing, reheat frozen popovers on a baking sheet in a 400° oven for 10 to 15 minutes.
- Assemble the Citrus Scallop Salad and serve it as a first course.
- For dessert, reheat the cranberry sauce, split the shortcakes in half horizontally and garnish.

honey-nut endive appetizers

(PICTURED AT RIGHT)

Sweet and savory flavors combine in this elegant appetizer. It's a nice, light option to serve before a big meal.

Carmel Gillogly | *FORT MILL, SC*

1/3 cup crumbled goat cheese

1/3 cup crumbled Gorgonzola cheese

1/3 cup pine nuts

1/3 cup chopped walnuts

1/3 cup golden raisins

4 bacon strips, cooked and crumbled

2 heads Belgian endive, separated into leaves

1/3 cup honey

In a small bowl, combine the first six ingredients. Spoon into endive leaves. Drizzle honey over cheese mixture. Serve immediately. **YIELD:** 1 dozen.

peppercorn beef top loin roast

(PICTURED ON PAGE 6)

*A red wine sauce complements the peppery brown sugar rub on the roast
in this inviting entree from our home economists. You can't go wrong with this down-home dish!*

1 boneless beef top loin roast (4 pounds)

1/3 cup packed brown sugar

3 tablespoons whole peppercorns, crushed

4 garlic cloves, minced

3/4 teaspoon salt

1 large onion, finely chopped

1 tablespoon olive oil

2 tablespoons tomato paste

2 teaspoons Worcestershire sauce

1-1/2 cups port wine

1-1/2 cups dry red wine

Trim fat from roast. In a small bowl, combine the brown sugar, peppercorns, garlic and salt. Rub over meat. Place in a shallow roasting pan.

Bake at 325° for 1 to 1-1/2 hours or until meat reaches desired doneness (for medium-rare, a meat thermometer should read 145°; medium, 160°; well-done, 170°). Let stand for 15 minutes before slicing.

Meanwhile, in a large saucepan, saute onion in oil until tender. Stir in tomato paste and Worcestershire sauce until blended. Add wines. Bring to a boil; cook until liquid is reduced to about 1-1/2 cups. Serve with roast. YIELD: 10 servings (1-1/2 cups sauce).

jarlsberg popovers

(PICTURED ON PAGE 6)

*When hosting holiday dinners, why not serve our Test Kitchen's cheesy popovers instead
of ordinary dinner rolls? They can be made ahead and reheated just before serving.*

4-1/2 teaspoons shortening

3 egg whites

2 eggs

1-1/2 cups milk

1/2 cup heavy whipping cream

2 cups all-purpose flour

1 tablespoon sugar

3/4 teaspoon salt

1/4 teaspoon white pepper

4 ounces Jarlsberg cheese, shredded

Using 1/2 teaspoon shortening for each cup, grease the bottom and sides of nine popover cups; set aside.

In a small bowl, beat egg whites and eggs; beat in milk and cream. Add the flour, sugar, salt and pepper; beat until smooth (do not overbeat). Fold in cheese. Fill prepared cups two-thirds full with batter. Fill empty cups two-thirds full with water.

Bake at 450° for 15 minutes. Reduce heat to 350° (do not open door). Bake 15 minutes longer or until deep golden brown (do not underbake). Immediately cut a slit in the top of each popover to allow steam to escape. YIELD: 9 servings.

citrus scallop salad

(PICTURED AT RIGHT)

With scallops, pears and citrus fruits, this deliciously different salad is an outstanding first course. It also makes a great main-dish salad for luncheons.

Sarah Geary | OKLAHOMA CITY, OK

2 packages (5 ounces each) spring mix salad greens

1 jar (24 ounces) refrigerated citrus salad

2 medium red pears, thinly sliced

1/2 cup all-purpose flour

16 sea scallops

2 tablespoons butter

2 tablespoons olive oil

1/2 cup balsamic vinaigrette

Divide salad greens among eight plates. Drain citrus salad, reserving syrup. Arrange citrus fruit on salads. In a small bowl, combine pear slices and reserved syrup. Using a slotted spoon, remove pears and arrange on salads. Discard syrup.

Place flour in a shallow bowl. Roll scallops in flour. In a large skillet, heat butter and oil over medium heat. Add scallops; cook for 2 minutes on each side or until scallops are firm and opaque. Top each salad with scallops. Drizzle with vinaigrette. YIELD: 8 servings.

zesty broccolini

(PICTURED ON PAGE 6)

*Garlic, gingerroot and red pepper flakes give this side dish from our Test Kitchen a little kick.
The long, elegant spears are so attractive on a dinner plate.*

3 packages (6 ounces each) Broccolini or 18 ounces broccoli spears

1/2 teaspoon salt

2 garlic cloves, minced

1/2 teaspoon grated fresh gingerroot

3 tablespoons olive oil

1/8 teaspoon crushed red pepper flakes

Place Broccolini and salt in a large skillet; cover with water. Bring to a boil. Reduce heat; cover and simmer for 5-7 minutes or until tender. Drain well. Remove and keep warm.

In the same skillet, saute garlic and ginger in oil until tender. Add Broccolini and pepper flakes; saute for 1-2 minutes or until heated through. **YIELD:** 6 servings.

BROCCOLINI BASICS

Broccolini is the trademarked name of the hybrid vegetable that's a cross between broccoli and Chinese kale. It's also called baby broccoli.

The long, slender stalks are topped with small buds that resemble a miniature broccoli head. The flavor is slightly sweet with a subtle peppery taste.

Broccolini is rich in vitamins A and C, iron, fiber and potassium.

garlic baby potatoes

(PICTURED ON PAGE 6)

Our home economists suggest this recipe when you need a classic potato dish that pairs well with a variety of meaty entrees. It's assembled in a snap, then roasts in the oven for an aromatic side dish.

6 tablespoons olive oil

12 garlic cloves, minced

1/4 cup minced fresh oregano

4-1/2 teaspoons balsamic vinegar

3 teaspoons kosher salt

1-1/2 teaspoons paprika

3/4 teaspoon lemon-pepper seasoning

24 small red or fingerling potatoes, halved

In a large bowl, combine the first seven ingredients. Add potatoes; toss to coat. Transfer potatoes to a greased 9-in. square baking pan; drizzle with garlic mixture. Cover and bake at 350° for 40 minutes, stirring every 10 minutes. Uncover, bake 10-20 minutes longer or until potatoes are tender. **YIELD:** 8 servings.

coconut cranberry shortcakes

(PICTURED AT RIGHT)

Our Test Kitchen's twist on strawberry shortcake features a tender coconut-flavored cake and a slightly tart cranberry sauce. It's a lovely dessert for the Christmas season.

3 cups all-purpose flour

1/3 cup sugar

4 teaspoons baking powder

1 teaspoon salt

2 cups coconut milk

TOPPING:

1 package (12 ounces) fresh or frozen cranberries

1 cup sugar

1/2 cup coconut milk

1/2 cup cranberry juice

Whipped cream, flaked coconut and fresh mint leaves, optional

In a large bowl, combine the flour, sugar, baking powder and salt. Stir in coconut milk just until moistened. Drop by 1/3 cupfuls 1 in. apart onto a greased baking sheet. Bake at 400° for 15-20 minutes or until lightly browned.

For topping, in a large saucepan, combine the cranberries, sugar, coconut milk and cranberry juice. Cook over medium heat until the berries pop, about 15 minutes. Split warm shortcakes in half horizontally. Spoon topping over bottoms and tops of shortcakes. Garnish with whipped cream, coconut and mint if desired. **YIELD:** 9 servings.

onion-topped cheese spread

I love to cook all kinds of dishes, but I'm known for my appetizers. In this robust spread, a cream cheese base is topped with caramelized onions. Cooking the onions in sugar mellows the flavor so they aren't overpowering.

Carol Bess White | PORTLAND, OR

2-1/2 pounds large sweet onions, coarsely chopped

1-1/2 teaspoons sugar

1/2 teaspoon salt

2 bay leaves

2 tablespoons olive oil

2 tablespoons butter

2 tablespoons white wine or chicken broth

2 packages (8 ounces each) cream cheese, softened

Assorted crackers

In a large skillet, cook the onions, sugar, salt and bay leaves in oil and butter over medium heat for 45-50 minutes or until onions are golden brown, stirring frequently.

Add wine, stirring to loosen browned bits from pan. Cook until wine is reduced by half. Remove and discard bay leaves. Cool slightly. Pour over cream cheese. Serve with crackers. YIELD: 2 cups spread (1-2/3 cups topping).

creamed mushrooms

If you're looking for a way to break from the usual Christmas sides, look no further. Fresh mushrooms are sauteed to tender perfection, then accompanied by a rich, creamy sauce. It's one dish that's full of comforting flavor.

Lois Telloni | LORAIN, OH

1 medium onion, sliced

3 tablespoons butter

1 pound sliced fresh mushrooms

1 tablespoon minced fresh parsley

1 teaspoon paprika

1/2 teaspoon salt

1 cup (8 ounces) sour cream

2 tablespoons milk

1 tablespoon all-purpose flour

In a large skillet, saute onion in butter until tender. Stir in the mushrooms, parsley, paprika and salt. Cook over medium heat for 10 minutes or until tender. Combine the sour cream, milk and flour. Gradually stir into mushroom mixture; heat through. YIELD: 6 servings.

luminous lantern centerpiece

(PICTURED ABOVE)

Bring the light of the Christmas season to your table with lanterns and candles.

Purchase lanterns in two different sizes in a color that coordinates with your dishes. Remember that an odd number will look more appealing.

Place pillar candles in the large lanterns and votive candles in the small ones.

If desired, put a candle wreath inside each lantern or simply add small beads as shown. Set a runner down the length of your table. For added color, you can place some Christmas greens in the center. Arrange the lanterns on top of the greens.

For an even more glorious glow, put a small, votive-filled clear glass container at each place setting. Wrap each candle holder with a ribbon and a coordinating strand of tiny beads.

Christmas dinner doesn't have to be fancy in order to be festive...or to be flavorful! You can host a special holiday meal for a crowd with very little fuss.

With seafood and mushrooms, Crab Macaroni & Cheese goes beyond the ordinary for unforgettable Yuletide fare.

Mushroom Spinach Salad is a hard-to-resist, updated classic, especially when topped with savory Cheese Croutons.

To round out the mouthwatering menu, pass a basket brimming with tender homemade Parmesan Potato Breadsticks.

PASTA IS PERFECT

(PICTURED AT RIGHT)

Crab Macaroni & Cheese (p. 20)
Parmesan Potato Breadsticks (p. 22)
Mushroom Spinach Salad (p. 22)
with Cheese Croutons (p. 20)

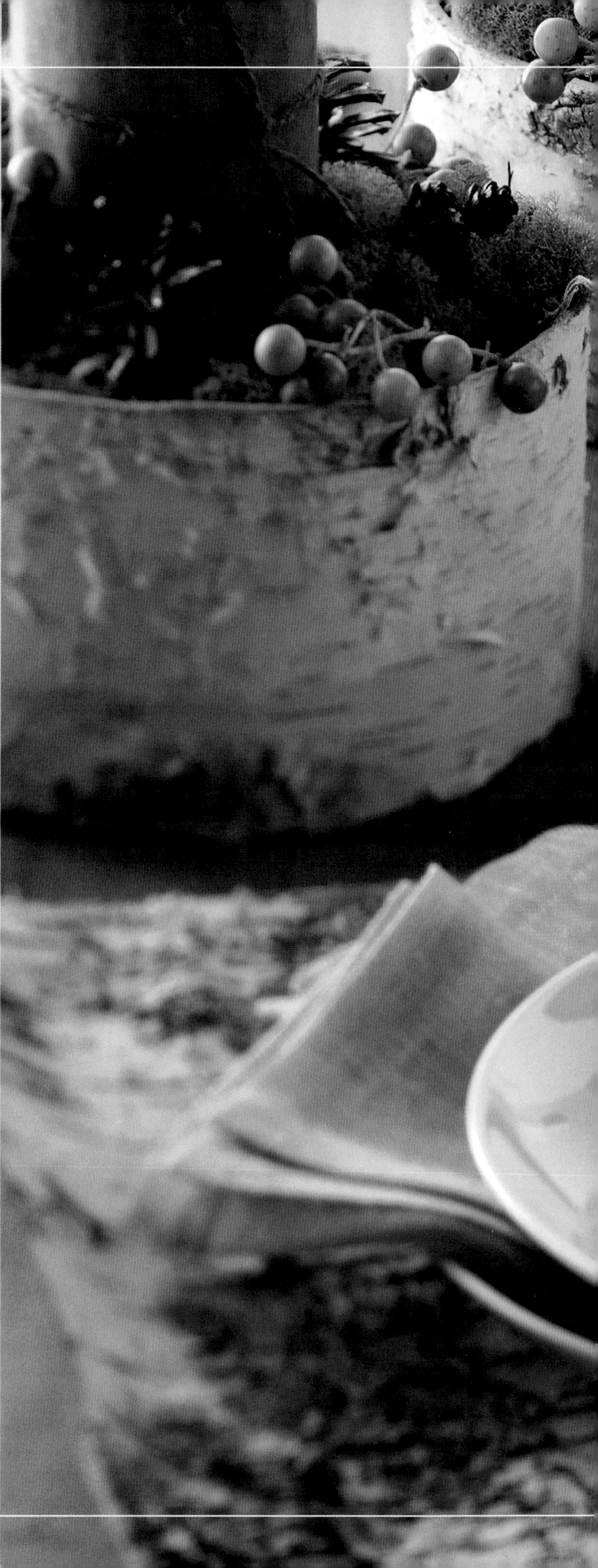

casual
CHRISTMAS DINNER

Casual Christmas
Party Plan

A Few Weeks Before:
- Prepare two grocery lists—one for nonperishable items to purchase now and one for perishable items to purchase a few days before Christmas.
- Bake Parmesan Potato Breadsticks and Cheese Croutons; cool. Transfer to separate heavy-duty, resealable plastic bags; seal and freeze.
- Gather supplies for the Birch Bark Centerpiece and Birch Place Cards. (See page 23.)

Two Days Before:
- Buy remaining grocery items, including the snow crab legs.
- Make the hard-cooked eggs for Mushroom Spinach Salad; refrigerate.

The Day Before:
- Set the table.
- For the Crab Macaroni & Cheese, cook, drain and rinse the macaroni; remove the meat from the crab legs. Place in separate airtight containers and refrigerate.
- For Mushroom Spinach Salad, slice red onion, tear spinach and slice the eggs; place in separate resealable plastic bags and chill. Toast the walnuts; store in an airtight container at room temperature.
- Make Ginger Chocolate Temptation, but don't garnish; cover with plastic wrap and refrigerate.

Christmas Day:
- In the morning, thaw the Cheese Croutons at room temperature. When defrosted, place on an ungreased baking sheet; bake at 450° for 5 minutes. Cool; store in an airtight container.
- Thaw Parmesan Potato Breadsticks at room temperature.
- Make the Puffy Lobster Turnovers 1 to 2 hours before the party; cover with plastic wrap and refrigerate. Bake as guests arrive.
- Assemble the Crab Macaroni & Cheese; bake as directed.
- If desired, wrap the breadsticks in foil and reheat at 350° for 10 minutes. Serve with butter.
- Prepare the Mushroom Spinach Salad; top with Cheese Croutons.
- Garnish Ginger Chocolate Temptation just before serving.

puffy lobster turnovers

(PICTURED AT RIGHT)

Tender bits of lobster are nestled in golden brown puff pastry for an easy, elegant appetizer. Get ready to hand out the recipe to party guests!

Benny Diaz | *AZUSA, CA*

1 cup fresh or frozen lobster, cut into chunks

1/4 cup finely chopped onion

1 teaspoon minced fresh basil

1 teaspoon minced fresh thyme

1 teaspoon paprika

1 garlic clove, minced

1 teaspoon tomato paste

1/8 teaspoon salt

1/8 teaspoon pepper

2 packages (17.3 ounces each) frozen puff pastry, thawed

1 egg, beaten

In a small skillet, combine the first nine ingredients. Cook and stir over medium heat for 4-5 minutes or until lobster is firm and opaque; set aside.

Unfold puff pastry. Using a 4-in. round cookie cutter, cut out four circles. Place on a greased baking sheet. Repeat with remaining pastries. Spoon 1 tablespoon lobster mixture in the center of each circle.

Brush edges with egg; fold dough over filling. Press edges to seal. Bake at 400° for 8-10 minutes or until puffy and golden brown. Serve warm. **YIELD:** 16 appetizers.

crab macaroni & cheese

(PICTURED ON PAGE 17)

Crab and mushrooms put a deliciously different spin on classic macaroni and cheese.
It's an upscale casserole for special occasions...but my family could eat it every day!

Angela Ochoa | *LAKE ELSINORE, CA*

1 package (16 ounces) elbow macaroni

6 baby portobello mushrooms

2 green onions, sliced

1 tablespoon plus 1/4 cup butter, divided

1/4 cup all-purpose flour

1 teaspoon ground mustard

1 teaspoon pepper

1/2 teaspoon salt

1/4 teaspoon paprika

2-1/2 cups half-and-half cream

1-1/2 cups (6 ounces) shredded part-skim mozzarella cheese, divided

1-1/2 cups (6 ounces) shredded medium cheddar cheese, divided

TOPPING:

1/2 cup panko (Japanese) bread crumbs

3 tablespoons butter, melted

1 tablespoon dried basil

1-1/2 pounds cooked snow crab legs, meat removed

4 thin slices Swiss cheese

1/4 cup grated Parmesan cheese

Cook macaroni according to package directions. Drain pasta and rinse in cold water.

Meanwhile, in a large skillet, saute mushrooms and onions in 1 tablespoon butter until tender; set aside.

In a large saucepan, melt remaining butter. Stir in the flour, mustard, pepper, salt and paprika until smooth; gradually add cream. Bring to a boil; cook and stir for 2 minutes or until thickened. Stir in 3/4 cup each mozzarella and cheddar cheeses until blended. Remove from the heat; fold in macaroni.

In a small bowl, combine the bread crumbs, butter and basil. Transfer half of the macaroni mixture into a greased 13-in. x 9-in. baking dish. Layer with reserved mushroom mixture, remaining macaroni mixture, mozzarella and cheddar cheeses. Top with crab and Swiss cheese. Sprinkle with crumb mixture and Parmesan cheese.

Bake at 350° for 15-20 minutes or until golden brown. Let stand for 5 minutes before serving. **YIELD:** 10 servings.

cheese croutons

(PICTURED ON PAGE 17)

This old family recipe is very popular. We also use them to top our favorite Italian Wedding Soup.

Anita DelSignore | *NORTH FORT MYERS, FL*

3 eggs

2 cups (8 ounces) shredded Swiss cheese

1/4 cup all-purpose flour

2 tablespoons grated Romano cheese

1-1/2 teaspoons Italian seasoning

1/4 teaspoon baking powder

In a large bowl, beat eggs. In another bowl, combine the remaining ingredients; gradually add to eggs. Spread evenly into a parchment paper-lined 9-in. square baking pan.

Bake at 350° for 25-30 minutes or until lightly browned. Cool for 10 minutes before removing from pan; cut into 1-in. cubes. Increase temperature to 450°. Place cubes on an ungreased baking sheet. Bake 10 minutes longer, turning once. Transfer to a wire rack to cool completely. **YIELD:** 4 cups.

ginger chocolate temptation

(PICTURED AT RIGHT)

Chocolate-covered candied ginger is one of my favorite treats, so I knew this recipe was for me! Every bite of this cool, creamy custard is rich, smooth and decadent.

Elise Lalor | ISSAQUAH, WA

2 cups heavy whipping cream

1 vanilla bean, split lengthwise

8 squares (1 ounce each) bittersweet chocolate, chopped

6 egg yolks, beaten

1/4 cup candied or crystallized ginger, minced, divided

Heavy whipping cream, whipped, optional

In small heavy saucepan, combine cream and vanilla bean. Bring to a boil. Reduce heat; simmer, uncovered, for 5 minutes. Remove the vanilla bean and scrape the inside of the bean to remove the seeds; add seeds to the pan. Discard vanilla bean. Stir in chocolate until melted. Stir 1/2 cup chocolate mixture into egg yolks; return all to the pan. Cook and stir until mixture reaches 160° and coats the back of a metal spoon. Remove from the heat. Stir in 2 tablespoons ginger.

Pour into 12 demitasse or espresso cups. Refrigerate for at least 1 hour. Just before serving, garnish with the whipped cream if desired and the remaining ginger. **YIELD:** 12 servings.

parmesan potato breadsticks

(PICTURED ON PAGE 17)

*More than 20 years ago, our son was looking through an old, county fair cookbook and came across this recipe.
I've made adjustments to it over time, resulting in these soft and tender breadsticks.*

Katie Koziolek | HARTLAND, MN

1 tablespoon active dry yeast

1-1/2 cups warm water (110° to 115°)

6 tablespoons mashed potato flakes

6 tablespoons butter, cubed

1/4 cup sugar

3 tablespoons nonfat dry milk powder

3/4 teaspoon salt

4 to 4-1/2 cups all-purpose flour

2 tablespoons butter, melted

1 tablespoon grated Parmesan cheese

2 teaspoons sesame seeds

1 teaspoon poppy seeds

1 teaspoon kosher salt

In a large bowl, dissolve yeast in warm water. Add the potato flakes, butter, sugar, milk powder, salt and 2 cups flour. Beat until smooth. Stir in enough remaining flour to form a stiff dough.

Turn onto a floured surface; knead until smooth and elastic, about 6-8 minutes. Place in a greased bowl, turning once to grease the top. Cover and let rise in a warm place until doubled, about 1 hour.

Punch dough down. Turn onto a lightly floured surface; divide into 24 pieces. Roll each into a 5-in. rope. Place 2 in. apart on greased baking sheets. Cover and let rise until doubled, about 30 minutes.

Brush with melted butter. Sprinkle with cheese, seeds and kosher salt. Bake at 375° for 10-12 minutes or until golden brown. Remove from pans to wire racks to cool. **YIELD:** 2 dozen.

mushroom spinach salad

(PICTURED ON PAGE 17)

*I had this salad at a restaurant one night and couldn't stop raving about it. The updated dressing
nicely coats the lettuce, while bacon, mushrooms, blue cheese, walnuts and eggs add extra interest.*

Dolores Brigham | INGLEWOOD, CA

8 bacon strips, diced

1-1/2 cups thinly sliced fresh mushrooms

1 medium red onion, thinly sliced

1/4 cup balsamic vinegar

1 package (10 ounces) fresh spinach, torn

1/4 cup chopped walnuts, toasted

1/4 cup crumbled blue cheese

2 hard-cooked eggs, sliced

In a large skillet, cook bacon over medium heat until crisp. Using a slotted spoon, remove to paper towels to drain. Saute mushrooms and onion in drippings. Stir in vinegar.

In a large bowl, combine the spinach, walnuts, cheese and bacon; toss with mushroom mixture. Top with egg slices. **YIELD:** 12 servings.

birch bark centerpiece

(PICTURED AT RIGHT)

You don't have to chop down a tree to create this woody winter wonderland!

We found 8-inch-high birch bark cylinders online and cut them in half crosswise to make two 4-inch-high cylinders. Insert an 8-in. Styrofoam circle inside each cylinder.

(You could also glue a sheet of birch bark around the Styrofoam circles. If you can't find birch bark cylinders or sheets, use birch bark-patterned scrapbook paper.)

Place a 9-in. tall pillar candle in the center of each Styrofoam circle. Add green reindeer moss, pinecones and bunches of small artificial green berries around each candle.

If desired, lay a sheet of birch bark or birch bark scrapbook paper on the table. Set the candle-filled birch bark cylinders on top. Place a third pillar candle on the sheet; add berries and pinecones around the base of the candle.

Birch bark sheets or scrapbook paper can also be used as place mats (as shown in the photo on page 16).

BIRCH PLACE CARDS

Go out on a limb and fashion a forest-inspired place card for each of your dinner guests this Christmas season!

Cut a 3/4-in.-thick slice from a 1-1/2-in.-diameter birch branch. Drill a hole in the center with a 1/8-in. bit. Insert a juniper sprig into the drilled hole. With a 1-1/4-in.-high star paper punch, punch a star shape from a thin layer of birch bark or bark-patterned scrapbook paper. Use a black fine-line marker to write a guest's name on the star. Glue the star to top of the juniper sprig.

$\mathcal{S}$leeping in on Christmas morning just isn't an option, especially for the little ones in the family!

Leave tired old cereal in the cupboard and celebrate the dawn of this special day with a sunny selection of breakfast and brunch goodies.

As the kids unwrap pretty packages from Santa, they can sip cold milk and nibble on tender Coconut Crescent Rolls topped with a sweet glaze.

Meanwhile, adults can indulge in refreshing Peach Wine Coolers!

Tasty takes on the traditional, Eggplant Eggs Benedict and Banana Hazelnut Waffles will make the morning meal even merrier!

MORNING MENU
(PICTURED AT RIGHT)

bright eyed
CHRISTMAS BRUNCH

Do-Ahead
Brunch Ideas

Don't be daunted by early-day dining. All of the mouthwatering recipes in this chapter have elements that can be done in advance.

- Coconut Crescent Rolls. Bake and freeze rolls two to three weeks in advance. Thaw at room temperature on Christmas Eve.

- Gingerbread Muffins. Bake and freeze two to three weeks beforehand. Thaw at room temperature on Christmas Eve. In the morning, wrap the muffins in foil and reheat at 350° for 10-15 minutes.

- Banana Hazelnut Waffles. Days before, combine the dry ingredients and chop hazelnuts; store in separate airtight containers.

- Crumb-Topped Cranberry Cake. Prepare the day before; store in the refrigerator.

- Eggplant Eggs Benedict. You can make the hollandaise sauce the day before; cover and refrigerate. Reheat just before using.

- Ham in Cider Sauce. During the day on Christmas Eve, prepare the sauce; cover and chill. Reheat before pouring over the ham steak.

- Prosciutto Egg Panini. The day before, scramble the eggs; cover and chill. Reheat in the microwave before preparing sandwiches. Combine mustard and syrup; place in a covered bowl in the refrigerator.

- Spiced Tomato Beverage. Combine the first 12 ingredients a day ahead; bring to a boil. Remove and discard the cinnamon stick. Chill.

- Strawberry Fruit Dip. Prepare the night before and refrigerate.

- Peach Wine Coolers. Early Christmas morning, combine peach slices, brandy, honey, lemon slices and wine; refrigerate.

crumb-topped cranberry cake

(PICTURED AT RIGHT)

This dessert has something for everyone—moist yellow cake, cream cheese filling and cranberry-coconut topping. Serve it at breakfast, lunch and dinner.

Darlene Brenden | *SALEM, OR*

2 cups plus 2 tablespoons all-purpose flour

2/3 cup sugar

1/2 teaspoon baking powder

1/2 teaspoon baking soda

1 package (8 ounces) cream cheese, divided

2 eggs

3/4 cup milk

2 tablespoons canola oil

1 teaspoon vanilla extract

1/2 cup flaked coconut

1 cup whole-berry cranberry sauce

TOPPING:

6 tablespoons all-purpose flour

2 tablespoons sugar

2 tablespoons cold butter

In a large bowl, combine the flour, sugar, baking powder and baking soda; cut in 3 ounces cream cheese until the mixture resembles fine crumbs. In another bowl, whisk 1 egg, milk and oil; stir into the crumb mixture just until moistened. Spread batter into a greased and floured 9-in. springform pan; set aside.

In a small bowl, beat the remaining cream cheese. Beat in vanilla and remaining egg; carefully spread over batter. Sprinkle with coconut. Dollop with cranberry sauce. In a small bowl, combine flour and sugar; cut in butter until crumbly. Sprinkle over the top.

Bake at 350° for 50-55 minutes or until golden brown. Cool on a wire rack for 15 minutes. Carefully run a knife around edge of pan to loosen. Remove sides of pan. Cool completely. Store in the refrigerator. **YIELD:** 12 servings.

coconut crescent rolls

(PICTURED ON PAGE 24)

These rich, tender and slightly sweet rolls are a nice accompaniment to both brunch and dinner menus.

Mildred Bickley | BRISTOL, VA

1-1/8 teaspoons active dry yeast

2 tablespoons warm water (110° to 120°)

1/2 cup warm heavy whipping cream, (110° to 120°)

2 tablespoons plus 2 teaspoons sugar

1 egg

1-2/3 cups all-purpose flour, divided

1/4 teaspoon salt

1/4 cup cold butter

FILLING:

2 tablespoons butter, softened

1/4 cup confectioners' sugar

1/4 cup flaked coconut

GLAZE:

1 egg

2 tablespoons milk

1/4 cup flaked coconut

In a small bowl, dissolve yeast in warm water. Stir in the warm cream, sugar, egg and 1/4 cup flour. Place salt and remaining flour in a large bowl; cut in butter until crumbly. Fold in yeast mixture just until blended. (Do not knead.) Cover and refrigerate for at least 2 to 3 hours or overnight.

For filling, combine butter and confectioners' sugar. Stir in coconut; set aside.

Punch dough down. Divide dough in half. Turn onto a lightly floured surface. Roll each portion into a 12-in. circle. Spread with filling mixture. Cut each circle into eight wedges. Roll up wedges from the wide end and place with pointed side down 2 in. apart on greased baking sheets. Curve ends to form a crescent shape. Cover and let rise in a warm place until doubled, about 1 hour.

For glaze, combine egg and milk. Brush over dough. Sprinkle with coconut. Bake at 375° for 13-18 minutes or until golden brown. Remove from pans to wire racks to cool. YIELD: 16 rolls.

peach wine coolers

(PICTURED ON PAGE 24)

The fantastic flavors of honey, wine and brandy come through to make a special drink for Easter brunch. It's like sunshine in a glass!

Annie Hendricks | BURBANK, CA

2 cups frozen unsweetened peach slices, thawed

1/2 cup brandy

1/3 cup honey

3 lemon slices, halved

1 bottle (750 milliliters) dry white wine

1-1/2 cups sparkling water, chilled

In a 2-qt. pitcher, combine the peach slices, brandy, honey and lemon slices; stir in wine. Refrigerate for 2-4 hours or until chilled.

Just before serving, stir in sparkling water. Serve in glasses. YIELD: 9 servings.

prosciutto egg panini

(PICTURED AT RIGHT)

With mustard, maple syrup and prosciutto, this is a yummy twist on the usual bacon-and-egg sandwich. Your family will agree that this is one breakfast worth waking up for!

Erin Renouf Mylroie | SANTA CLARA, UT

3 eggs

2 egg whites

6 tablespoons milk

1 green onion, thinly sliced

1 tablespoon Dijon mustard

1 tablespoon maple syrup

8 slices sourdough bread

8 thin slices prosciutto or deli ham

1/2 cup shredded sharp cheddar cheese

8 teaspoons butter

In a small bowl, whisk the eggs, egg whites, milk and onion. Coat a large skillet with cooking spray and place over medium heat. Add egg mixture; cook and stir over medium heat until completely set.

Combine the mustard and syrup; spread over four bread slices. Layer with the scrambled eggs, prosciutto and cheese; top with the remaining bread. Butter outsides of sandwiches.

Cook on a panini maker or indoor grill for 3-4 minutes or until bread is browned and cheese is melted. Cut each panini in half to serve. **YIELD:** 8 servings.

eggplant eggs benedict

(PICTURED ON PAGE 25)

Instead of ordinary scrambled eggs, make beautiful eggs Benedict.
The lemon hollandaise sauce pairs well with the salmon.

Ameerah Lydick | *LANCASTER, CA*

2 tablespoons olive oil

1/4 teaspoon salt

1/4 teaspoon white pepper

8 slices eggplant (1 inch thick)

1 teaspoon white vinegar

8 eggs

4 English muffins, split and toasted

8 ounces smoked salmon fillet, flaked

1/2 cup sour cream

HOLLANDAISE SAUCE:

3 egg yolks

1/4 cup water

2 tablespoons lemon juice

3/4 cup butter, melted

1 teaspoon salt

1/4 teaspoon white pepper

2 tablespoons minced chives

In a small bowl, combine the oil, salt and pepper; brush over both sides of eggplant. Place in an ungreased 15-in. x 10-in. x 1-in. baking pan. Broil 4-6 in. from the heat for 5-7 minutes on each side or until tender and lightly browned.

Meanwhile, place 2-3 in. of water in a large skillet with high sides; add vinegar. Bring to a boil; reduce heat and simmer gently. Break cold eggs, one at a time, into a custard cup or saucer; holding the cup close to the surface of the water, slip each egg into water. Cook, uncovered, until whites are completely set and yolks begin to thicken (but are not hard), about 4 minutes. With a slotted spoon, lift each egg out of the water.

Top each muffin half with an eggplant slice, egg, 3 tablespoons salmon and 1 tablespoon sour cream. Set aside and keep warm.

In a double boiler over simmering water, constantly whisk the egg yolks, water and lemon juice until mixture begins to thicken and coats the back of a metal spoon. Reduce heat to low. Slowly drizzle in melted butter, whisking constantly. Whisk in salt and pepper.

Spoon 3 tablespoons sauce onto eight serving plates. Top with a prepared muffin; sprinkle with chives. **YIELD:** 8 servings.

ham in cider sauce

If you don't want the hassle of making a whole ham,
prepare these tasty ham steaks instead. I like to serve them with scalloped potatoes.

Deborah Maki | *KAMLOOPS, BC*

1 tablespoon whole cloves

2 boneless fully cooked ham steaks (1 inch thick and 1 pound each)

2 tablespoons brown sugar

1/4 cup butter, cubed

1/4 cup all-purpose flour

2-1/2 cups apple cider or juice

1/3 cup raisins

Insert cloves into edges of ham steaks; rub steaks with brown sugar. Place in a greased 13-in. x 9-in. baking dish.

Bake, uncovered, at 400° for 20 minutes. Meanwhile, in a large saucepan, melt butter over medium heat; stir in flour until smooth. Gradually stir in apple cider and raisins. Bring to a boil; cook and stir for 2 minutes or until thickened. Pour over ham steaks. Bake, uncovered, 15-20 minutes longer or until heated through. Discard cloves before serving. **YIELD:** 8 servings.

strawberry fruit dip

(PICTURED AT RIGHT)

*Served with a strawberry-flavored dip,
fresh fruit tastes even better.
I turn to this recipe for just about
every family gathering.*

Dawn Brandt | *KALBASHA, MI*

1 package (8 ounces) cream cheese, softened

1 carton (6 ounces) yogurt

1 package (10 ounces) frozen sweetened
sliced strawberries, thawed

Assorted fresh fruit

In a small bowl, beat the cream cheese and
yogurt until blended. Add the strawberries. Serve with fresh fruit. Cover and
refrigerate leftovers. **YIELD:** 2-1/2 cups.

gingerbread muffins

*My mom would always have these muffins on hand when I was growing up.
They were a special, sweet little treat any time of day!*

Ann Bush | *KANSAS CITY, MO*

3/4 cup butter, softened

1/2 cup sugar

2 eggs

1/2 cup buttermilk

1/2 cup molasses

2 cups all-purpose flour

1 teaspoon salt

1 teaspoon ground ginger

3/4 teaspoon baking soda

3/4 teaspoon ground nutmeg

1/8 teaspoon ground allspice

3/4 cup chopped dates

1/2 cup chopped black walnuts

In a large bowl, cream butter and sugar until light and fluffy. Add
eggs, one at a time, beating well after each addition. Stir in buttermilk and molasses. Combine the flour, salt, ginger, baking soda,
nutmeg and allspice; add to creamed mixture just until moistened
Fold in dates and walnuts.

Fill paper-lined muffin cups three-fourths full. Bake at 350° for
20-25 minutes or until a toothpick comes out clean. Cool for
5 minutes before removing from the pan to a wire rack. Serve the
muffins warm. **YIELD:** 1 dozen.

banana hazelnut waffles

(PICTURED ON PAGE 25)

This recipe was created from my love of hazelnuts. My family really enjoys these light, crisp waffles.
Karen Bomberger | *AUBURN, AL*

1 cup all-purpose flour

1/2 cup whole wheat flour

2 tablespoons flaxseed

1-1/2 teaspoons baking powder

1/2 teaspoon salt

3 eggs, separated

1 cup milk

1/2 cup mashed ripe banana

2 tablespoons orange juice

1 tablespoon butter, melted

1 teaspoon vanilla extract

1/2 cup chopped hazelnuts

1-1/2 cups maple pancake syrup

1 tablespoon hazelnut coffee drink mix

Sliced ripe bananas and hazelnuts, optional

In a large bowl, combine the flours, flax, baking powder and salt. In a large bowl, whisk the egg yolks, milk, banana, orange juice, butter and vanilla. Stir into the dry ingredients just until moistened. Stir in the hazelnuts.

In a large bowl, beat egg whites until stiff peaks form. Fold into batter. Bake in a preheated waffle iron according to manufacturer's directions until golden brown.

Meanwhile, in a small saucepan, combine syrup and coffee drink mix; heat through. Serve with waffles. Garnish with bananas and hazelnuts if desired. **YIELD:** 12 waffles (1-1/2 cups syrup).

spiced tomato beverage

This zesty beverage recipe from my Uncle Merle will awaken all your senses! Skip the vodka for a nonalcoholic drink.
Ron Roth | *THREE RIVERS, MI*

8 cups tomato juice

3 tablespoons white vinegar

1 tablespoon sugar

1 tablespoon Worcestershire sauce

2 beef bouillon cubes

1 teaspoon salt

1/2 teaspoon onion powder

1/2 teaspoon celery salt

1/2 teaspoon pepper

1/4 teaspoon garlic powder

2 to 6 drops hot pepper sauce

1 cinnamon stick (3 inches)

Ice cubes

16 ounces vodka, optional

8 celery ribs, optional

In a large saucepan, combine the first 12 ingredients. Bring to a boil. Remove and discard cinnamon stick. Serve warm or cover and refrigerate until chilled.

If desired, place ice in a glass. Fill a shaker three-fourths full with ice. Add 2 ounces vodka and 1 cup tomato mixture to shaker; cover and shake for 10-15 seconds or until condensation forms on outside of shaker. Strain into prepared glass. Garnish with a celery rib. Repeat with the remaining vodka, tomato mixture and celery. **YIELD:** 8 servings.

festive glass vase fillers

(PICTURED AT RIGHT)

Decorating for the holidays doesn't have to be an expensive endeavor. Although there's no denying the outstanding beauty of poinsettias, amaryllis and other Christmas flowers, the pretty plants only last so long...especially if you don't have a green thumb!

But it is worth investing in several clear glass containers in various shapes and sizes. Hunt for them throughout the year on sale or on clearance at department stores. You can also pick them up at bargain prices at discount stores, flea markets and rummage sales.

Put the versatile vessels to work all year long in countless decorating displays. Below we offer three ideas for the Christmas season. Use these photos as inspiration to create your own seasonal decorations.

EDIBLE CENTERPIECE. For a display that has both form and function, fill clear vases with Christmas candy...then encourage hungry guests to dig in! For a spectacular striped look, we used a variety of peppermints including sticks, circles and rectangles.

BEAUTIFUL BAUBLES. Bright, shiny ornaments are always eye-catching on a table. We separated round glass ornaments by color, and then put each color in a different vase. You could also fill the containers with the same color of ornaments or use ornaments with different shapes (such as stars).

NATURAL WONDERS. An impressive centerpiece is as easy as the nearest pine tree! Collect small, medium and large pinecones. You could even purchase white-tipped pinecones from a craft store.

$\mathcal{W}$here there's good food, people gather. Make sure your next holiday party is the place to be by serving the best-of-the-season appetizers celebrated here.

From standard party munchies to more elegant selections, you'll find this merry-making collection fit for any Yuletide festivity.

Whether hosting an upscale holiday soiree or a casual tree-trimming get-together, pass around a tray of Curried Beef Satay, White Bean Crostini, Goat Cheese Wontons and Pesto Chicken Polenta Bites. Don't forget to set out bowls filled with Spicy Peanuts for your guests to munch while mingling.

FESTIVE FINGER FOODS
(PICTURED AT RIGHT)

Spicy Peanuts (p. 38)
Goat Cheese Wontons (p. 38)
Curried Beef Satay (p. 36)
White Bean Crostini (p. 40)
Pesto Chicken Polenta Bites (p. 40)

seasonal
PARTY STARTERS

curried beef satay

(PICTURED ON PAGE 35)

Here's a hearty addition to your appetizer tray. Tender strips of beef sirloin are marinated in a spicy curry sauce, then threaded onto skewers and broiled to juicy perfection. Served with Thai peanut sauce, it's one tasteful way to begin your event.

Zakia Zoummane | *SUN PRAIRIE, WI*

1/2 cup soy sauce

1/4 cup white vinegar

1/4 cup peanut oil

2 tablespoons chili powder

1 tablespoon curry powder

1/4 teaspoon ground chipotle pepper

1 pound boneless beef sirloin steak, cut into 1/8-inch strips

3/4 cup Thai peanut sauce, warmed

In a small bowl, combine the first six ingredients. Set aside 1/4 cup for basting. Pour remaining mixture into a large resealable plastic bag; add the beef. Seal bag and turn to coat; refrigerate for at least 30 minutes.

Drain and discard marinade. Thread beef onto 12 metal or soaked wooden skewers. Place skewers in two greased 15-in. x 10-in. baking pans. Broil 3-4 in. from the heat for 2-4 minutes on each side or until meat reaches desired doneness, basting occasionally with reserved marinade. Serve with peanut sauce. **YIELD:** 12 skewers.

garlic phyllo bundles

Our home economists wrap flaky phyllo dough around wonderful roasted garlic for an appetizer that simply melts in your mouth. Walnuts add a surprising crunch to these bite-sized bundles.

10 sheets phyllo dough (14 inches x 9 inches)

1/3 cup butter, melted

20 garlic cloves, peeled

7 tablespoons finely chopped walnuts

1/4 cup seasoned bread crumbs

Lightly brush one sheet of phyllo with butter; place another sheet of phyllo on top and brush with butter. (Keep remaining phyllo covered with plastic wrap and a damp towel to prevent it from drying out.)

Cut the two layered sheets into four 14-in. x 2-1/4-in. strips. Place one garlic clove on lower corner of each strip; sprinkle 1 teaspoon walnuts over length of strip.

Fold dough over garlic, forming a triangle. Fold triangle up, then fold triangle over, forming another triangle. Continue folding, like a flag, until you come to the end of the strip. Brush end of dough with butter and press onto triangle to seal. Place bread crumbs in a small shallow bowl. Brush both sides of triangle with butter; dip in bread crumbs. Place on a greased baking sheet. Repeat.

Bake at 350° for 15-18 minutes or until golden brown. Serve warm. **YIELD:** 20 appetizers.

chinese pork tenderloin

(PICTURED AT RIGHT)

Because I live in an area where there aren't many Chinese restaurants, I developed this Asian-inspired starter. A combination of soy and plum sauces, red wine, garlic and ginger create a full-bodied marinade that infuses every morsel with enticing flavor.

Delores Condon | PAYNESVILLE, MN

1/4 cup sugar

1/4 cup soy sauce

2 tablespoons plum sauce

2 tablespoons ketchup

1 tablespoon dry red wine or beef broth

1 garlic clove, minced

3/4 teaspoon finely chopped candied or crystallized ginger

2 pork tenderloins (3/4 pound each)

Toasted sesame seeds, Chinese-style mustard and additional plum sauce, optional

In a small bowl, combine the first seven ingredients. Pour 1/3 cup into a large resealable plastic bag; add the pork. Seal bag and turn to coat; refrigerate for 8 hours or overnight, turning several times. Cover and refrigerate remaining marinade for basting.

Drain and discard marinade. Place pork on a greased rack in a foil-lined roasting pan. Bake, uncovered, at 425° for 20-30 minutes or until a meat thermometer reads 160°, brushing occasionally with the reserved marinade.

Let stand for 5-10 minutes before slicing. Sprinkle with sesame seeds and serve with mustard and additional plum sauce if desired. **YIELD:** 10 servings.

goat cheese wontons

(PICTURED ON PAGE 35)

Tangy goat cheese and fresh herb flavors shine through in every bite of these crispy bundles.
The egg roll-like snacks are a simple but impressive addition to your holiday appetizer offerings.

Carla DeVelder | MISHAWAKA, IN

1 cup crumbled goat cheese

1 teaspoon each minced fresh basil, parsley and chives

1 garlic clove, minced

Dash salt and pepper

1 egg, beaten

1 tablespoon water

16 wonton wrappers

Oil for frying

In a small bowl, combine the cheese, herbs, garlic, salt and pepper. Beat egg and water.

Place 1 tablespoon cheese mixture in the center of a wonton wrapper. (Keep remaining wrappers covered with a damp paper towel until ready to use.) Fold bottom corner over filling. Fold sides toward center over filling. Moisten remaining corner with egg; roll up tightly to seal.

In an electric skillet or deep-fat fryer, heat oil to 375°. Fry wontons, a few at a time, for 30-60 seconds on each side or until golden brown. Drain on paper towels. YIELD: 16 wontons.

GIFT OF GOOD HEALTH

Treat your health-conscious guests to Goat Cheese Wontons that are baked instead of deep-fried. Here's how: Spritz both sides of wonton wrappers with refrigerated butter-flavored spray. Press into mini-muffin cups and bake at 350° for 4 to 5 minutes or until lightly browned, then add filling and bake 5 minutes longer. You'll get the same crispy, savory snack, but with less fat and calories.

spicy peanuts

(PICTURED ON PAGE 34)

It's always nice to have something simple for guests to nibble on while mingling. These special peanuts
are just the thing. Crushed red pepper flakes and chili powder turn up the heat on this classic party fare.

Phyllis Schmalz | KANSAS CITY, KS

3 tablespoons olive oil

1 tablespoon crushed red pepper flakes

1 can (12-1/2 ounces) Spanish peanuts (skin on)

1 can (12 ounces) salted peanuts

4 garlic cloves, minced

1 teaspoon chili powder

1/4 teaspoon salt

In a large heavy skillet, heat oil and pepper flakes over medium heat for 1 minute. Add peanuts and garlic. Cook and stir for 3-5 minutes or until lightly browned. Drain on paper towels.

Transfer to a large bowl. Sprinkle with chili powder and salt; toss to coat. Cool completely. Store in an airtight container. YIELD: 4-1/2 cups.

mediterranean dip with garlic pita chips

(PICTURED AT RIGHT)

This deliciously different dip is one of those recipes that's so good, you keep trying to find new ways to use it. The chunky, veggie-laden mixture of eggplant, onion and sweet peppers is terrific on pita chips as a starter, or served over pasta, chicken or fish as an entree.

Sarah Geary | OKLAHOMA CITY, OK

2 medium eggplants, peeled

1 large sweet red pepper

1 large sweet yellow pepper

1 large red onion

1/4 cup olive oil

1 teaspoon salt

1/4 teaspoon pepper

2 garlic cloves, minced

4 teaspoons tomato paste

PITA CHIPS:

1/4 cup olive oil

2 tablespoons grated Parmesan cheese

2 garlic cloves, minced

1 teaspoon dried basil

1 teaspoon dried thyme

1/2 teaspoon salt

1/2 teaspoon dried tarragon

1/4 teaspoon coarsely ground pepper

1 package (12 ounces) whole pita breads

Cut the eggplants, peppers and onion into 1-in. pieces; place in a large bowl. Add the oil, salt and pepper; toss to coat. Transfer to two greased 15-in. x 10-in. baking pans.

Bake at 400° for 40 minutes, stirring once. Stir in garlic; bake 5-10 minutes longer or until vegetables are tender. Cool for 10 minutes. Place vegetables and tomato paste in a food processor; cover and process until desired consistency.

For pita chips, in a small bowl, combine the oil, cheese, garlic and seasonings. Place pita breads on baking sheets; brush with half of oil mixture. Bake at 350° for 7 minutes. Turn over; brush with remaining mixture. Bake 7-9 minutes longer or until crisp. Cut each pita into six wedges. Serve with dip. **YIELD:** 2-1/2 cups dip (30 chips).

pesto chicken polenta bites

(PICTURED ON PAGE 35)

Simple to make but elegant in appearance, these pretty, handheld treats feature the unique flavor combination of robust pesto and sweet dried cranberries. Expect an empty tray—and several recipe requests!

Betty Fulks | ONIA, AK

2-1/2 cups water, divided

3/4 teaspoon salt

1/4 teaspoon pepper

1 cup yellow cornmeal

1/2 cup heavy whipping cream

TOPPING:

2 cups shredded cooked rotisserie chicken

2/3 cup prepared pesto

1/4 teaspoon pepper

1/2 cup dried cranberries

In a small heavy saucepan, bring the water, salt and pepper to a boil. Reduce heat to a gentle boil; slowly whisk in cornmeal. Cook and stir with a wooden spoon for 15-20 minutes or until polenta is thickened and pulls away cleanly from the sides of the pan (mixture will be very thick). Gradually stir in cream during the last 2 minutes of cooking.

Pour into a greased 15-in. x 10-in. pan. Let stand until firm, about 30 minutes. Cut polenta with a scalloped 2-in. cookie cutter.

Combine the chicken, pesto and pepper; spoon 1 tablespoon of the mixture over each polenta cutout. Sprinkle with the cranberries. **YIELD:** 32 appetizers.

white bean crostini

(PICTURED ON PAGE 35)

A buttery bean puree showcasing the fresh flavors of garlic and thyme tops golden slices of French bread. The versatile appetizer never fails to win the approval of my guests.

Nancee Melin | TUCSON, AZ

1 can (15 ounces) white kidney or cannellini beans, rinsed and drained

1/4 cup plus 2 tablespoons olive oil, divided

2 garlic cloves, peeled

1/4 teaspoon salt

1/8 teaspoon pepper

2 tablespoons chopped ripe olives

2 tablespoons minced fresh thyme or 2 teaspoons dried thyme

24 slices French bread baguette (1/2 inch thick)

Sliced ripe olives and additional fresh thyme, optional

In a food processor, combine the beans, 1/4 cup oil, garlic, salt and pepper. Cover and process until smooth. Add olives and thyme; process until blended.

Place bread on an ungreased baking sheet. Brush with remaining oil. Broil 3-4 in. from the heat for 1-2 minutes or until golden brown. Cool slightly. Spread each slice with 1 tablespoon bean mixture. Garnish with olives and thyme if desired. **YIELD:** 2 dozen.

PLANNING YOUR APPETIZER MENU

Look for recipes with make-ahead aspects to prevent last-minute fuss. Have a variety of tastes, textures and colors to please your guests' palates. Avoid foods that require a lot of cutting.

chili shrimp

(PICTURED AT RIGHT)

This spicy shrimp dish is a hit at every buffet I host. The fiery sauce clings to the succulent shrimp, which look so pretty arranged on a festive platter. Best of all, the shrimp can be easily prepared the day before your event.

Beth Schaefer | *SHERWOOD, OH*

3 tablespoons ketchup

1 tablespoon sugar

1 tablespoon white wine vinegar

1 tablespoon soy sauce

1/8 to 1/2 teaspoon crushed red pepper flakes

1 pound uncooked medium shrimp, peeled and deveined

1 tablespoon canola oil

1 tablespoon minced fresh gingerroot

3 garlic cloves, minced

1 green onion, sliced

1/2 teaspoon sesame oil

Combine the first five ingredients; set aside. In a large skillet or wok, stir-fry the shrimp in oil for 2 minutes. Add ginger and garlic; stir-fry 2-3 minutes longer or until the shrimp turn pink.

Add ketchup mixture to the pan and heat through. Stir in onion and sesame oil. Serve warm. **YIELD:** about 3 dozen.

walnut pastry roll-ups

The flaky, nutty texture and hint of blue cheese guarantee that these cute bites will win raves every time. The simple appetizers can be made ahead of time, then baked just before guests arrive.

Margaret Minnich | COLUMBUS, OH

1 sheet refrigerated pie pastry

2/3 cup finely chopped walnuts

1/3 cup crumbled blue cheese

2 tablespoons minced fresh parsley, divided

1/4 teaspoon pepper

1 tablespoon milk

2 teaspoons grated Parmesan cheese

On a lightly floured surface, unroll pastry. Combine the walnuts, blue cheese, 1 tablespoon parsley and pepper; sprinkle over pastry. Cut into 12 wedges. Roll up wedges from the wide ends and place point side down 2 in. apart on a greased baking sheet. Brush with milk; sprinkle with Parmesan cheese.

Bake at 425° for 12-15 minutes or until golden brown. Sprinkle with remaining parsley. Serve warm. **YIELD:** 1 dozen.

chicken puffs

My neighborhood has a progressive dinner before Christmas each year. These delightful puffs were served one year to everyone's enjoyment. The cheesy flavor and creamy texture of the chicken salad mixture is wonderful inside the tender puffs.

Donna Kittredge | WESTBOROUGH, MA

1-1/4 cups water

1/4 cup butter, cubed

1/2 teaspoon salt

1 cup all-purpose flour

4 eggs

1 cup (4 ounces) shredded Swiss cheese

FILLING:

2 cups finely chopped cooked chicken

1 cup (4 ounces) shredded Swiss cheese

3/4 cup chopped celery

1/2 cup mayonnaise

1/2 teaspoon salt

1/2 teaspoon prepared yellow mustard

1/8 teaspoon pepper

In a large saucepan, bring the water, butter and salt to a boil. Add flour all at once and stir until a smooth ball forms. Remove from the heat; let stand for 5 minutes. Add eggs, one at a time, beating well after each addition. Continue beating until mixture is smooth and shiny. Stir in cheese.

Drop by tablespoonfuls 2 in. apart onto greased baking sheets. Bake at 400° for 20-25 minutes or until golden brown. Remove to wire racks. Immediately split puffs open; remove tops and set aside. Discard soft dough from inside. Cool puffs.

Meanwhile, in a large bowl, combine the filling ingredients. Spoon into puffs; replace tops. Serve immediately. **YIELD:** 3 dozen.

mini beef wellingtons

(PICTURED AT RIGHT)

I discovered this lovely starter at a wedding I attended. After sampling one, I decided I had to try duplicating the recipe at home. I think my version is a bit easier and faster to prepare, but just as elegant in appearance and just as crowd pleasing in flavor.

Annie De La Hoz | DELTA, CO

1 boneless beef chuck roast (3 to 4 pounds)

14 tablespoons butter, divided

1 can (10-1/2 ounces) condensed beef broth, undiluted, divided

1 cup Madeira or marsala wine, divided

1/2 pound medium fresh mushrooms, finely chopped

1 garlic clove, minced

3 tablespoons minced fresh parsley

2 tablespoons cornstarch

1/2 teaspoon salt

1/4 teaspoon pepper

5 tubes (16.3 ounces each) large refrigerated flaky biscuits

In a Dutch oven, brown roast on all sides in 4 tablespoons butter. Pour 1/2 cup broth and 1/2 cup wine over roast. Cover and bake at 325° for 1-1/4 to 1-1/2 hours or until tender. Remove roast and cool slightly; shred meat with two forks.

In a small skillet, saute mushrooms in 2 tablespoons butter until tender. Add the garlic; cook 1 minute longer. Stir in the parsley; set aside.

In a large saucepan, bring remaining broth and 1 tablespoon butter to a boil. Combine cornstarch and remaining wine until smooth; gradually stir into the pan. Bring to a boil; cook and stir for 2 minutes or until thickened. Stir in the meat, mushroom mixture, salt and pepper.

Press each biscuit into a 4-in. circle. Place 2 tablespoons meat mixture on half of each circle. Bring edges of biscuit over mixture and pinch seam to seal. Place on greased baking sheets. Bake at 400° for 15-20 minutes or until golden brown. Melt remaining butter; brush over appetizers. **YIELD:** 40 appetizers.

baked brie in a bread bowl

This rich treat gets wonderful flavor from ripe pears, fresh thyme,
crunchy almonds and velvety Brie. Once baked, it cuts nicely into savory wedges.

Mary Lou Timpson | *COLORADO CITY, AZ*

1/3 cup dry white wine

1/2 teaspoon brown sugar

1/2 teaspoon minced fresh thyme or
1/8 teaspoon dried thyme

1/8 teaspoon salt

1/8 teaspoon pepper

2 shallots, thinly sliced

1 tablespoon butter

2 medium pears, peeled and thinly sliced

1 round loaf (1 pound) sourdough bread

1 round Brie cheese (8 ounces), halved
horizontally

1/2 cup slivered almonds

In a small bowl, combine the wine, brown sugar and seasonings. In a large skillet over medium heat, cook shallots in butter until tender. Add the pears; cook and stir 3 minutes longer. Add the wine mixture; bring to a boil. Cook and stir for 10 minutes or until the liquid is evaporated.

Cut the top fourth off of the loaf of bread; carefully hollow out enough of bread from the bottom so cheese will fit (discard removed bread or save for another use). Layer half of the cheese, pear mixture and almonds in bread. Repeat layers. Replace the bread top. Wrap in a large piece of heavy-duty foil.

Bake at 350° for 45-50 minutes or until cheese is melted. Let stand for 10 minutes. Cut into wedges. YIELD: 16 servings.

herbed feta dip

Guests can't get enough of this thick, zesty dip that bursts with fresh Mediterranean flavor.
The feta cheese and fresh mint complement each other beautifully, creating the perfect sidekick
for crunchy carrots, toasted pita chips, sliced baguettes or any other dipper you fancy.

Rebecca Ray | *CHICAGO, IL*

1/2 cup packed fresh parsley sprigs

1/2 cup fresh mint leaves

1/2 cup olive oil

2 garlic cloves, peeled

1/2 teaspoon pepper

4 cups (16 ounces) crumbled feta cheese

3 tablespoons lemon juice

Assorted fresh vegetables

In a food processor, combine the first five ingredients; cover and pulse until finely chopped. Add cheese and lemon juice; process until creamy. Serve with vegetables. YIELD: 3 cups.

COLORFUL BUFFET

When serving healthier appetizers such as fresh vegetables with low-fat dip, dress up the serving platter. Cut off the tops of red or green peppers; remove the seeds and membranes. Then fill the pepper cups with the dip. This is a great way to add color to your buffet table.

smoked salmon appetizer crepes

(PICTURED AT RIGHT)

*A creamy filling featuring
smoked salmon and fresh chives
is tucked inside golden, tender crepes.
A splash of brandy adds impeccable flavor.
Folded into quarters and cut in half,
the cute snacks are never passed up.*

Karen Sue Garback-Pristera | ALBANY, NY

1 cup milk

2 eggs

2 egg yolks

2 tablespoons butter, melted

2 tablespoons brandy or unsweetened apple juice

1 cup all-purpose flour

1/2 teaspoon salt

FILLING:

2 packages (3 ounces each) cream cheese, softened

3 tablespoons heavy whipping cream

4 teaspoons minced chives

1 package (4 ounces) smoked salmon or lox

In a small bowl, combine the first five ingredients. Add flour and salt; mix well. Cover and refrigerate for 1 hour.

Heat a lightly greased 8-in. nonstick skillet over medium heat; pour 3 tablespoons batter into the center of skillet. Lift and tilt pan to coat bottom evenly. Cook until top appears dry; turn and cook 15-20 seconds longer. Remove to a wire rack. Repeat with the remaining batter, greasing skillet as needed. When cool, stack the crepes with waxed paper or paper towels in between.

For filling, in a large bowl, beat the cream cheese, cream and chives until fluffy. Stir in salmon.

To serve, spread each crepe with about 2 tablespoons filling. Fold the crepes into quarters; cut each folded crepe into two wedges. **YIELD:** 20 appetizers.

A Christmas feast isn't complete without special, tried-and-true side dishes. As time goes by, those timeless recipes become almost as important as the Christmas ham itself. But every once in a while, it's nice to add a new tradition by introducing fresh takes on the classics.

Put a deliciously different spin on your holiday menu with taste twists such as Sage Mashed Potatoes with Corn, Sweet & Sour Beets and Mushroom Wild Rice.

Brimming with crave-worthy flavors and textures, the recipes featured here for veggies, stuffing, salads and more will soon become treasures for years to come.

TASTY TRIMMINGS
(PICTURED AT RIGHT)

Sweet & Sour Beets (p. 48)
Sage Mashed Potatoes with Corn (p. 52)
Mushroom Wild Rice (p. 50)

sparkling
YULETIDE SIDES

curried rice

*I've been cooking this simple rice dish for more than 40 years. The pleasant curry flavor
is especially nice with roasted chicken, turkey or duck, making it the perfect addition to a holiday spread.*

Bess Placha | *CHICAGO, IL*

1-1/2 cups uncooked long grain rice

1 medium onion, chopped

3 tablespoons butter

3 cups chicken broth

3/4 teaspoon each dried basil, marjoram, thyme and sage

1/2 teaspoon salt

1/2 teaspoon curry powder

In a large saucepan, saute rice and onion in butter for 5 minutes. Stir in broth and seasonings. Bring to a boil. Reduce heat; cover and simmer for 18-22 minutes or until rice is tender. **YIELD**: 7 servings.

sweet & sour beets

(PICTURED ON PAGE 46)

*With a slight sweet-sour flavor and hint of orange found in every bite,
these beets are hard to resist. They're a must on my family's Christmas menu.*

Dottie Kilpatrick | *WILMINGTON, NC*

1-3/4 pounds whole fresh beets

1/2 cup sugar

1 tablespoon cornstarch

1/4 teaspoon salt

1/2 cup cider vinegar

2 tablespoons orange marmalade

1 tablespoon butter

Place beets in a large saucepan; cover with water. Bring to a boil. Reduce heat; cover and cook for 25-30 minutes or until tender. Drain and cool slightly. Peel and quarter beets; keep warm.

Meanwhile, in another large saucepan, combine the sugar, cornstarch and salt; stir in vinegar. Bring to a boil over medium heat; cook and stir for 1 minute or until thickened. Stir in marmalade and butter until melted. Reduce heat to low. Add beets; heat through. **YIELD**: 6 servings.

THE BASICS OF BEETS

Select firm, deep, red, round beets with unwilted green tops. The skin should be unblemished and unbroken.

Remove the greens before storing. Place uncooked beets in an open plastic bag in your refrigerator's crisper drawer for up to 2 weeks.

Gently wash beets before using, but don't peel or trim. Adding a small amount of vinegar to the cooking water will keep the brilliant color from fading.

To prevent your hands from staining, wear plastic gloves when peeling and slicing beets.

risotto-stuffed portobello mushrooms

(PICTURED AT RIGHT)

These elegant, stuffed mushroom caps make a lovely special-occasion side dish. Green and red sweet peppers add festive color to the creamy and tender risotto.

Christie Szabo | HELOTES, TX

1 cup balsamic vinaigrette

8 large portobello mushrooms (4 to 4-1/2 inches), stems removed

4 cups chicken broth, divided

2 large sweet onions, chopped

1 medium green pepper, diced

1 medium sweet red pepper, diced

1 tablespoon pine nuts

2 garlic cloves, minced

3 tablespoons butter

2 cups uncooked arborio rice

1/2 cup plus 2 tablespoons grated Parmesan cheese, divided

1/4 cup minced fresh parsley

1/4 teaspoon pepper

Place the vinaigrette in a large resealable plastic bag; add the mushrooms. Seal the bag and turn to coat; refrigerate for at least 30 minutes.

Drain and discard marinade. Place mushroom caps in a 15-in. x 10-in. baking pan. Bake, uncovered, at 425° for 15-20 minutes or until tender.

Meanwhile, in a small saucepan, heat broth and keep warm. In a Dutch oven, saute the onions, peppers, pine nuts and garlic in butter until tender, about 3 minutes. Add rice; cook and stir for 2-3 minutes. Carefully stir in 1 cup warm broth. Cook and stir until all of the broth is absorbed.

Add remaining broth, 1/2 cup at a time, stirring constantly. Allow the liquid to absorb between additions. Cook until risotto is creamy and rice is almost tender. (Cooking time is about 20 minutes.)

Stir in 1/2 cup cheese, parsley and pepper. Place 3/4 cup risotto in each mushroom cap. Sprinkle with remaining cheese; serve immediately. **YIELD:** 8 servings.

mushroom wild rice

(PICTURED ON PAGE 47)

With its nutty texture and visual appeal, you'll turn to this hearty side whenever a rice dish is in order. I've served it for more than 30 years and, over time, have learned to make enough to be sent home with family members.

Virginia Peter | WINTER, WI

4 cups chicken broth

1-1/2 cups uncooked wild rice

1/2 teaspoon salt

1/4 teaspoon pepper

3 bacon strips, cut into 1/2-inch pieces

2 cups sliced fresh mushrooms

1 small onion, chopped

1/2 cup sliced almonds

In a large saucepan, bring broth to a boil. Stir in the rice, salt and pepper. Reduce heat to low; cover and simmer for 55 minutes or until rice is tender. Remove from the heat.

Meanwhile, in a large skillet, cook the bacon over medium heat until crisp. Using a slotted spoon, remove to paper towels to drain. Saute the mushrooms, onion and almonds in drippings until the vegetables are tender; stir into the rice mixture. Add the bacon. **YIELD:** 10 servings.

creamy pepper penne

A flavorful sour cream sauce nicely coats penne in this pleasing pasta. To turn it into an entree, stir in some cubed cooked chicken or cooked shrimp.

Deborah Wolf | PALMYRA, NY

2 cups uncooked penne pasta

1 large sweet red pepper, julienned

1 medium onion, finely chopped

2 garlic cloves, minced

2 teaspoons olive oil

2 plum tomatoes, seeded and chopped

3/4 cup sour cream

2 tablespoons heavy whipping cream

1/4 teaspoon salt

1/4 teaspoon hot pepper sauce

1/8 teaspoon paprika

1/8 teaspoon pepper

Cook pasta according to package directions. Meanwhile, in a large skillet, saute the red pepper, onion and garlic in oil until tender. Add tomatoes; saute 1 minute longer.

In a small bowl, combine the remaining ingredients. Drain the pasta; place in a serving bowl. Add the red pepper and sour cream mixtures; toss to coat. Serve immediately. **YIELD:** 6 servings.

sausage bread dressing

(PICTURED AT RIGHT)

My husband and father go crazy for this dressing. Although leftovers are rare, it freezes quite well. To save time, chop the veggies and prepare the stuffing mix ahead of time.

Bette Votral | BETHLEHEM, PA

4 cups seasoned stuffing cubes

1 cup corn bread stuffing mix

1/2 pound bulk Italian sausage

1 large onion, chopped

1 large tart apple, peeled and chopped

1-1/3 cups sliced fresh shiitake mushrooms

1-1/4 cups sliced fresh mushrooms

1 celery rib, chopped

1/8 teaspoon salt

1/8 teaspoon pepper

3 tablespoons butter

1 can (14-1/2 ounces) chicken broth

1 cup pecan halves

1/2 cup minced fresh parsley

1 tablespoon fresh sage or 1 teaspoon dried sage leaves

In a large bowl, combine the stuffing cubes and stuffing mix; set aside. In a large skillet, cook the sausage, onion, apple, mushrooms, celery, salt and pepper in butter over medium heat until the sausage is no longer pink. Add to the stuffing mixture. Stir in the broth, pecans, parsley and sage; toss to coat.

Transfer to a greased 3-qt. baking dish. Cover and bake at 325° for 30 minutes. Uncover; bake 10 minutes longer or until lightly browned. **YIELD**: about 12 cups.

sage mashed potatoes with corn

(PICTURED ON PAGE 47)

*Mashed potatoes seem to be a staple at any holiday meal—now here's a way
to jazz them up a bit! The flavor is simply tantalizing, and the corn adds pretty flecks of color.
The heavenly aroma alone is enough to draw people to the table.*

Julie Foppes | *VERONA, NY*

6 medium potatoes, peeled and cubed

1 cup frozen corn, thawed

2 teaspoons canola oil

1/2 cup heavy whipping cream

1/4 cup butter, cubed

1/4 cup minced fresh sage

1 teaspoon salt

1/4 teaspoon pepper

Place potatoes in a large saucepan and cover with water. Bring to a boil. Reduce heat; cover and cook for 15-20 minutes or until tender. Meanwhile, in a small skillet, saute corn in oil until lightly browned; set aside. In a small saucepan, combine cream and butter. Cook, uncovered, over medium heat until butter is melted. Drain potatoes; mash. Add the cream mixture, sage, salt and pepper. Stir in corn. **YIELD:** 6 servings.

MAKE OVER YOUR MASHED POTATOES

It's hard to improve on a classic dish like mashed potatoes. But there are ways to add spark to a standard recipe. In addition to stirring in herbs and vegetables (like in Sage Mashed Potatoes with Corn), try these ideas:

- Instead of regular milk, substitute evaporated milk or half-and-half cream for a richer flavor.
- A few ounces of cream cheese makes mashed potatoes a decadent treat. Experiment with flavors like garlic and herb or chive and onion.
- For Garlic Mashed Potatoes, add a few whole peeled garlic cloves to the cooking water. Mash the garlic with the potatoes.
- Give "spuds" a nutritional boost! Stir in cooked sweet potatoes, parsnips or turnips and mash.

- After the potatoes have been mashed, fold in shredded cheese (like cheddar or mozzarella) and cooked, crumbled bacon.
- Replace the butter with sour cream. Then mix in chopped, sauteed mushrooms and onions.
- Bring a taste of the tropics to your table. Mash some ripe banana with your potatoes.
- Diced kalamata olives add a slight salty flavor.
- Chopped sweet onion and peeled, diced cucumber impart a refreshing, crunchy texture.
- Slice some shallots; saute in olive oil until crisp. Add to your mashed potato mixture.
- For an Italian twist, use olive oil instead of butter. Season with Parmesan cheese, basil and oregano.

herb-roasted vegetables

(PICTURED AT RIGHT)

I grow my own onions, and this is one way I like to showcase my harvest. Thyme, oregano and rosemary create the perfect seasoning blend for the slow-roasted vegetable medley.

Lisa Jane Morwald | *HAMILTON, ON*

1 small rutabaga, peeled and cut into 3/4-inch pieces

4 medium potatoes, cut into 1-inch pieces

4 medium carrots, cut into 1-inch pieces

1 medium onion, cut into 1-inch pieces

1/4 cup butter, melted

1 teaspoon salt

1/2 teaspoon dried oregano

1/2 teaspoon dried thyme

1/2 teaspoon dried rosemary, crushed

1/4 teaspoon pepper

In a large bowl, combine rutabaga, potatoes, carrots and onion. Add remaining ingredients; toss to coat. Arrange in a single layer in a greased 15-in. x 10-in. baking pan.

Bake, uncovered, at 400° for 45-55 minutes or until tender, stirring occasionally. **YIELD:** 8 servings.

three-grain side dish

Starring long grain rice, bulgur and barley, this is a deliciously different dressing. The unique texture and unbeatable blend of seasonings make it better than any box version I've tried. I think you'll agree!

Shirley Bedzis | SAN DIEGO, CA

3/4 cup sliced green onions

3/4 cup chopped celery

1/2 cup chopped dried apricots

1/2 cup golden raisins

3 tablespoons sherry

2 tablespoons butter

1 cup uncooked long grain rice

1 cup bulgur

1/2 cup quick-cooking barley

4 cups chicken broth

1-1/2 teaspoons poultry seasoning

1 teaspoon dried savory

1/2 teaspoon salt

1/4 cup minced fresh parsley

In a nonstick saucepan, saute the onions, celery, apricots and raisins in sherry and butter for 2 minutes or until sherry has evaporated. Stir in the rice, bulgur and barley; saute for 3 minutes.

Add the broth, poultry seasoning, savory and salt. Bring to a boil. Reduce heat; cover and simmer for 15-20 minutes or until rice is tender. Stir in parsley. **YIELD:** 10 servings.

creole bread dressing

I'm not known to be much of a cook, but I can make this recipe with success. When I take it to my company's holiday potluck, I always come home with an empty dish.

Terri Udy | COLORADO SPRINGS, CO

1 package (14 ounces) seasoned stuffing cubes

1 cup chopped pecans

1 small onion, chopped

1 celery rib, chopped

1/4 cup butter, cubed

1 pound uncooked large shrimp, peeled, deveined and cut into bite-size pieces

3 to 5 drops hot pepper sauce

1 can (14-1/2 ounces) chicken broth

1/4 cup egg substitute

1/2 teaspoon poultry seasoning

In a large bowl, combine stuffing cubes and pecans; set aside. In a large skillet, saute onion and celery in butter until tender. Add shrimp; cook and stir for 3 minutes or until the shrimp turn pink. Sprinkle with hot pepper sauce.

Add to stuffing mixture and toss to combine. Add the broth, egg substitute and poultry seasoning; toss to coat.

Spoon into a greased shallow 3-qt. baking dish. Bake, uncovered, at 350° for 30-35 minutes or until a thermometer inserted near the center reads 165°. The dressing may be stuffed into poultry if desired. **YIELD:** 10 cups.

golden au gratin potatoes

(PICTURED AT RIGHT)

With its golden, crunchy topping and gooey, cheesy interior, this comforting spin on a classic side dish is brimming with robust flavors. Horseradish and nutmeg add that extra-special touch.

Janice Elder | *CHARLOTTE, NC*

2 large onions, thinly sliced

2 tablespoons butter

1 cup half-and-half cream

1 cup canned pumpkin

1 tablespoon prepared horseradish

1/2 teaspoon ground nutmeg

1 teaspoon salt

1/2 teaspoon pepper

2-1/4 pounds potatoes, peeled and cut into 1/4-inch slices

2 cups soft bread crumbs

8 ounces Gruyere or Swiss cheese, shredded

2 tablespoons chopped fresh sage

In a large skillet, cook the onions in butter over medium heat for 15-20 minutes or until the onions are golden brown, stirring frequently.

In a large bowl, combine the cream, pumpkin, horseradish, nutmeg, salt and pepper. In a greased 13-in. x 9-in. baking pan, layer potato slices and onions. Spread with pumpkin mixture. Cover and bake at 350° for 1-1/4 hours.

Increase temperature to 400°. In a large bowl, combine the bread crumbs, cheese and sage. Sprinkle over top. Bake, uncovered, 15-20 minutes longer or until golden brown. **YIELD:** 15 servings.

WHAT IS AU GRATIN?

Au gratin is a French term meaning "with scrapings." Back in the day when cooks never let anything go to waste, dried bits of bread were scraped from the bottom of the baking pan. The crumbs were mixed with grated cheese and used to top dishes.

creamy sausage risotto

I have fond memories of standing at the stove cooking this hearty Italian rice dish with my Nona. I've altered the recipe a bit to save on time, but it still delivers just as much home-cooked love.

Amanda Cable | *BOXFORD, MA*

3 cans (14-1/2 ounces each) chicken broth

1 pound bulk Italian sausage

1/2 pound medium fresh mushrooms, quartered

1 medium onion, finely chopped

1 garlic clove, minced

Dash saffron threads

1 tablespoon butter

1 tablespoon canola oil

2 cups uncooked arborio rice

1/2 cup grated Parmesan cheese

1/2 cup heavy whipping cream

In a small saucepan, heat broth and keep warm. Meanwhile, in a large nonstick skillet, cook sausage over medium heat until meat is no longer pink; drain. Set aside and keep warm.

In the same skillet, saute the mushrooms, onion, garlic and saffron in butter and oil until tender, about 3 minutes. Add rice; cook and stir for 2-3 minutes. Carefully stir in 1 cup warm broth. Cook and stir until all of the liquid is absorbed.

Add remaining broth, 1/2 cup at a time, stirring constantly. Allow the liquid to absorb between additions. Cook until risotto is creamy and rice is almost tender. (Cooking time is about 20 minutes.) Add reserved sausage; heat through. Remove from the heat. Stir in cheese and cream. Serve immediately. **YIELD:** 12 servings.

easy caesar salad

Fans of Caesar salad will find the dressing used in this tasty version one of the best. My sister, Jan, developed the recipe and was nice enough to share her secret with me.

Dianne Nash | *KASLO, BC*

1/4 cup grated Parmesan cheese

1/4 cup mayonnaise

2 tablespoons milk

1 tablespoon lemon juice

1 tablespoon Dijon-mayonnaise blend

1 garlic clove, minced

Dash cayenne pepper

1 bunch romaine, torn

Salad croutons and additional grated Parmesan cheese, optional

In a small bowl, combine the first seven ingredients. Place romaine in a large bowl. Drizzle with dressing and toss to coat. Serve with salad croutons and additional cheese if desired. **YIELD:** 8 servings.

brussels sprouts in wine sauce

(PICTURED AT RIGHT)

Of all my favorite Christmas side dishes, this one stands above the rest. The wine sauce adds a lovely, rich flavor that makes every bite divine.

Stella Sargent | *ALEXANDRIA, VA*

1 package (16 ounces) frozen brussels sprouts

1/4 cup butter, cubed

1/4 cup all-purpose flour

1/2 teaspoon salt

1/4 teaspoon pepper

1 cup half-and-half cream

2/3 cup white wine or chicken broth

1 jar (16 ounces) whole onions, drained

2 tablespoons chopped almonds

1 tablespoon minced fresh parsley

1 tablespoon sliced almonds

Place brussels sprouts and a small amount of water in a microwave-safe dish. Cover and microwave on high for 2 minutes. Stir; microwave 1-2 minutes longer or until partially cooked. Let stand 5 minutes; drain and set aside.

In a large saucepan, melt butter. Stir in the flour, salt and pepper until smooth. Combine cream and wine. Gradually whisk into flour mixture. Bring to a boil. Cook and stir for 1-2 minutes or until thickened and bubbly. Stir in the onions, chopped almonds, parsley and reserved brussels sprouts.

Transfer to a greased 1-1/2-qt. baking dish. Sprinkle with sliced almonds. Bake, uncovered, at 400° for 20-25 minutes or until bubbly and brussels sprouts are tender. **YIELD:** 6 servings.

EDITOR'S NOTE: This recipe was tested in a 1,100-watt microwave.

pecan-mandarin tossed salad

*I enjoy making this fruity, crunchy salad for special events
and holiday dinners. Because of its mouthwatering blend of flavors and textures,
I've been asked to bring the salad to events for the past 25 years!*

Linda Curtis | RIPON, CA

4-1/2 teaspoons butter

2 cups pecan halves

2 tablespoons sugar

2 bunches romaine, torn

3 cups seedless red grapes

2 cups mandarin oranges, drained

4 celery ribs, chopped

6 green onions, chopped

DRESSING:

1 cup canola oil

1/2 cup white vinegar

6 tablespoons sugar

1 teaspoon salt

1 teaspoon ground mustard

1/2 teaspoon garlic powder

In a large heavy skillet, melt butter. Add pecans; cook over medium heat until nuts are toasted, about 4 minutes. Sprinkle with the sugar. Cook and stir for 2-4 minutes or until sugar is melted. Spread on foil to cool.

In a large salad bowl, combine romaine, grapes, oranges, celery and green onions. In a jar with a tight-fitting lid, combine the dressing ingredients; shake well. Drizzle over salad. Add pecans; toss to coat. **YIELD:** 22 servings (1 cup each).

raspberry-mallow sweet potatoes

*My idea of fun is taking old, reliable recipes and creating new taste twists from them. This is one such success story.
A classic holiday vegetable gets a delightful pick-me-up from raspberry preserves and marshmallow creme.*

Darlene Godschalx | PRESCOTT, AZ

4-1/2 pounds sweet potatoes, peeled and chopped (about 8 large)

1/4 cup packed brown sugar

1/4 cup maple syrup

2 tablespoons butter

1 jar (7 ounces) marshmallow creme

1/2 cup seedless raspberry jam, melted

Fresh raspberries, optional

Place sweet potatoes in a large saucepan. Cover with water. Bring to a boil. Reduce heat. Cover and simmer for 20-25 minutes or until the potatoes are tender; drain. Transfer to a large bowl; mash. Combine the brown sugar, syrup and butter; beat into the potatoes until smooth.

Spread potato mixture into a greased 13-in. x 9-in. baking dish. Drop marshmallow creme by tablespoonfuls over potatoes. Drizzle with jam. Cut through marshmallow creme with a knife to swirl. Cover and bake at 325° for 20-25 minutes or until heated through. Garnish with raspberries if desired. **YIELD:** 16-20 servings.

swiss chard bundles

(PICTURED AT RIGHT)

Tired of sauteed greens, I created this unique "stuffed" side dish that features Swiss chard. A robust blend of seasonings and two types of cheese pack the tender bundles with loads of flavor.

Laurie Bock | LYNDEN, WA

1 bunch Swiss chard

3 medium potatoes (about 1 pound), peeled and cubed

1 medium onion, chopped

6 garlic cloves, minced

1 tablespoon olive oil

1/4 cup white wine or chicken broth

1/4 cup minced fresh oregano

1/2 teaspoon crushed red pepper flakes

1/3 cup sour cream

1/4 cup grated Parmesan cheese

3 tablespoons shredded cheddar cheese

1/4 teaspoon salt

1/4 teaspoon pepper

2 medium tomatoes, chopped

1/4 cup shredded Parmesan cheese

Cook Swiss chard in boiling water for 2-3 minutes or until tender. Drain and pat dry. Cut out the thick vein from the bottom of eight leaves, making a V-shaped cut; set aside. (Refrigerate remaining Swiss chard for another use.)

Place potatoes in a large saucepan and cover with water. Bring to a boil. Reduce heat; cover and cook 15-20 minutes or until potatoes are tender.

Meanwhile, in a small skillet, cook the onion and garlic in oil until tender. Stir in the wine, oregano and pepper flakes. Bring to a boil; set aside.

Drain potatoes and mash. Stir in the wine mixture, sour cream, grated Parmesan cheese, cheddar cheese, salt and pepper. Overlapping cut ends of leaves, place about 1/3 cup potato mixture on each leaf. Fold in sides. Roll up completely to enclose filling.

Place seam side down in a greased 8-in. square baking dish. Cover and bake at 350° for 25 minutes. Sprinkle with the tomatoes and shredded Parmesan cheese. Bake, uncovered, 10-15 minutes longer or until the Swiss chard is tender and the cheese is melted. **YIELD:** 8 servings.

Friends and family will be dreaming of a white Christmas when you set your dessert table with a snowy selection of sweets.

These gorgeous treats may be light on color but they're heavy on unforgettable flavor!

Topped with a fluffy frosting and flaked coconut, Coconut Cake Supreme will be the star of any Christmas celebration.

Elegant Cannoli Cupcakes will make your holidays merry and bright, especially when served alongside Frosty Pineapple Punch.

TASTY TREATS
(PICTURED AT RIGHT)

Coconut Cake Supreme (p. 62)
Frosty Pineapple Punch (p. 64)
Cannoli Cupcakes (p. 64)

white christmas
DESSERTS

coconut cake supreme

(PICTURED ON PAGE 61)

When I need an impressive dessert for special occasions, this is the recipe I depend on. And guests are glad I do!
Edna Hoffman | *HEBRON, IN*

3/4 cup butter, softened

1-1/2 cups sugar, divided

1 teaspoon almond extract

1 teaspoon vanilla extract

2-3/4 cups cake flour

4 teaspoons baking powder

3/4 teaspoon salt

1 cup milk

4 egg whites

FROSTING:

2 cups sugar

3 egg whites

1/2 cup water

1 teaspoon vanilla extract

3 cups flaked coconut

In a large bowl, cream butter and 1 cup sugar until light and fluffy. Beat in extracts. Combine the flour, baking powder and salt; add to the creamed mixture alternately with milk.

In another bowl, beat egg whites until soft peaks form. Gradually add remaining sugar, 1 tablespoon at a time, beating until stiff peaks form. Fold into batter.

Pour into three greased and floured 9-in. round baking pans. Bake at 350° for 13-17 minutes or until a toothpick inserted near the center comes out clean. Cool for 10 minutes before removing from pans to wire racks to cool completely.

For frosting, in a heavy saucepan, combine the sugar, egg whites and water. With a portable mixer, beat mixture on low speed for 1 minute. Continue beating on low over low heat until frosting reaches 160°, about 10 minutes. Pour into a large bowl; add vanilla. Beat on high until frosting forms stiff peaks, about 7 minutes. Spread between layers and over top and sides of cake. Sprinkle with coconut. Store in the refrigerator. **YIELD:** 12 servings.

white cranberry-lime sorbet

Our Test Kitchen created this sorbet as a refreshing way to end heavy holiday meals. The sweet-tart combination of flavors is fantastic.

4 cups white cranberry juice

1 cup sugar

1/4 cup lime juice

1 teaspoon grated lime peel

In a large saucepan, bring cranberry juice and sugar to a boil. Cook and stir until sugar is dissolved. Remove from the heat; stir in lime juice and peel. Refrigerate until chilled.

Fill cylinder of ice cream freezer; freeze according to manufacturer's directions. Transfer sorbet to a freezer container; freeze for 4 hours or until firm. **YIELD:** 1-1/4 quarts.

italian lemon frozen dessert

(PICTURED AT RIGHT)

Lemon fans will favor the flavor of this invigorating dessert. I sometimes top individual servings with fresh berries.

Sally Sibthorpe | *SHELBY TOWNSHIP, MI*

5 eggs

1 cup sugar

1 cup ricotta cheese

1/2 cup plus 3 tablespoons butter, melted, divided

1 cup lemon juice

1 tablespoon grated lemon peel

1-1/2 cups heavy whipping cream

1 cup amaretti cookie crumbs

In a large bowl, beat the eggs, sugar and ricotta cheese; slowly add 1/2 cup butter. Stir in lemon juice and peel. Transfer to a large saucepan. Cook and stir over medium heat until mixture reaches at least 160° and coats the back of a metal spoon. Transfer to a large bowl; cool completely.

Line a 9-in. x 5-in. loaf pan with plastic wrap. In a small bowl, whip the cream until soft peaks form. Fold into cooled lemon mixture. Pour into prepared pan. Combine cookie crumbs and remaining butter; sprinkle over lemon mixture. Cover and freeze for several hours or overnight.

Remove from the freezer 10 minutes before serving. Using plastic wrap, lift dessert out of pan. Invert onto a serving platter; discard plastic wrap. Cut into slices. **YIELD:** 8 servings.

cannoli cupcakes

(PICTURED ON PAGE 60)

These jumbo cupcakes from our Test Kitchen feature a fluffy, creamy cannoli-like filling. White chocolate curls on top are the crowning touch.

1 package (18-1/4 ounces) white cake mix

3/4 cup heavy whipping cream, divided

1 cup ricotta cheese

1 cup confectioners' sugar

1/2 cup Mascarpone cheese

1/4 teaspoon almond extract

1/2 cup chopped pistachios

4 ounces white baking chocolate, chopped

White chocolate curls

Prepare cake mix batter according to package directions. Fill paper-lined jumbo muffin cups three-fourths full. Bake according to package directions for 24-28 minutes or until a toothpick inserted near the center comes out clean. Cool for 10 minutes before removing from pans to wire racks to cool completely.

In a small bowl, beat 1/2 cup cream until stiff peaks form; set aside. In a large bowl, combine the ricotta cheese, confectioner's sugar, Mascarpone cheese and extract until smooth. Fold in pistachios and reserved whipped cream.

Cut the top off of each cupcake. Spread or pipe cupcakes with cheese mixture; replace tops. In a small saucepan, melt white baking chocolate with remaining cream over low heat; stir until smooth. Remove from the heat. Cool to room temperature. Spoon over the cupcakes; sprinkle with the chocolate curls. Refrigerate leftovers. **YIELD:** 8 cupcakes.

frosty pineapple punch

(PICTURED ON PAGE 61)

This fun, refreshing punch has a nice combination of coconut and pineapple. The flavor is reminiscent of pina coladas.

Charlene Tennant | UPPER TRACT, WV

1 can (46 ounces) unsweetened pineapple juice, chilled

1 can (15 ounces) cream of coconut

1 quart vanilla ice cream

1 bottle (1 liter) club soda, chilled

In a punch bowl, combine pineapple juice and cream of coconut. Add scoops of ice cream; gradually pour in club soda. Serve immediately. **YIELD:** 16 servings (3 quarts).

DRIED PINEAPPLE GARNISH

Our home economists garnished Frosty Pineapple Punch with dried pineapple rings (see photo on page 61). If you can't find them at specialty grocery stores, make your own.

Peel a fresh pineapple. Cut into thin slices; remove core from the center of each slice. Place slices in a single layer on a parchment paper-lined baking sheet. Bake at 250° for 2 to 3 hours or until the pineapple slices are no longer juicy but not yet crunchy. Remove to a wire rack to cool. Store in an airtight container at room temperature.

berries with champagne cream

(PICTURED AT RIGHT)

This recipe came from a cooking class I attended at a local department store. I first served it to my husband on Valentine's Day, but now I make it for Christmas as well.

Michele Fehring | FISHERS, IN

8 egg yolks

1/2 cup sugar

1 cup champagne

1 cup heavy whipping cream, whipped

1 pint fresh raspberries

1 pint fresh strawberries

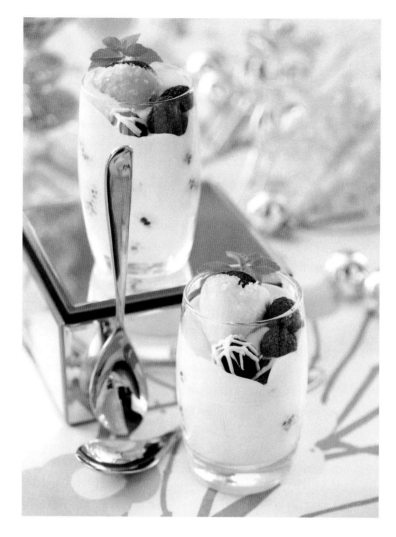

In a heavy saucepan, beat egg yolks and sugar with a portable mixer until thick and lemon-colored. Gradually beat in champagne. Place the saucepan over low heat. With a portable mixer, beat on low speed for 1 minute. Continue beating over low heat until mixture reaches 160°, about 5-6 minutes.

Cool quickly by placing pan in a bowl of ice water; stir for 2 minutes. Press plastic wrap onto surface of custard. Refrigerate until chilled.

Fold in whipped cream. Spoon three-quarters of the champagne cream into stemmed glasses. Top with berries. Spoon remaining champagne cream over berries. **YIELD:** 6 servings.

eggnog custard

Our home economists give a twist to traditional eggnog by using it to make individual, creamy custards.

5 egg yolks

1/3 cup sugar

2 cups eggnog

1/4 cup spiced rum

1 teaspoon vanilla extract

1/4 teaspoon salt

In a small bowl, whisk egg yolks and sugar. In a small saucepan, heat eggnog over medium heat until bubbles form around sides of pan. Remove from the heat; stir a small amount of eggnog into egg yolk mixture. Return all to the pan, stirring constantly. Stir in the rum, vanilla and salt.

Transfer to six 6-oz. ramekins or custard cups. Place ramekins in a baking pan; add 1 in. of boiling water to pan. Bake, uncovered, at 325° for 25-30 minutes or until centers are just set (mixture will jiggle). Remove ramekins from water bath; cool for 10 minutes. Cover and refrigerate for at least 4 hours. **YIELD:** 6 servings.

EDITOR'S NOTE: This recipe was tested with commercially prepared eggnog.

pineapple chiffon cake

My tall, moist cake makes quite an impression on a dessert table. Pineapple is a nice addition to the cake and frosting.

Joyce Maynard | *ST. IGNATIUS, MT*

2 cups all-purpose flour

1-3/4 cups sugar

3 teaspoons baking powder

1 teaspoon salt

8 eggs, separated

3/4 cup pineapple juice

1/2 cup canola oil

2 teaspoons vanilla extract

1/2 teaspoon cream of tartar

FROSTING:

3/4 cup butter, softened

2-1/2 cups confectioners' sugar

3 teaspoons vanilla extract

1 can (8 ounces) crushed pineapple, drained

In a large bowl, combine the flour, sugar, baking powder and salt. In another bowl, whisk the egg yolks, pineapple juice, oil and vanilla; add to dry ingredients. Beat until well blended. In another bowl, beat egg whites and cream of tartar until stiff peaks form; fold into batter.

Spoon into an ungreased 10-in. tube pan. Bake at 325° for 50-55 minutes or until top springs back when lightly touched. Immediately invert cake onto a wire rack; cool completely. Remove cake to a serving platter.

In a large bowl, cream the butter, confectioners' sugar and vanilla. Stir in pineapple. Frost cake. Store in the refrigerator. **YIELD:** 12-16 servings.

toffee crunch cheesecake

(PICTURED AT RIGHT)

This delectable cheesecake features chocolate-covered toffee bits in the crust and topping. It's the perfect dessert for any celebration.

Laura Mahaffey | ANNAPOLIS, MD

1-1/2 cups graham cracker crumbs

2 tablespoons brown sugar

1/3 cup butter, melted

1/2 teaspoon vanilla extract

1 cup milk chocolate English toffee bits

FILLING:

3 packages (8 ounces each) cream cheese, softened

1 cup sugar

1 cup (8 ounces) sour cream

3 teaspoons vanilla extract

4 eggs, lightly beaten

TOPPING:

1-1/2 cups sour cream

1/4 cup sugar

1 teaspoon vanilla extract

1/2 cup milk chocolate English toffee bits

In a small bowl, combine the cracker crumbs, brown sugar, butter and vanilla. Press onto the bottom and 2 in. up the sides of a greased 9-in. springform pan. Bake at 350° for 6-8 minutes or until set; cool on a wire rack. Sprinkle with toffee bits.

In a small bowl, beat cream cheese and sugar until smooth. Beat in sour cream and vanilla. Add eggs; beat on low speed just until combined. Pour into crust. Place pan on a baking sheet.

Bake at 350° for 50-60 minutes or until center is almost set. Cool on a wire rack for 10 minutes. Carefully run a knife around the edge of pan to loosen.

For topping, combine the sour cream, sugar and vanilla; spread over the cheesecake. Bake 5 minutes longer. Cool on a wire rack for 1 hour. Refrigerate overnight. Remove sides of pan. Sprinkle with toffee bits. **YIELD:** 12-14 servings.

white chocolate fudge

(PICTURED AT FAR RIGHT)

A small bite of this rich candy is all you need to satisfy a sweet tooth.
My family prefers it to the more common chocolate fudge.

Linda Wilkens | MAPLE GROVE, MN

1-1/2 teaspoons plus 1/2 cup butter, divided

2 cups sugar

1 can (12 ounces) evaporated milk

8 squares (1 ounce each) white baking chocolate, coarsely chopped

1 cup miniature marshmallows

1/2 cup flaked coconut

1/2 cup coarsely chopped walnuts

1 teaspoon vanilla extract

Line a 9-in. square pan with foil and grease the foil with 1-1/2 teaspoons butter; set aside. In a large heavy saucepan, combine the sugar, milk and remaining butter. Bring to a boil over medium-low heat, stirring constantly. Cook and stir for 30-40 minutes or until a candy thermometer reads 234° (soft-ball stage).

Remove from the heat; stir in white chocolate and marshmallows until melted. Stir in the coconut, nuts and vanilla. Pour into prepared pan. Let stand at room temperature until cool.

Using foil, lift fudge out of pan; cut into 1-in. squares. Store in an airtight container in the refrigerator. **YIELD:** 2 pounds.

EDITOR'S NOTE: We recommend that you test your candy thermometer before each use by bringing water to a boil; the thermometer should read 212°. Adjust your recipe temperature up or down based on your test.

coconut lace cookies

Delicate, crisp cookies such as these are a lovely addition to a Christmas cookie tray.
Every taste has great coconut flavor.

Clara Coulston Minney | WASHINGTON COURT HOUSE, OH

1-3/4 cups confectioners' sugar

1/3 cup all-purpose flour

1/3 cup coconut milk

1 teaspoon vanilla extract

1 cup flaked coconut

1/3 cup butter, melted

In a large bowl, combine the confectioners' sugar and flour. Stir in coconut milk and vanilla. Add coconut and butter; mix well. Cover and refrigerate for at least 30 minutes.

Drop by scant teaspoonfuls 3 in. apart onto foil-lined baking sheets. Bake at 350° for 6-7 minutes or until lacy and edges are golden brown. Allow cookies to cool completely before carefully removing from foil. **YIELD:** 4 dozen.

vanilla meringue cookies

(PICTURED AT RIGHT)

Holiday dinners often feature decadent, heavy desserts. So our home economists suggest you also offer these, light, airy morsels.

3 egg whites

1-1/2 teaspoons clear vanilla extract

1/4 teaspoon cream of tartar

Dash salt

3/4 cup sugar

Place egg whites in a small bowl; let stand at room temperature for 30 minutes. Add the vanilla, cream of tartar and salt; beat on medium speed until soft peaks form. Gradually beat in sugar, 1 tablespoon at a time, on high until stiff glossy peaks form and sugar is dissolved, about 7 minutes.

Cut a small hole in the corner of a pastry or plastic bag; insert a #32 star tip. Fill bag with egg white mixture. Pipe 1-1/4-in.-diameter cookies onto parchment paper-lined baking sheets.

Bake at 250° for 40-45 minutes or until set and dry. (Turn oven off; leave cookies in oven for 1 hour.) Carefully remove from parchment paper. Store in an airtight container. **YIELD**: about 5 dozen.

MAKING MERINGUE

1. In a large mixing bowl, beat the egg whites, cream of tartar, vanilla and salt on medium speed until the egg whites begin to increase in volume and soft peaks form. To test for soft peaks, the peaks of the egg whites should curl down when you lift up the beaters.

2. Add sugar, 1 tablespoon at a time, beating on high speed until stiff peaks form and sugar is dissolved. To test for stiff peaks, the peaks should stand straight up when you lift up the beaters; if you tilt the bowl, the whites should not slide around. Sugar is dissolved when the mixture feels silky-smooth between your fingers.

candy cane ice cream

I've become known for making all kinds of ice cream. At Christmas, family and friends request this minty treat.

Sandra McKenzie | BRAHAM, MN

1 cup milk

1/2 cup honey

1/8 teaspoon salt

2 eggs, beaten

2 cups heavy whipping cream

2 teaspoons peppermint extract

1/2 cup finely crushed peppermint candy

In a large heavy saucepan, heat milk to 175°; stir in honey and salt until combined. Whisk a small amount of the hot mixture into the eggs. Return all to the pan, whisking constantly. Cook and stir over low heat until mixture reaches at least 160° and coats the back of a metal spoon.

Remove from the heat. Cool quickly by placing pan in a bowl of ice water; stir for 2 minutes. Stir in whipping cream and extract. Press waxed paper onto surface of custard. Refrigerate for several hours or overnight.

Fill cylinder of ice cream freezer two-thirds full; freeze according to the manufacturer's directions. Add candy the last 3 minutes of freezing. When ice cream is frozen, transfer to a freezer container; freeze for 2-4 hours before serving. **YIELD:** 1 quart.

creamy coconut snowballs

My grandmother made these cheesecake-like bites for years.
They store nicely in the refrigerator so you can keep them on hand for drop-in holiday guests.

Yvonne Schaney | ALLIANCE, OH

1/2 teaspoon plus 1/2 cup butter, softened, divided

1-3/4 cups flaked coconut, divided

4 ounces cream cheese, softened

3-3/4 cups confectioners' sugar

8 ounces white candy coating, chopped

2 tablespoons shortening

Line a 9-in. x 5-in. loaf pan with foil and grease the foil with 1/2 teaspoon butter; set aside. Place 3/4 cup coconut in a food processor; cover and process into small pieces. Add cream cheese and remaining butter; cover and process until blended. Gradually add confectioners' sugar and process until blended. Press into prepared pan. Cover and refrigerate for at least 3 hours.

In a microwave-safe bowl, melt candy coating and shortening; stir until smooth. Cool slightly. Using foil, lift coconut mixture out of pan. Gently peel off foil; cut into 36 pieces. Roll each piece into a ball, a few at a time (keeping remaining pieces refrigerated).

Using a toothpick, completely dip the balls, one at a time, in the melted coating mixture, allowing excess to drip off. Roll in the remaining coconut; place on waxed paper-lined baking sheets. Refrigerate until set. Store in an airtight container in the refrigerator. **YIELD:** 1-1/2 pounds.

white christmas table

(PICTURED AT RIGHT)

To tie into the cool colors of the eye-catching desserts, set a pretty table using white, off-white and silver items.

First lay down a light-colored tablecloth. Choose clear glass, white or silver serving dishes for the desserts.

A floral arrangement and large white bottle-brush Christmas tree can star as the centerpieces in your display.

For simple party favors, purchase or make Christmas poppers.

Candles are a must at an evening holiday gathering. Place taper candles in glass candle holders. When shopping, look for white tree candles.

In addition to displaying white and silver ornaments, set silver tree toppers on the table, making sure they sit flat. As the finishing touch, fill bowls or apothecary jars with fragrant potpourri.

WHITE ELEPHANT GIFT EXCHANGE

Add a little lighthearted fun to your dessert party by incorporating a White Elephant Gift Exchange (also known as a Yankee Swap).

Ask each guest to bring a wrapped "gag" gift. It's usually funny, ugly or out of date. It can be something from your attic, a discount store or a garage sale. Think old workout videos, hideous jewelry, weird knick-knacks and fad items (like a pet rock). The more strange it is, the more laughs it'll get!

Have each guest draw a number. The first number picks a gift from the pile and opens it. Each succeeding person can either pick a new gift from the pile or take someone else's unwrapped gift. If someone's unwrapped gift is taken, that person gets to choose another wrapped or unwrapped gift. Play continues until the last gift from the pile is selected and unwrapped.

Oftentimes, people set rules to the game. For instance, an item can't immediately be stolen back from the person who took it by the person it was taken from. Gifts are "frozen" after three owners.

*T*he family is snug in their beds. Their stockings are hung with care...and filled to the brim with tempting cookies and candies.

The joy of Christmas goodies goes beyond eating them. True holiday cheer is shared by giving the homemade confections away as lip-smacking stocking stuffers.

Imagine the delight of waking up Christmas morning to such tasty treats as buttery, chocolaty Ben's English Toffee and melt-in-your-mouth Cinnamon Crescent Cookies.

A festive stocking that holds a decorative tin filled with pretty Chocolate-Nut Pinwheel Cookies and other sweet surprises makes the perfect last-minute gift, hostess thank-you or solution for the hard-to-buy-for family member.

SWEET STOCKING STUFFERS
(PICTURED AT RIGHT)

Ben's English Toffee (p. 74)
Cinnamon Crescent Cookies (p. 76)
Chocolate-Nut Pinwheel Cookies (p. 74)

christmas
COOKIES & CANDIES

ben's english toffee

(PICTURED ON PAGE 72)

*This rich, buttery toffee is covered in chocolate and sprinkled with nuts.
The melt-in-your-mouth texture makes this candy a favorite of everyone who tries it.*

Ben Lohse | WORCESTER, PA

2 teaspoons plus 1/2 cup butter, cubed

1-3/4 cups sugar

1/8 teaspoon cream of tartar

1 cup heavy whipping cream

1 teaspoon rum extract

1 cup milk chocolate chips

1 cup mixed nuts, chopped and toasted

Grease a 15-in. x 10-in. pan with 2 teaspoons butter; set aside.

In a large heavy saucepan, combine sugar and cream of tartar; stir in cream and remaining butter. Cook and stir over medium heat until a candy thermometer reads 300° (hard-crack stage). Remove from the heat; stir in extract. Quickly pour into prepared pan. Let stand at room temperature until cool.

In a microwave, melt chocolate chips; stir until smooth. Spread over toffee. Sprinkle with nuts. Let stand until set, about 1 hour. Break into pieces. Store in an airtight container. **YIELD:** 1-3/4 pounds.

EDITOR'S NOTE: We recommend that you test your candy thermometer before each use by bringing water to a boil; the thermometer should read 212°. Adjust your recipe temperature up or down based on your test.

chocolate-nut pinwheel cookies

(PICTURED ON PAGE 73)

The chocolate and almond flavors packed into these pretty cookies make them stand out among other sweet treats. The dough is easy to handle and slices nicely for a beautiful pinwheel appearance.

Sedonie Zeitler | LUXEMBURG, WI

2/3 cup butter, softened

3/4 cup sugar

1 egg

1 teaspoon vanilla extract

1-3/4 cups all-purpose flour

1/2 teaspoon baking powder

1/4 teaspoon salt

1/3 cup ground almonds

1/4 teaspoon almond extract

1/4 cup baking cocoa

In a large bowl, cream butter and sugar until light and fluffy. Beat in egg and vanilla. Combine the flour, baking powder and salt; gradually add to creamed mixture and mix well. Divide dough in half; add almonds and almond extract to one portion. Add cocoa to remaining portion.

Roll out each portion between two sheets of waxed paper into a 16-in. x 8-in. rectangle. Refrigerate for 30 minutes. Remove waxed paper. Place almond layer over chocolate dough. Roll up tightly jelly-roll style, starting with a long side; wrap in plastic wrap. Refrigerate overnight or until firm.

Unwrap and cut into 1/4-in. slices. Place 2 in. apart on ungreased baking sheets. Bake at 350° for 9-11 minutes or until set. Remove to wire racks to cool. **YIELD:** about 5 dozen.

reindeer snack mix

(PICTURED AT RIGHT)

Sweet white chocolate coats a yummy combination of pretzels, peanuts and peanut butter-flavored cereal. Because it takes only 15 minutes to make, it's a simple, last-minute gift.

Lisa Bianco | *PALM COAST, FL*

4-1/2 cups puffed peanut butter and chocolate cereal

4 cups miniature pretzels

1 can (12 ounces) salted peanuts

1 package (12 ounces) vanilla or white chips

In a large bowl, combine the cereal, pretzels and peanuts. In a microwave, melt the chips; stir until smooth. Pour over the cereal mixture and toss to coat. Immediately spread onto waxed paper-lined baking sheets; let stand until set, about 20 minutes. Break into pieces. Store in an airtight container. **YIELD:** 3 quarts.

CANDY-MAKING POINTERS

It's actually quite simple to make candy from scratch if you keep in mind these pointers. Always test your candy thermometer before each use, and be sure to measure and assemble all ingredients for a recipe before beginning. It's best to use heavy-gauge saucepans that are deep enough to allow candy mixtures to boil freely without boiling over and to use wooden spoons with long handles for stirring.

santa's fruit & nut cookies

(PICTURED AT FAR RIGHT)

This recipe is a delightful Yuletide treat a co-worker shared with me. Since then, I've made them for every Christmas party I've been invited to. The yummy cookies haven't failed me once!

Sherry Turner | MIAMI, FL

1-1/2 cups all-purpose flour

1/4 cup sugar

1-1/2 teaspoons baking powder

1/4 teaspoon salt

1/3 cup shortening

1/2 cup milk

1 cup chopped mixed candied fruit

1/2 cup chopped walnuts

ICING:

1 cup confectioners' sugar

1 to 2 tablespoons milk

In a large bowl, combine the flour, sugar, baking powder and salt. Cut in shortening until crumbly. Stir in milk just until moistened. Stir in fruit and nuts.

On a floured surface, roll or pat the dough into a 12-in. x 6-in. rectangle. Cut into 4-in. x 1/2-in. strips. Form into "S" shapes; place 1 in. apart on greased baking sheets.

Bake at 425° for 6-8 minutes or until lightly browned. Cool on wire racks. Combine the confectioners' sugar and enough milk to achieve a drizzling consistency; drizzle over the cookies. **YIELD:** 3 dozen.

cinnamon crescent cookies

(PICTURED ON PAGE 73)

These light, delicate gems are among my favorite Christmas goodies. I enjoy them with coffee or hot tea, but Santa can relish them with a tall glass of milk.

Theresa Jarabak | JOHNSTOWN, PA

4 cups all-purpose flour

3/4 cup cold butter

1 cup sour cream

3 egg yolks

2 teaspoons vanilla extract

2 egg whites

2 tablespoons water

1 cup sugar

3 teaspoons ground cinnamon

Place flour in a large bowl; cut in butter until mixture resembles coarse crumbs. In a small bowl, whisk the sour cream, egg yolks and vanilla; add to crumb mixture and mix until dough forms a ball. Cover and refrigerate for 4 hours or overnight.

Divide dough into fourths. On a lightly floured surface, roll each portion into a 10-in. circle.

Whisk egg whites and water; brush over dough. Combine sugar and cinnamon; set aside 1/4 cup. Sprinkle remaining cinnamon-sugar over the dough. Cut each circle into eight wedges.

Roll up each wedge from the wide end; roll in reserved cinnamon-sugar. Place point side down 1 in. apart on greased baking sheets. Curve ends to form crescents.

Bake at 375° for 15-17 minutes or until lightly browned. Remove to wire racks to cool. Store in an airtight container. **YIELD:** 32 cookies.

hazelnut cutout cookies

(PICTURED AT RIGHT)

The recipe for these thin, crispy cutouts is my grandmother's. We'd always enjoy a batch at Christmastime. The lovely hazelnut flavor is wonderful.

Alice LeBlanc | ALBURG, VT

1 cup butter, softened

2 cups sugar

1 egg white

2 cups all-purpose flour

Dash baking soda

2 cups ground hazelnuts

1/4 cup confectioners' sugar or vanilla sugar

In a large bowl, cream butter and sugar until light and fluffy. Beat in egg white. Combine flour and baking soda; gradually add to creamed mixture and mix well. Beat in hazelnuts. Cover and refrigerate overnight or until easy to handle.

On a lightly floured surface, roll out to 1/4-in. thickness. Cut with floured 2-in. cookie cutters. Place 1 in. apart on ungreased baking sheets. Bake at 350° for 6-8 minutes or until the edges are lightly browned. Remove to wire racks to cool.

Dust with confectioners' sugar. Store in an airtight container. **YIELD:** 6 dozen.

turtle candies

Sweet, chewy caramel and salty, crunchy pecans are a match made in heaven in these homemade delights. Prepare a batch of the gooey clusters to add to your dessert offerings or as yummy stocking stuffers.

Carole Wiese | *NEW BERLIN, WI*

1 pound pecan halves, toasted

1 can (14 ounces) sweetened condensed milk

3/4 cup light corn syrup

1/2 cup sugar

1/3 cup packed brown sugar

1/4 cup butter, cubed

1-1/2 teaspoons vanilla extract

1 pound milk chocolate candy coating, chopped

On waxed paper-lined baking sheets, arrange pecans in small clusters of four to five pecans each.

For caramel, in a small saucepan, combine the milk, corn syrup and sugars. Cook and stir over medium heat until a candy thermometer reads 238° (soft-ball stage). Remove from the heat. Stir in butter and vanilla. Working quickly, spoon caramel onto pecan clusters. Let stand until set.

In a microwave, melt candy coating; stir until smooth. Spoon over caramel. Chill for 10 minutes or until set. Store in an airtight container. **YIELD:** 4 dozen.

EDITOR'S NOTE: We recommend that you test your candy thermometer before each use by bringing water to a boil; the thermometer should read 212°. Adjust your recipe temperature up or down based on your test.

slice & bake chocolate pecan cookies

Toasting the pecans makes all the difference in this holiday favorite. The chocolate drizzle satisfies the chocolate-lovers in my family and makes the cookies look like they're from the best bakery in town.

Lindsay Weiss | *OVERLAND PARK, KS*

1-1/2 cups butter, softened

2-1/4 cups confectioners' sugar

1 egg

3 teaspoons vanilla extract

3-1/4 cups all-purpose flour

1/2 cup baking cocoa

1/2 teaspoon baking powder

1-2/3 cups chopped pecans, toasted

1 cup (6 ounces) semisweet chocolate chips

1 cup vanilla or white chips

In a large bowl, cream butter and confectioners' sugar until light and fluffy. Beat in egg and vanilla. Combine the flour, cocoa and baking powder; gradually add to creamed mixture and mix well. Stir in the pecans.

Shape into four 6-in. logs; wrap in plastic wrap. Refrigerate for 2 hours or until firm. Unwrap the dough and cut into 1/4-in. slices. Place 2 in. apart on ungreased baking sheets. Bake at 375° for 10-12 minutes or until firm. Remove to wire racks to cool.

In a microwave, melt semisweet chocolate chips; stir until smooth. Drizzle over cookies. Repeat with vanilla chips. Let stand until set. Store in an airtight container. **YIELD:** 8 dozen.

dark chocolate orange truffles

(PICTURED AT RIGHT)

I love chocolate truffles, so you can imagine my delight when I came across the recipe for these dark and decadent confections. The hint of orange makes them deliciously different from other candies.

Theresa Young | MCHENRY, IL

1 package (12 ounces) dark chocolate chips

3/4 cup heavy whipping cream

1 teaspoon orange extract

1/3 cup sugar

In a microwave, melt chocolate; stir until smooth. Gradually stir in cream until blended. Stir in extract. Cool to room temperature, stirring occasionally. Refrigerate until firm. Shape into 3/4-in. balls. Roll in sugar.
YIELD: 2-1/2 dozen.

SANTA HAT-TOPPED TRUFFLES

If you thought truffles couldn't get any cuter, we found a way to dress them up! For an extra-special touch—and to complement the candy's slight citrus flavor—roll Dark Chocolate Orange Truffles in orange-colored sugar. Then top truffles with miniature Santa hats. Turn the truffles into a placeholder by tucking in a slip of paper with each guest's name.

peppermint truffle bars

(PICTURED AT FAR RIGHT)

The combination of textures created by the creamy chocolate layer and flaky shortbread crust is nothing short of extraordinary. The mint flavor comes through with every bite, making these bars a holiday favorite.

Alysha Braun | ST. CATHARINES, ON

1 teaspoon plus 3/4 cup cold butter

1-1/2 cups all-purpose flour

3/4 cup confectioners' sugar

1/4 teaspoon salt

1/2 teaspoon vanilla extract

FILLING:

16 squares (1 ounce each) semisweet chocolate, chopped

3/4 cup milk

1/2 cup butter, cubed

4 eggs

2/3 cup sugar

1 teaspoon peppermint extract

Line a 13-in. x 9-in. baking pan with foil; grease the foil with 1 teaspoon butter. In a large bowl, combine the flour, confectioners' sugar and salt. Add vanilla and remaining butter; cut in butter until mixture resembles fine crumbs. Pat into prepared pan.

Bake at 325° for 20-25 minutes or until edges are lightly browned. Cool on a wire rack.

In a large saucepan, combine the chocolate, milk and butter. Cook and stir over low heat until smooth; set aside.

In a large bowl, beat eggs and sugar until thick and lemon-colored. Beat in extract and chocolate mixture. Pour over crust. Bake for 30-35 minutes or until center is almost set. Cool completely in pan on a wire rack.

Refrigerate overnight. Using foil, lift bars out of pan; cut into triangles. Store in the refrigerator. **YIELD:** 7 dozen.

lemon shortbread cookies

My cousin tried to duplicate the cookies she loves so much at a favorite restaurant and this was the mouthwatering result. Sparkling with sunny lemon flavor, they disappear quickly!

Lorie Miner | KAMAS, UT

1/2 cup butter, softened

1/3 cup sugar

4 teaspoons grated lemon peel

1 teaspoon vanilla extract

1 cup all-purpose flour

2 tablespoons plus 1-1/2 teaspoons cornstarch

1/4 teaspoon ground nutmeg

1/8 teaspoon salt

DRIZZLE:

1/2 cup confectioners' sugar

2 to 3 teaspoons lemon juice

In a small bowl, cream butter and sugar until light and fluffy. Beat in lemon peel and vanilla. Combine the flour, cornstarch, nutmeg and salt; gradually add to creamed mixture and mix well. (Dough will be crumbly.) Shape into a ball.

On a lightly floured surface, press dough to 1/2-in. thickness. Cut with a floured 1-in. fluted cookie cutter; place 1 in. apart on ungreased baking sheets. Prick cookies with a fork. Reroll scraps if desired. Bake at 350° for 12-15 minutes or until firm. Cool for 2 minutes before carefully removing to wire racks to cool completely.

Combine confectioners' sugar and lemon juice; drizzle over cookies. Store in an airtight container. **YIELD:** 2 dozen.

coconut rocky road treats

(PICTURED AT RIGHT)

This sweet, chocolaty treat is a welcome addition to your assortment of Christmas sweets. The simple, tasty recipe was given to me by my sister, and continues to be one she makes every year.

Dawn Supina | *EDMONTON, AB*

1 cup butterscotch chips

1 cup semisweet chocolate chips

1 package (8 ounces) cream cheese, cubed

2 cups miniature marshmallows

1/2 cup chopped walnuts

2 cups flaked coconut

Line a baking sheet with waxed paper; set aside. In a saucepan, combine the butterscotch chips, chocolate chips and cream cheese. Cook and stir over low heat until smooth. Remove from the heat; stir in marshmallows and nuts. Cool slightly.

Shape into 1-in. balls and roll in the coconut. Place on prepared baking sheet. Refrigerate for 1 hour or until firm. Store in an airtight container in the refrigerator. **YIELD:** about 4-1/2 dozen.

nutty maple cookies

I make these sweet, small indulgences every Yuletide season.
The rich maple taste adds wonderful variety to a platter of Christmas cookies.

Lillian Anderson | WEBSTER, WI

2/3 cup butter, softened

1/3 cup confectioners' sugar

1 tablespoon water

1 teaspoon maple flavoring

1-3/4 cups all-purpose flour

1/2 teaspoon salt

1 cup chopped walnuts

FROSTING:

1/4 cup butter, softened

1-1/2 cups confectioners' sugar

2 tablespoons heavy whipping cream

1 teaspoon maple flavoring

Additional chopped walnuts, optional

In a large bowl, cream butter and confectioners' sugar until light and fluffy. Beat in water and flavoring. Combine flour and salt; gradually add to creamed mixture and mix well. Stir in walnuts.

Roll into 1-in. balls; flatten to 1/2-in. thickness with a fork. Place 2 in. apart on ungreased baking sheets. Bake at 350° for 10-12 minutes or until lightly browned. Cool on wire racks.

For frosting, in a small bowl, beat the butter, confectioners' sugar, cream and flavoring until smooth. Frost cookies. Sprinkle with additional walnuts if desired. YIELD: 3 dozen.

peanut caramel delights

I enjoy making goodies as gifts for the holidays, and this one is perfect to give away
to friends and family. The flavor is reminiscent of a popular candy bar.

Kathy Albright | READING, MI

1 teaspoon plus 2 tablespoons butter, softened

1/4 cup light corn syrup

2 tablespoons creamy peanut butter

1 tablespoon vanilla extract

1/4 teaspoon salt

3 cups confectioners' sugar

1 package (14 ounces) caramels

2 tablespoons water

1 cup unsalted dry roasted peanuts

3 cups milk chocolate chips

Line an 8-in. square dish with foil; grease foil with 1 teaspoon butter and set aside.

In a large bowl, combine the corn syrup, peanut butter, vanilla, salt and remaining butter. Beat on high speed for 1 minute. Gradually add confectioners' sugar and mix well. Press into prepared pan.

In a large microwave-safe bowl, melt caramels with water; stir until smooth. Stir in peanuts. Pour over corn syrup mixture. Refrigerate for 1-1/2 hours or until firm.

Using foil, lift the candy out of pan. Invert onto a cutting board; cut into 1-in. pieces. In a microwave, melt the chocolate chips; stir until smooth. Dip the candy in chocolate, allowing excess to drip off. Place on waxed paper; let stand until set. Store in the refrigerator. YIELD: 2-3/4 pounds.

homemade candy canes

(PICTURED AT RIGHT)

As a fun way to get into the Christmas spirit, invite friends and family over to make homemade candy canes! Our home economists used peppermint and spearmint extracts, but feel free to experiment with different flavored extracts to suit your family's taste.

1 teaspoon butter

1 cup sugar

1 cup water

1 cup light corn syrup

1/4 teaspoon cream of tartar

1 teaspoon peppermint or spearmint extract

6 drops red or green food coloring

Grease two baking sheets with butter; set aside. In a large saucepan, bring the sugar, water, corn syrup and cream of tartar to a boil. Cook, without stirring, until a candy thermometer reads 280° (soft-crack stage).

Remove from the heat; stir in the extract and food coloring. Immediately pour onto prepared pans in eight 8-in. strips. Let stand just until cool enough to handle, about 1-2 minutes.

Working quickly, roll each strip into a 10-in. log. Cut each into two 5-in. lengths. Curve the top of each to form the handle of a cane. Cool completely. Store in an airtight container. **YIELD:** 16 canes.

EDITOR'S NOTE: We recommend that you test your candy thermometer before each use by bringing water to a boil; the thermometer should read 212°. Adjust your recipe temperature up or down based on your test.

*L*ooking for a unique party idea this Christmas season? Consider a progressive dinner party, whereby a group of friends plan a meal together. Then each couple prepares and serves one course at their home. The party moves from place to place during the night.

The five courses featured in this chapter are: appetizers and cocktails; soup and salad; entree and side dish; dessert; after-dinner drinks and cookies.

MOVING MEAL

progressive
DINNER PARTY

zucchini saltimbocca

(PICTURED AT FAR RIGHT)

These unique, sandwich-like snacks have the best of both worlds...a crunchy outside and a cheesy inside!
Even folks who don't like zucchini will gobble them up. For even more savory flavor,
serve them with heated marinara sauce.

Janet Rinehart | CHILLICOTE, OH

1 medium zucchini

2 ounces Asiago cheese, thinly sliced

8 fresh sage leaves

8 thin slices prosciutto or deli ham

1/2 cup all-purpose flour

3 egg whites, lightly beaten

1 cup seasoned bread crumbs

Cut zucchini lengthwise into eight 1/4-in. slices; discard ends. Layer cheese and sage on four zucchini slices; top with remaining zucchini. Wrap two pieces of prosciutto around each zucchini stack. Carefully cut each stack widthwise into fourths.

Place the flour, egg whites and bread crumbs in separate shallow bowls. Dip stacks in flour, egg whites, then bread crumbs. Place on a greased baking sheet. Bake, uncovered, at 425° for 10-15 minutes or until golden brown, turning once. YIELD: 16 servings.

holiday cocktail

(PICTURED AT FAR RIGHT)

With sweet vermouth, scotch and brandy, this cocktail from our Test Kitchen
will warm the souls of your dinner guests! Add a bit more club soda if the drink is stronger than you like.
A maraschino cherry garnish would add a bit of color and sweetness.

Ice cubes

1-1/2 ounces Scotch

1 ounce brandy

1/2 ounce sweet vermouth

1/2 ounce chilled club soda

Splash grenadine syrup

Fill a rocks glass with ice cubes. Add the remaining ingredients. YIELD: 1 serving.

blue cheese spread

(PICTURED AT RIGHT)

When entertaining during the holidays, it's nice to have make-ahead recipes like this. Crunchy toasted walnuts complement the creamy spread.

Carol Bess White | PORTLAND, OR

3 shallots, finely chopped

2 teaspoons butter

2 cups (8 ounces) crumbled blue cheese

2 packages (8 ounces each) cream cheese, softened

1/2 cup sour cream

2 tablespoons Cognac or brandy

1/4 teaspoon salt

1/4 teaspoon white pepper

1/2 cup chopped walnuts, toasted

Assorted crackers

In a small skillet, saute shallots in butter until tender. Remove from the heat; cool.

Meanwhile, in a large bowl, combine the cheeses, sour cream, Cognac, salt and pepper. Add shallots and mix well. Line a 3-cup bowl with plastic wrap. Spread cheese mixture into prepared bowl. Cover and refrigerate for at least 1 hour.

Unmold onto a serving plate; garnish with walnuts. Serve with crackers. **YIELD:** 3 cups.

APPETIZER AGENDA

The host of the Progressive Dinner Party's first course has a little less pressure to get things done in advance. But there are some do-ahead elements that will make entertaining even easier.

• Make the Blue Cheese Spread early in the day and refrigerate. Just before guests arrive, unmold, garnish with walnuts and serve with crackers.

• For the Zucchini Saltimbocca, you can assemble the stacks 1 to 2 hours before the party. Bake them as guests arrive at your house.

• Have the ingredients for Holiday Cocktails ready to go on your counter. But make the drinks as requested by guests.

mushroom-spinach cream soup

(PICTURED AT FAR RIGHT)

*Fresh mushrooms are a surprise for the palate in creamy spinach soup.
You can make it in advance and reheat it just before serving.*

Patricia Kile | GREENTOWN, PA

1 pound sliced fresh mushrooms

2 small onions, chopped

6 tablespoons butter, cubed

1/2 cup all-purpose flour

2 teaspoons Italian seasoning

1/2 teaspoon onion powder

1/2 teaspoon pepper

1/8 teaspoon paprika

4 cups milk

1 carton (32 ounces) chicken broth

2 packages (10 ounces each) frozen chopped spinach, thawed and squeezed dry

In a large saucepan, saute the mushrooms and onions in butter until tender. Stir in the flour and seasonings until blended; gradually add the milk and broth. Bring to a boil; cook and stir for 2 minutes or until thickened.

Stir in spinach. Reduce heat; cover and simmer for 5 minutes or until heated through. **YIELD:** 10 servings (2-1/2 quarts).

endive watercress salad

(PICTURED AT RIGHT)

Two kinds of greens, cucumber and orange slices are coated with a light ginger dressing in this recipe from our Test Kitchen.

10 cups watercress

4 cups thinly sliced Belgian endive

3 medium navel oranges, peeled and sliced

1 medium cucumber, halved and thinly sliced

10 slices red onion, separated into rings

DRESSING:

2/3 cup canola oil

1/4 cup lemon juice

1/4 cup rice vinegar

1/4 cup olive oil

4 teaspoons Dijon mustard

2 teaspoons ground ginger

1-1/2 teaspoons sugar

1/2 teaspoon salt

1/4 teaspoon pepper

Divide the watercress and endive among 10 salad plates. Arrange the oranges, cucumber and onion over salad greens. In a jar with a tight-fitting lid, combine the dressing ingredients; shake well. Drizzle over the salads. **YIELD:** 10 servings.

SPEEDY SOUP & SALAD

Doing your slicing, chopping and thawing well in advance will prevent lots of last-minute rush.

- Two days before, thaw the spinach for Mushroom-Spinach Cream Soup in the refrigerator. The morning of the party, drain the spinach; cover and chill. Also, prepare the soup up to the point of stirring in the spinach. When you return to your house, reheat the soup over low heat and stir in the spinach.
- For Endive Watercress Salad, make the dressing the day before; refrigerate. Slice the endive, oranges, cucumber and red onion; store in separate containers until ready to assemble.

MAKE-AHEAD MAIN COURSE

The main course can be the most challenging part of a progressive dinner. But with a slow-cooked brisket and quick-cooking orzo, dinner can be served in a dash.

- Prepare the dressing for the Orzo with Feta & Almonds the day before; cover and chill. Chop the onion, toast the almonds and grate the lemon; store in separate containers. The day of the party, finish the recipe while the beef is standing.

- A day ahead of time, make the barbecue sauce for the Zippy Barbecued Beef Brisket and marinate the meat. Place in the oven at 325° before heading out for the first course.

orzo with feta & almonds

(PICTURED AT FAR RIGHT)

Quick-cooking orzo pasta is the secret to getting this side dish on the table in a jiffy. It pairs well with a variety of entrees.

Clara Coulston Minney | *WASHINGTON COURT HOUSE, OH*

1 package (16 ounces) orzo pasta

1 large onion, chopped

8 tablespoons olive oil, divided

2 cups (8 ounces) crumbled feta cheese

1 cup sliced almonds, toasted

1/2 cup dried currants

3 tablespoons minced fresh parsley

2 tablespoons minced fresh oregano or 2 teaspoons dried oregano

2 tablespoons lemon juice

2 teaspoons grated lemon peel

1/4 teaspoon salt

1/4 teaspoon pepper

Cook orzo according to package directions. Meanwhile, in a large skillet, saute onion in 1 tablespoon oil until tender. Drain orzo; transfer to a large bowl. Add the cheese, almonds, currants, parsley, oregano and onion.

In a small bowl, whisk the lemon juice, peel, salt, pepper and the remaining olive oil. Drizzle over orzo mixture; toss to coat. **YIELD:** 12 servings.

zippy barbecued beef brisket

(PICTURED AT RIGHT)

This is an authentic Texas dish from a good friend. The tangy sauce not only helps tenderize the meat but also provides fantastic flavor.

Joan Hallford | NORTH RICHLAND HILLS, TX

1 cup ketchup

3 celery ribs, finely chopped

1/2 cup water

1/2 cup cider vinegar

1/4 cup butter, cubed

1/4 cup Worcestershire sauce

3 bay leaves

2 tablespoons finely chopped onion

1 tablespoon paprika

1 garlic clove, minced

1 teaspoon sugar

1 teaspoon chili powder

Dash pepper

MARINADE:

2 tablespoons Liquid Smoke, optional

1 tablespoon teriyaki sauce

2 teaspoons celery seed

2 teaspoons pepper

1 teaspoon each salt, garlic salt and onion salt

1 fresh beef brisket (about 5 pounds)

For barbecue sauce, in a large saucepan, combine the first 13 ingredients. Bring to a boil. Reduce heat; simmer, uncovered, for 15 minutes, stirring occasionally. Remove from the heat. Strain sauce, discarding bay leaves and vegetable pulp; set aside.

For marinade, in a large resealable plastic bag, combine the Liquid Smoke if desired, teriyaki sauce, celery seed, pepper, salts and 1 cup reserved barbecue sauce. Add the brisket. Seal bag and turn to coat; refrigerate for 8 hours or overnight, turning occasionally. Cover and refrigerate remaining barbecue sauce.

Drain and discard marinade. Place brisket on a large sheet of heavy-duty foil; seal tightly. Place in a greased 15-in. x 10-in. x 1-in. baking pan. Bake at 325° for 3-4 hours or until meat is tender.

Remove brisket to a serving platter; let stand for 15 minutes. Reheat reserved sauce. Thinly slice meat across the grain. Serve with sauce. **YIELD:** 10 servings.

EDITOR'S NOTE: This is a fresh beef brisket, not corned beef.

citrus-banana ice cream

Of all the homemade ice creams I make, this is my favorite.
The combination of banana and citrus flavors is simply delicious.

Sharon Dearden | HENEFER, UT

3 cups milk

3 cups sugar

3 medium ripe bananas, mashed

1-1/3 cups orange juice

2/3 cup lemon juice

3 cups heavy whipping cream

In a large saucepan, heat the milk to 175°; stir in the sugar until dissolved. Cool quickly by placing the pan in a bowl of ice water; stir for 2 minutes.

In a large bowl, combine the bananas, orange juice and lemon juice; stir in cream and milk mixture.

Fill the cylinder of ice cream freezer two-thirds full; freeze according to the manufacturer's directions. Refrigerate the remaining mixture until ready to freeze. When the ice cream is frozen, transfer to a freezer container; freeze for 2-4 hours before serving. **YIELD:** about 3 quarts.

chocolate mint cake

This lovely layered cake takes some time to prepare, but cake mix gives it a head start.
The mint flavor is so refreshing after a holiday meal.

Debbie Taylor | WHITE BLUFF, TN

1 package (18-1/4 ounces) devil's food cake mix

1-1/3 cups water

3 eggs

1/2 cup canola oil

1 teaspoon mint extract

FILLING:

1/2 cup shortening

2 tablespoons water

1/4 teaspoon vanilla extract

1/4 teaspoon butter flavoring

2 cups confectioners' sugar

15 chocolate-covered peppermint patties

FROSTING:

2 cups shortening

2/3 cup baking cocoa

1/4 cup water

1 teaspoon mint extract

1/2 teaspoon vanilla extract

1/2 teaspoon butter flavoring

4 cups confectioners' sugar

In a large bowl, combine the cake mix, water, eggs, oil and extract; beat on low speed for 30 seconds. Beat on medium for 2 minutes.

Pour into three greased and floured 9-in. round baking pans. Bake at 350° for 18-22 minutes or until a toothpick inserted near the center comes out clean. Cool for 10 minutes before removing from pans to wire racks to cool completely.

For filling, combine the shortening, water, vanilla and flavoring; gradually add confectioners' sugar and mix well. Mash patties; stir into filling.

For frosting, in a large bowl, combine the shortening, cocoa, water, extracts and flavoring until smooth; gradually add the confectioners' sugar and mix well.

Place one cake layer on a serving plate; spread with half of the filling. Repeat layers. Top with remaining cake layer. Frost top and sides of cake. Store in the refrigerator. **YIELD:** 16 servings.

peppermint grasshopper torte

(PICTURED AT RIGHT)

This three-layer ice cream cake takes a bit of time to prepare, but it can be done in advance. Guests will rave about each minty, cool slice.

Eileen Putsey | CESAREA, ON

2 cups chocolate wafers (about 40)

1/3 cup butter, melted

1 pint vanilla ice cream, softened

5 drops green food coloring

1 jar (7 ounces) marshmallow creme

1/4 cup milk

1/2 teaspoon peppermint extract

2 drops red food coloring

2 cups heavy whipping cream, whipped

Chocolate curls, peppermint candies and mint sprigs, optional

In a small bowl, combine cookie crumbs and butter. Press onto the bottom of a 9-in. springform pan. Refrigerate for 30 minutes. Tint ice cream with green food coloring. Spread over crust. Cover and freeze for 2 hours or until firm.

Meanwhile, in a bowl, combine the marshmallow creme and milk. Add the extract and red food coloring. Fold in the whipped cream. Spread over ice cream. Cover and freeze until firm. Remove from the freezer 10 minutes before serving. Garnish with chocolate curls, candies and mint if desired. **YIELD:** 12 servings.

DAZZLING DESSERTS

The dessert course is great to host because sweet treats can be made in advance.

- Make the Citrus-Banana Ice Cream and Peppermint Grasshopper Torte two days in advance.
- Bake Chocolate Mint Cake the day before.
- Remove the torte from the freezer 10 minutes before serving and garnish as desired.

viennese cookies

(PICTURED AT FAR RIGHT)

A Swedish friend shared this recipe with me many years ago.
A chocolate glaze tops tender cookies filled with apricot jam.

Beverly Stirrat | MISSION, BC

1-1/4 cups butter, softened

2/3 cup sugar

2-1/4 cups all-purpose flour

1-2/3 cups ground almonds

1 cup apricot jam

2 cups (12 ounces) semisweet chocolate chips

2 tablespoons shortening

In a large bowl, cream butter and sugar until light and fluffy. Combine flour and ground almonds; gradually add to creamed mixture and mix well. Cover and refrigerate for 1 hour.

On a lightly floured surface, roll dough to 1/4-in. thickness. Cut with a floured 2-1/4-in. round cookie cutter. Place 2 in. apart on ungreased baking sheets. Bake at 350° for 7-9 minutes or until edges are lightly browned. Remove to wire racks to cool completely.

Spread jam on the bottoms of half of the cookies; top with remaining cookies. In a microwave, melt chocolate chips and shortening; stir until smooth. Dip half of each sandwich cookie into chocolate mixture; place on waxed paper until set. Store in an airtight container. **YIELD:** about 3 dozen.

sweet kahlua coffee

This beverage is brewing in my slow cooker at my annual Christmas open house. I set out the whipped cream and grated chocolate in pretty dishes so guests can help themselves. It's a great way to end a festive night.

Ruth Gruchow | YORBA LINDA, CA

2 quarts hot water

1/2 cup Kahlua

1/4 cup creme de cacao

3 tablespoons instant coffee granules

2 cups heavy whipping cream

1/4 cup sugar

1 teaspoon vanilla extract

2 tablespoons grated chocolate

In a 4-qt. slow cooker, combine the water, Kahlua, creme de cacao and coffee granules. Cover and cook on low for 3-4 hours or until heated through.

In a large bowl, beat cream until it begins to thicken. Add sugar and vanilla; beat until stiff peaks form.

Ladle coffee into mugs. Garnish with whipped cream and grated chocolate. **YIELD:** 9 servings (2-1/4 quarts).

irish creme drink

(PICTURED AT RIGHT)

We top off holiday celebrations with this creamy beverage. With sweetened condensed milk and ice cream, it's like a liquid dessert!

Fred Schneider | *STURGEON BAY, WI*

3-1/2 cups vanilla ice cream, softened

3/4 cup vodka

1/2 cup eggnog

1/3 cup sweetened condensed milk

1 tablespoon chocolate syrup

1 teaspoon instant coffee granules

1/2 teaspoon vanilla extract

1/4 teaspoon almond extract

Grated chocolate and additional chocolate syrup

In a large bowl, combine the first eight ingredients; beat until smooth. Set aside.

Place grated chocolate and additional chocolate syrup in separate shallow bowls. Hold each glass upside down and dip rim in chocolate syrup, then dip in grated chocolate. Pour drink mixture into prepared glasses.

Serve immediately. **YIELD:** 10 servings (1/2 cup each).

EDITOR'S NOTE: This recipe was tested with commercially prepared eggnog. Melted ice cream should not be stored in the refrigerator, so discard any leftover mixture.

LAST COURSE LESSONS

End the evening on a sweet note with after-dinner drinks and apricot jam-filled cookies.

- A few weeks in advance, bake Viennese Cookies but don't dip in melted chocolate; freeze. Thaw cookies at room temperature the day before. Dip in chocolate as directed; store in an airtight container.
- In the morning, prepare the glasses to be used for the Irish Creme Drink; refrigerate. Remove the ice cream as soon as you get home. When softened, combine with other ingredients; serve in prepared glasses.
- Before leaving for the first house, start Sweet Kahlua Coffee in the slow cooker and grate the chocolate. Whip the cream and refrigerate. Stir the cream before using.

*I*f the flurry of holiday duties has you flustered, call up friends for a little wintertime fun!

Blow off some steam by heading outdoors for an afternoon of skiing, sledding, snowshoeing and snowball fights! (If you don't have snow in your area, plan on meeting at an indoor ice skating rink.)

Afterwards, offer frozen folks a chance to warm up at your home with down-home, hearty foods like Shredded Pork Sandwiches, Manicotti Crepes and Tortellini Meatball Stew.

HOT & HEARTY
(PICTURED AT RIGHT)

let it snow
CELEBRATION

manicotti crepes

(PICTURED ON PAGE 97)

This entree may lack meat but it's loaded with three cheeses! Using homemade crepes instead of manicotti shells makes it special for holidays and other gatherings.

Lori Henry | *ELKHART, IN*

2 cans (28 ounces each) diced tomatoes, undrained

1-1/2 cups finely chopped onions

1 can (6 ounces) tomato paste

1/3 cup olive oil

4 garlic cloves, minced

2 tablespoons dried parsley flakes

1 tablespoon sugar

1 tablespoon salt

1 teaspoon minced fresh oregano

1 teaspoon minced fresh basil

1/4 teaspoon pepper

CREPES:

6 eggs

1-1/2 cups water

1-1/2 cups all-purpose flour

Dash salt

2 tablespoons canola oil, divided

FILLING:

2 cartons (15 ounces each) ricotta cheese

2 cups (8 ounces) shredded part-skim mozzarella cheese

1 cup shredded Parmesan cheese

2 eggs

1 tablespoon dried parsley flakes

1 teaspoon salt

1/4 teaspoon pepper

In a large saucepan; combine the first 11 ingredients. Bring to a boil. Reduce heat; simmer, uncovered, for 1-1/2 to 2 hours or until sauce is reduced to 5 cups, stirring occasionally.

Meanwhile, in a large bowl, beat eggs and water. Combine flour and salt; add to egg mixture and mix well. Cover and refrigerate for 1 hour. In a large bowl, combine the filling ingredients. Cover and refrigerate.

Heat 3/4 teaspoon oil in an 8-in. nonstick skillet. Stir crepe batter; pour a scant 3 tablespoons into center of skillet. Lift and tilt pan to coat bottom evenly. Cook until top appears dry; turn and cook 15-20 seconds longer. Remove to a wire rack. Repeat with remaining batter, using remaining oil as needed. When cool, stack crepes with waxed paper or paper towels in between.

Spread about 1/4 cup filling down the center of each crepe; roll up and place 12 crepes in each of two greased 13-in. x 9-in. baking dishes. Spoon sauce over top. Cover and bake at 350° for 45-50 minutes or until a thermometer reads 160°. **YIELD:** 12 servings.

homemade crisp crackers

(PICTURED AT RIGHT)

Store-bought crackers have nothing on these cheesy crisps created in our Test Kitchen. Make them in advance and keep them handy in an airtight container for anytime snacking.

1-3/4 cups all-purpose flour

1/2 cup cornmeal

1/2 teaspoon baking soda

1/2 teaspoon sugar

1/2 teaspoon salt

1/2 teaspoon garlic powder

1/4 teaspoon Italian seasoning

1/2 cup cold butter

1-1/2 cups (6 ounces) shredded Colby-Monterey Jack cheese

1/2 cup plus 2 tablespoons cold water

2 tablespoons cider vinegar

In a large bowl, combine the first seven ingredients; cut in butter until crumbly. Stir in cheese. Gradually add water and vinegar, tossing with a fork until dough forms a ball. Wrap in plastic wrap and refrigerate for 1 hour or until firm.

Divide into six portions. On a lightly floured surface, roll each portion into an 8-in. circle. Cut into eight wedges and place on greased baking sheets. Bake at 375° for 17-20 minutes or until edges are lightly browned. Cool on wire racks. Store in an airtight container. **YIELD:** 4 dozen.

hot crab dip

(PICTURED ABOVE)

One batch of this slow-cooked appetizer isn't enough for my family so I often double the recipe.
Terri Perrier | SIMONTON, TX

1 package (8 ounces) cream cheese, softened

1/2 cup finely chopped sweet onion

1/4 cup grated Parmesan cheese

1/4 cup mayonnaise

2 garlic cloves, minced

2 teaspoons sugar

1 can (6 ounces) crabmeat, drained, flaked and cartilage removed

Assorted crackers

In a 1-1/2-qt. slow cooker, combine the first six ingredients; stir in crab. Cover and cook on low for 2-3 hours or until heated through. Serve with crackers. **YIELD:** 2 cups.

tortellini meatball stew

(PICTURED ON PAGE 96)

Loaded with meatballs, tortellini, tomatoes and kidney beans, this hearty stew is sure to warm you up on cold winter days. Sprinkle servings with shredded Parmesan for even more flavor.

Lori Martin | MARYSVILLE, MI

1 egg, lightly beaten

1 package (10 ounces) frozen chopped spinach, thawed and squeezed dry

1/4 cup seasoned bread crumbs

1/2 teaspoon salt

1/4 teaspoon pepper

1 pound lean ground beef

2 tablespoons canola oil, divided

1 large onion, chopped

1 cup chopped celery

1 cup chopped carrots

4 cups beef broth

1 can (16 ounces) kidney beans, rinsed and drained

1 can (14-1/2 ounces) Italian diced tomatoes, undrained

1/2 teaspoon dried basil

1/2 teaspoon dried oregano

1 package (9 ounces) refrigerated cheese tortellini

1/4 cup shredded Parmesan cheese

In a large bowl, combine the egg, spinach, bread crumbs, salt and pepper. Crumble beef over mixture and mix well. Shape into 3/4-in. balls.

In a large saucepan, brown meatballs in batches in 1 tablespoon oil; drain. Remove meatballs and keep warm.

In the same pan, saute onion in remaining oil for 2 minutes. Add celery and carrots; saute 2 minutes longer. Stir in the broth, beans, tomatoes, basil and oregano. Add meatballs; bring to a boil. Reduce heat; cover and simmer for 10 minutes.

Return to a boil. Add tortellini; cook for 7-9 minutes or until tender, stirring several times. Garnish with Parmesan cheese. **YIELD:** 6 servings (2-1/2 quarts).

shredded pork sandwiches

(PICTURED ON PAGE 96)

I like to share this dish at potlucks because it can be made ahead, which I especially appreciate during the busy holiday season. The sweet-and-spicy sauce is always a hit.

Martha Anne Carpenter | MESA, AZ

1 boneless whole pork loin roast (4 pounds)

1 can (14-1/2 ounces) beef broth

1/3 cup plus 1/2 cup Worcestershire sauce, divided

1/3 cup plus 1/4 cup hot pepper sauce, divided

1 cup ketchup

1 cup molasses

1/2 cup prepared mustard

10 kaiser rolls, split

Cut roast in half; place in a 5-qt. slow cooker. Combine the broth, 1/3 cup Worcestershire sauce and 1/3 cup pepper sauce; pour over roast. Cover and cook on low for 7-8 hours or until tender.

Remove pork; shred with two forks. Drain and discard cooking liquid. Return shredded pork to the slow cooker. For sauce, combine the ketchup, molasses, mustard and the remaining Worcestershire sauce and pepper sauce. Pour over pork.

Cover and cook on high for 30 minutes or until heated through. Serve on rolls. **YIELD:** 10 servings.

EDITOR'S NOTE: This recipe was tested with Frank's Red Hot Sauce.

marshmallow pops

(PICTURED AT RIGHT)

Homemade marshmallows are fun to eat on a stick or to stir in hot chocolate. Their melt-in-your-mouth texture appeals to the young and the young at heart.

Jennifer Andrzejewski | *GRIZZLY FLATS, CA*

1/2 cup cold water

3 envelopes unflavored gelatin

2 cups sugar

1 cup light corn syrup

1/2 cup water

1/4 teaspoon salt

1 teaspoon almond extract

1/2 cup confectioners' sugar, divided

Lollipop sticks

In a large bowl, combine cold water and gelatin; set aside.

Meanwhile, in a large heavy saucepan over medium heat, combine the sugar, corn syrup, water and salt. Bring to a boil, stirring occasionally. Cover and cook for 2 minutes to dissolve sugar crystals; uncover and cook on medium-high heat, without stirring, until a candy thermometer reads 240° (soft-ball stage).

Remove from the heat and gradually add to gelatin. Beat on medium speed for 14 minutes. Add extract; beat 1 minute longer. Meanwhile, sprinkle 2 tablespoons confectioners' sugar into a greased 13-in. x 9-in. pan.

With greased hands, spread marshmallow mixture into the prepared pan. Sprinkle 2 tablespoons confectioners' sugar over the top. Cover and cool at room temperature for 6 hours or overnight.

Cut 15 snowflakes with a greased 2-1/2-in. snowflake-shaped cookie cutter; toss in remaining confectioners' sugar. Gently press lollipop stick into each snowflake. Store in an airtight container in a cool dry place. **YIELD:** 15 pops.

EDITOR'S NOTE: We recommend that you test your candy thermometer before each use by bringing water to a boil; the thermometer should read 212°. Adjust your recipe temperature up or down based on your test.

PLAY WITH THE FLAVOR

Have fun experimenting with different flavors of Marshmallow Pops. Instead of almond extract, use vanilla, peppermint or even lemon. To the confectioners' sugar, stir in flaked coconut, miniature chocolate chips or crushed peppermint candy.

holiday corn 'n' turkey casserole

*I create this comforting casserole in minutes using leftover holiday turkey.
It's a family-favorite recipe that I've relied on for years.*

Edie DeSpain | LOGAN, UT

1 small onion, finely chopped

1/4 cup butter, cubed

1/4 cup all-purpose flour

3/4 teaspoon salt

1/2 teaspoon ground mustard

1/2 teaspoon pepper

3/4 cup milk

2 cups frozen corn, thawed

1 package (9 ounces) frozen broccoli cuts, thawed and chopped

2 cups cubed cooked turkey

1 cup (4 ounces) shredded cheddar cheese

2 eggs, lightly beaten

1/3 cup sliced almonds

In a large saucepan, saute onion in butter until tender. Combine the flour, salt, mustard and pepper; stir into onion mixture until blended. Gradually add milk. Bring to a boil over medium heat. Cook and stir for 2 minutes or until thickened. Remove from the heat.

In a large bowl, combine the corn, broccoli, turkey and cheese. Whisk eggs into onion mixture. Pour over turkey mixture; stir until combined. Transfer to a greased 1-1/2-qt. baking dish. Sprinkle with almonds. Bake, uncovered, at 350° for 25-30 minutes or until bubbly. **YIELD:** 8 servings.

nacho cheese twists

*I like to serve these zesty twists as an appetizer. But they would also pair well with a bowl of chili.
Frozen puff pastry makes them easy to prepare.*

Tammy Miller | LARGO, FL

1 cup (4 ounces) shredded cheddar cheese

1/4 cup salsa

2 tablespoons finely chopped ripe olives

1 package (17.3 ounces) frozen puff pastry, thawed

1 egg, beaten

1 tablespoon water

1/2 teaspoon chili powder

In a small bowl, combine the cheese, salsa and olives. Unfold one pastry sheet on a lightly floured surface; spread half of cheese mixture over half of pastry. Fold plain half over filling; press gently to seal.

Repeat with remaining pastry and cheese mixture. Cut each rectangle into twelve 3/4-in.-wide strips. Twist strips several times; place 2 in. apart on greased baking sheets.

Combine egg and water; brush over twists. Lightly sprinkle with chili powder. Bake at 400° for 14-16 minutes or until golden brown. Serve warm. **YIELD:** 2 dozen.

snowmen cookies

(PICTURED AT RIGHT)

While my family loves the subtle cheesecake flavor of these cookies, I like the fact that I don't need to use a cookie cutter to shape them. The scrumptious snowmen look so cute on a cookie tray.

Cathy Medley | CLYDE, OH

1 cup butter, softened

1 package (8 ounces) cream cheese, softened

2-1/4 cups sugar, divided

1 egg

1 teaspoon vanilla extract

1/4 teaspoon almond extract

3-1/2 cups all-purpose flour

1 teaspoon baking powder

1 teaspoon salt

50 pretzel sticks

Frosting of your choice

In a large bowl, cream the butter, cream cheese and 2 cups sugar until light and fluffy. Beat in egg and extracts. Combine the flour, baking powder and salt; gradually add to creamed mixture and mix well. Cover and refrigerate dough for at least 30 minutes or until easy to handle.

Shape the dough into 1-in., 3/4-in. and 1/2-in. balls. For each snowman, gently press one of each size ball together; gently roll in the remaining sugar. Place 2 in. apart on ungreased baking sheets. Break the pretzel sticks in half; press into the sides of each cookie, the forming arms.

Bake at 325° for 15-18 minutes or until bottoms are lightly browned. Cool 1 minute before removing to wire racks. Decorate as desired. **YIELD**: about 4 dozen.

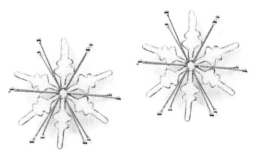

veggie-sausage cheese soup

I took this soup to a potluck at work, where it was well received...and was the only dish prepared by a guy! The great combination of textures and flavors had everyone asking for the recipe.

Richard Grant | HUDSON, NH

2 medium onions, finely chopped

1 each medium green and sweet red pepper, chopped

2 celery ribs, chopped

4 garlic cloves, minced

1 tablespoon olive oil

1 pound smoked kielbasa or Polish sausage, cut into 1/4-inch slices

2 medium potatoes, diced

1 can (14-3/4 ounces) cream-style corn

1 can (14-1/2 ounces) chicken broth

1 can (10-3/4 ounces) condensed cream of mushroom soup, undiluted

2 medium carrots, sliced

1 cup whole kernel corn

1 cup sliced fresh mushrooms

1 tablespoon Worcestershire sauce

1 tablespoon Dijon mustard

1 tablespoon dried basil

1 tablespoon dried parsley flakes

1/2 teaspoon pepper

2 cups (8 ounces) shredded sharp cheddar cheese

1 can (12 ounces) evaporated milk

In a large skillet, saute the onions, peppers, celery and garlic in oil until tender. Transfer to a 5-qt. slow cooker. Stir in the sausage, potatoes, cream-style corn, broth, soup, carrots, corn, mushrooms, Worcestershire sauce, Dijon mustard and seasonings.

Cover and cook on low for 6-1/2 to 7-1/2 hours or until vegetables are tender. Stir in the cheese and milk. Cook on low 30 minutes longer or until the cheese is melted. Stir until blended. **YIELD:** 16 servings (4 quarts).

slow-cooked applesauce

This chunky, sweet applesauce is perfect alongside main entrees. Because it's prepared in a slow cooker, you can fix it and forget it before you and the family head out for some winter fun.

Susanne Wasson | MONTGOMERY, NY

6 pounds apples (about 18 medium), peeled and sliced

1 cup sugar

1 cup water

1 teaspoon salt

1 teaspoon ground cinnamon

1/4 cup butter, cubed

2 teaspoons vanilla extract

In a 5-qt. slow cooker, combine the apples, sugar, water, salt and cinnamon. Cover and cook on low for 6-8 hours or until tender.

Turn off heat; stir in butter and vanilla. Mash if desired. Serve warm or cold. **YIELD:** 12 cups.

snowball centerpiece

(PICTURED AT RIGHT)

Keep guests guessing why these "snowballs" aren't melting as fast as Frosty! For added fun, display them in an attractive ice bowl.

ICE BOWL:

1-quart and 2-1/2-quart freezer-safe glass nesting bowls

Ice cubes

Freezer tape

SNOWBALLS:

3-inch Styrofoam balls

Clear-drying craft glue

White decorator sand

For the ice bowl, fill the 2-1/2-qt. bowl with water. Place the 1-qt. bowl on top so there is about 1 in. of space between the bowls. Fill the smaller bowl with ice cubes. Place freezer tape across both bowls to hold them in place. Freeze overnight.

Remove freezer tape and ice cubes. Fill the 1-qt. bowl with lukewarm water; remove the bowl. Dip the 2-1/2-qt. bowl in water and twist to loosen. Remove the ice bowl and return to the freezer. When ready to use, place the bowl on a platter to catch the water as it melts.

For the snowballs, hold a Styrofoam ball in your hand and push it down on a flat surface. Turn the ball; repeat. Continue to do this until the ball is the shape and size of a snowball.

Coat the ball with glue and immediately roll it in sand. Place on a parchment paper-lined baking sheet until dry. Display in the ice bowl.

SNOWFLAKE INVITATION

Send out a warm welcome to your cool gathering! Fold a 5-in. x 7-in. piece of white paper in half crosswise to make a 3-1/2-inch x 5-inch piece. (This is the minimum size the post office will accept.) Open and write invitation on the inside. Fold a 5-in. x 7-in. piece of card stock or scrapbook paper in half. Place the white piece of paper inside. Apply rubber cement to one side of a homemade paper snowflake. Immediately sprinkle the snowflake with clear iridescent glitter. Let dry; shake off excess glitter. Glue snowflake to the front of the invitation; let dry.

GIVING *thanks*

A down-home turkey dinner with all the fixings is always favored by friends and family. The crowd-pleasing meal offers three recipes for cooking the beautiful bird. Round out your menu with a bounty of home-baked breads. For dessert, not much can top pumpkin pie. But why not think outside the box and feature the fabulous flavor of pumpkin in a variety of delicious desserts?

ear after year, folks look forward to a down-home dinner of turkey and all the fixings on Thanksgiving. At no other celebration are food and family the main focus of the day!

Such a special occasion calls for a showstopping entree like Herbed Turkey. (Two other pleasing poultry recipes in the chapter are Chai Turkey and Beer-Brined Turkey with Giblet Gravy.)

Instead of offering ordinary "spuds," serve your guests deliciously different Cauliflower Mashed Potatoes.

Chestnut Dressing is true comfort food that everyone will savor.

MEMORABLE MEAL
(PICTURED AT RIGHT)

Herbed Turkey (p. 114)
Cauliflower Mashed Potatoes (p. 112)
Chestnut Dressing (p. 116)

an elegant
THANKSGIVING

Thanksgiving Dinner
Agenda

A Few Weeks Before:
- Prepare two grocery lists—one for non-perishable items to purchase now and one for perishable items to purchase a few days before Thanksgiving Day.
- Order a fresh turkey or buy and freeze a frozen turkey.

Two to Three Days Before:
- Buy your remaining grocery items, including the fresh turkey if you ordered one.

The Day Before:
- Set the table.
- For Almond Butter-Stuffed Pears, make the almond filling; store in an airtight container at room temperature. Make the sauce; cover and chill.
- If using the Beer-Brined Turkey with Giblet Gravy or Chai Turkey recipe, prepare the brine and marinate the turkey. If making Herbed Turkey, process herbs in a food processor; cover and set aside.
- Steam cauliflower for Cauliflower Mashed Potatoes; drain and cool. Refrigerate in a covered container.
- For the Chestnut Stuffing, chop the celery and onion; shell and chop the chestnuts. Cover and chill. Cube the bread and store in an airtight container at room temperature.
- For Crunchy Pomegranate Salad, seed pomegranates; cover and refrigerate. Toast the pecans; place in an airtight container.

- Cook the carrots for Glazed Carrots with Rosemary. Drain and cool; refrigerate in a covered container.
- Make the Pear Squash Bisque with Cinnamon Cream; cover and chill the cinnamon cream and soup in separate containers.
- Cook the beets for Caramelized Onions and Beets. Place in an airtight container and refrigerate.
- Make the Vanilla Cranberry Sauce; cover and chill.

Thanksgiving Day:
- Peel and quarter the potatoes for Cauliflower Mashed Potatoes. Cover with cold water and refrigerate.
- If you brined the turkey; drain, pat dry and roast as directed. For Herbed Turkey, prepare turkey as directed and bake.
- Assemble and bake the Chestnut Stuffing.
- Make Glazed Carrots with Rosemary.
- Prepare the Caramelized Onions and Beets.
- Make the Cauliflower Mashed Potatoes.
- Cover the turkey and let stand for 15 minutes before carving. Prepare the gravy if desired.
- Reheat the Pear Squash Soup; garnish individual servings with cinnamon cream and spiced seeds.
- Assemble Crunchy Pomegranate Salad.
- Set out the Vanilla Cranberry Sauce.
- After dinner, stuff the pears and bake as directed. Meanwhile, reheat the sauce and serve on the side.

pear squash bisque with cinnamon cream

(PICTURED AT RIGHT)

This lightly sweet and fruity squash soup makes a lovely first course for Thanksgiving. The texture is creamy and smooth.

Elaine Sweet | DALLAS, TX

3/4 cup sour cream

1-1/2 teaspoons maple syrup

1/2 teaspoon ground cinnamon

2 medium butternut squash (3 pounds each)

1 tablespoon butter, melted

1-1/2 teaspoons Caribbean jerk seasoning

4-1/2 cups vegetable broth

4 medium pears, peeled and chopped

1/2 cup packed brown sugar

1-1/2 teaspoons ground cinnamon

1/2 teaspoon salt

1/2 teaspoon ground ginger

1/4 teaspoon ground nutmeg

1/4 teaspoon ground cloves

3/4 cup heavy whipping cream

For cinnamon cream, in a small bowl, combine the sour cream, maple syrup and cinnamon. Cover and refrigerate until serving.

Peel squash. Scoop out seeds and pulp; rinse and pat seeds dry. In a small bowl, combine the squash seeds, butter and jerk seasoning. Spread onto a greased 15-in. x 10-in. x 1-in. baking pan. Bake at 375° for 12-15 minutes or until lightly browned, stirring once. Cool on a wire rack.

Meanwhile, cut squash into cubes. In a large saucepan, combine the squash, broth and pears; bring to a boil. Reduce heat; cover and simmer for 10-15 minutes or until squash is tender. Cool slightly. In a blender, process squash mixture in batches until smooth; return to the pan. Add brown sugar and seasonings. Gradually stir in whipping cream. Garnish soup with cinnamon cream and spiced seeds. **YIELD:** 12 servings (3 quarts).

cauliflower mashed potatoes

(PICTURED AT FAR RIGHT AND ON PAGE 109)

*Mom used this recipe as a way to get my kids to eat a vegetable other than potatoes.
It's now a family favorite and a must for Thanksgiving!*

Carine Nadel | *LAGUNA HILLS, CA*

3-1/2 to 4 pounds medium potatoes, peeled and quartered

1 large head cauliflower, broken into florets

1/3 cup milk

1/3 cup butter, melted

1-1/4 teaspoons salt

1/2 teaspoon pepper

Place potatoes in a Dutch oven and cover with water. Bring to a boil. Reduce heat; cover and cook for 15-20 minutes or until tender.

Meanwhile, place cauliflower in a steamer basket; place in a large saucepan over 1 in. of water. Bring to a boil; cover and steam for 8-12 minutes or until very tender. Drain; cool slightly. Place in a blender; add the milk, butter, salt and pepper. Cover and process until smooth.

Drain potatoes and mash. Add cauliflower mixture and mix well. Transfer to a large serving bowl. **YIELD:** 12 servings.

glazed carrots with rosemary

(PICTURED AT FAR RIGHT)

*Caramelizing carrots results in a sweet and buttery side dish that even folks not fond
of vegetables will favor. Fresh rosemary adds the finishing touch.*

Helen Faddis | *GLOUCESTER, MA*

4 pounds medium carrots, cut into 1/2-inch slices

6 cups chicken broth

1/2 cup white wine or additional chicken broth

2 teaspoons salt

1/2 cup butter, cubed

1/4 cup packed brown sugar

2 tablespoons plus 2 teaspoons lemon juice

2 tablespoons minced fresh rosemary or 2 teaspoons dried rosemary, crushed

1 teaspoon white pepper

In a large saucepan, combine the carrots, broth, wine and salt. Bring to a boil. Reduce heat. Cover and simmer for 7-9 minutes or until crisp-tender. Drain and discard liquid.

Add the remaining ingredients. Cook and stir over low heat until glazed and heated through. **YIELD:** 13 servings (1/2 cup each).

chai turkey

(PICTURED AT RIGHT)

A chai tea mix is the tasty base for this brined turkey. The result is a slightly cinnamon and clove flavor that appeals to all palates.

Amanda Boe | LAKEVILLE, MN

5 quarts plus 1-1/4 cups water, divided

1 carton (32 ounces) chai tea latte concentrate

1 medium orange, quartered, divided

1 turkey (14 to 16 pounds)

2 turkey-size oven roasting bags

1 medium apple, quartered

1/4 cup canola oil

1 teaspoon salt

1/2 teaspoon pepper

2 tablespoons all-purpose flour

For marinade, in a large bowl, combine 5 quarts water, chai tea mix and two orange wedges. Remove giblets from turkey; (discard or save for another use). Place a turkey-size oven roasting bag inside a second roasting bag; add the turkey. Place in a roasting pan. Carefully pour marinade into bag. Squeeze out as much air as possible; seal bags and turn to coat. Refrigerate for 18-24 hours, turning several times.

Drain and discard marinade. Place apple and remaining orange slices in cavity of turkey. Rub oil over skin; season with salt and pepper. Skewer turkey openings; tie drumsticks together.

Place turkey breast side up on a rack in a roasting pan. Bake, uncovered, at 325° for 2-3/4 to 3-1/4 hours or until a meat thermometer reads 180°, basting occasionally with pan drippings. (Cover loosely with foil if turkey browns too quickly.) Cover and let stand for 15 minutes before carving. Discard orange and apple slices.

Add 1 cup water to the pan, scraping to loosen browned bits. Skim and discard fat; pour drippings into a small saucepan. Combine flour and remaining water until smooth; gradually stir into drippings. Bring to a boil; cook and stir for 2 minutes or until thickened. Serve with turkey. **YIELD:** 14-16 servings.

herbed turkey

(PICTURED ON PAGE 109)

*The aroma of this turkey roasting in the oven is simply wonderful. Better yet,
the meat turns out moist and delicious every time I make it.*

Mary Lou Timpson | *COLORADO CITY, AZ*

1 turkey (14 to 16 pounds)

3 tablespoons kosher salt

3 tablespoons dried marjoram

3 tablespoons dried thyme

3 tablespoons dried juniper berries, optional

1 tablespoon whole peppercorns, crushed

2 teaspoons aniseed

12 fresh rosemary sprigs

12 garlic cloves, peeled

1/2 cup butter, softened, divided

Pat turkey dry. Place the salt, marjoram, thyme, juniper berries if desired, peppercorns and aniseed in a small food processor; cover and process until blended. Sprinkle half of salt mixture over inside of cavity. Place rosemary and garlic inside cavity.

With fingers, carefully loosen skin from the turkey breast; rub half of the butter under the skin. Sprinkle skin with remaining salt mixture. Melt remaining butter; drizzle over turkey. Skewer turkey openings; tie drumsticks together. Place breast side up on a rack in a roasting pan.

Bake at 325° for 2-3/4 to 3-1/2 hours or until a meat thermometer reads 180°, basting occasionally with pan drippings. (Cover loosely with foil if turkey browns too quickly.) Cover and let stand for 20 minutes before carving. **YIELD:** 14-16 servings.

vanilla cranberry sauce

*My quick and easy cranberry sauce has the subtle flavors of vanilla and orange.
It's been featured on our Thanksgiving menu for years.*

Wilma Sue Sanders | *DIVIDE, CO*

1 package (12 ounces) fresh cranberries

1 cup sugar

1 cup orange juice

1 vanilla bean, split

In a large saucepan, combine the cranberries, sugar, orange juice and vanilla bean. Cook over medium heat until the berries pop, about 15 minutes.

Remove from the heat; remove bean halves. With a sharp knife, scrape the bean to remove the seeds; stir into sauce. Discard bean. Cover and refrigerate at least 1 hour or until chilled. **YIELD:** 3 cups.

crunchy pomegranate salad

(PICTURED AT RIGHT)

Thanksgivings here in Utah wouldn't be the same without this traditional, tasty salad. You can even stir in sliced bananas, mandarin oranges or pineapple tidbits.

Jan Olpin | SALT LAKE CITY, UT

2 cups heavy whipping cream

1/4 cup sugar

2 teaspoons vanilla extract

2-1/2 cups pomegranate seeds (about 3 large pomegranates)

2 medium apples, peeled and cubed

1 cup chopped pecans, toasted

In a large bowl, beat the cream until it begins to thicken. Add the sugar and vanilla; beat until stiff peaks form. Fold in the pomegranate seeds and apples. Sprinkle with the pecans. Serve immediately. **YIELD:** 16 servings (1/2 cup each).

chestnut dressing

(PICTURED ON PAGE 108)

I enjoyed this stuffing when I spent my first Thanksgiving with my husband, Mike. It's a family recipe his mother has been making for years. Italian seasoning and chestnuts add flavor and texture.

Sharon Brunner | MOHNTON, PA

4 celery ribs, chopped

1 large onion, chopped

1-1/2 cups butter, cubed

3 cups sweet chestnuts, shelled and coarsely chopped

3 tablespoons Italian seasoning

10 slices Italian bread (3/4 inch thick), cubed

In a large skillet, saute celery and onion in butter until tender. Add the chestnuts and Italian seasoning. Bring to a boil. Reduce heat; simmer, uncovered, for 10 minutes. Add bread cubes and stir to coat.

Transfer mixture to an ungreased 13-in. x 9-in. baking dish. Bake, uncovered, at 350° for 20-25 minutes until golden brown. **YIELD:** 18 servings (1/2 cup each).

BUYING AND STORING CHESTNUTS

December is the peak month for finding fresh chestnuts. Look for ones that are glossy and smooth. Avoid any with blemishes or that are cracked or shriveled. If the nut rattles inside the shell, it's dried out.

Store chestnuts in their shell in a cool, dry place and use within 1 week. Or place in a perforated plastic bag in the crisper drawer for up to 1 month. Chestnuts can also be frozen for 4 months.

caramelized onions and beets

As retired farmers, my husband and I enjoy delicious, down-home foods. These mildly flavored onions and beets complement a variety of main dishes.

Violet Klause | ONOWAY, AB

4 pounds whole fresh beets (about 12 medium), trimmed and cleaned

6 medium onions, sliced

3 tablespoons butter

1/4 cup sugar

1/4 cup red wine or cider vinegar

1 teaspoon salt

1/2 teaspoon pepper

Place the beets in a Dutch oven; cover with water. Bring to a boil; cover and cook for 35-40 minutes or until tender. Drain, reserving 1/4 cup of the cooking liquid; cool slightly. Peel and quarter the beets; set aside.

Meanwhile, in a large skillet, saute onions in butter until tender; add the sugar and vinegar. Cover and cook over medium heat for 15-20 minutes or until onions are golden brown, stirring frequently.

Add beets, salt, pepper and reserved cooking liquid to skillet; cover and cook for 5 minutes or until heated through. **YIELD:** 12 servings.

almond butter-stuffed pears

(PICTURED AT RIGHT)

*A formal dinner calls for an elegant dessert
like these stuffed pears from our home
economists. The nutty filling pairs well with
the tender, sweet fruit.*

2 cups unblanched whole almonds, toasted

1/4 teaspoon salt

2 tablespoons canola oil

2 cups pear juice

3 cups sweet white wine, divided

1/4 cup packed brown sugar

1 vanilla bean, split

12 medium pears

Combine the almonds and salt in a food
processor. Cover and process until almonds
are finely chopped. Add oil; cover and
process until blended. Set aside.

In a large saucepan, combine the pear
juice, 1 cup wine, brown sugar and vanilla
bean. Bring to a boil. Remove from the heat;
remove vanilla bean. With a sharp knife,
scrape the bean to remove the seeds; stir
into sauce. Discard the bean. Return to a
boil; cook, uncovered, over medium heat for
50-55 minutes or until mixture coats the
back of a metal spoon.

Meanwhile, slice 1 in. off the top of each
pear and set aside. Core the pears, leaving
bottoms intact. Fill with reserved almond
mixture. Place pears in a shallow roasting
pan; replace tops. Add remaining wine. Bake,
uncovered, at 400° for 30-35 minutes or
until pears are tender, basting occasionally.
Serve with sauce. **YIELD:** 12 servings.

CORING PEARS

You don't need a special tool to remove the pear cores when
making Almond Butter-Stuffed Pears. An everyday melon baller
does the trick!

beer-brined turkey with giblet gravy

Our relatives request this turkey every Thanksgiving, and I hate to disappoint them. Brining the turkey keeps the meat moist while roasting gives incredible flavor.

Jeff Locke | ARMA, KS

2 quarts apple cider or juice

1-1/2 cups kosher salt

1-1/2 cups packed brown sugar

3 tablespoons whole peppercorns

2 cinnamon sticks (3 inches)

4 bay leaves

1 tablespoon juniper berries, optional

1 teaspoon whole cloves

6 bottles (12 ounces each) dark beer, chilled

6 cups cold water

1 turkey (14 to 16 pounds)

2 turkey-size oven roasting bags

1 large onion, chopped

2 medium carrots, chopped

2 celery ribs, chopped

6 garlic cloves, minced

1 cup reduced-sodium chicken broth

1/2 cup butter, melted

1 tablespoon rotisserie chicken seasoning

GRAVY:

3 cups reduced-sodium chicken broth, divided

1 tablespoon olive oil

1 tablespoon butter

1/4 cup all-purpose flour

1/2 cup white wine or chicken broth

2 tablespoons fresh sage or 2 teaspoons dried sage leaves

In a large kettle, combine the first eight ingredients. Bring to a boil; cook and stir until salt and brown sugar are dissolved. Remove from the heat. Add cold beer and water to cool the marinade to room temperature.

Remove giblets from turkey; cover and refrigerate for gravy. Place a turkey-size oven roasting bag inside a second roasting bag; add turkey. Carefully pour cooled marinade into bag. Squeeze out as much air as possible; seal bags and turn to coat. Place in a roasting pan. Refrigerate for 18-24 hours, turning several times.

Drain and discard brine. Rinse turkey under cold water; pat dry. Place the onion, carrots, celery and garlic in both cavities. Skewer turkey openings; tie the drumsticks together. In a small bowl, combine the broth, butter and chicken seasoning.

Place turkey breast side up on a rack in a roasting pan. Bake, uncovered, at 325° for 3-1/2 to 4 hours or until a meat thermometer reads 180°, basting occasionally with broth mixture. (Cover loosely with foil if turkey browns too quickly.) Cover and let stand for 15 minutes before carving; discard vegetables or save for another use.

For gravy, add 1 cup broth to the pan, scraping to loosen browned bits. Skim and discard fat, reserving 1-1/2 cups pan drippings; pour into a small saucepan.

Chop giblets. In a large saucepan, cook giblets in oil and butter until browned. Add 1-1/4 cup pan drippings; cook and stir for 5 minutes. Combine flour and remaining drippings until smooth. Gradually stir into pan. Bring to a boil; cook and stir for 2 minutes or until thickened.

Add the wine, sage and remaining chicken broth. Bring to a boil. Reduce heat; simmer, uncovered, for 15-20 minutes or until liquid is reduced by half. Serve with turkey. **YIELD:** 14-16 servings.

EDITOR'S NOTE: This recipe was tested with Morton kosher salt and McCormick rotisserie chicken seasoning. It is best not to use a prebasted turkey for this recipe. However, if you do, omit the salt in the recipe.

decorate with pears

(PICTURED AT RIGHT)

From lovely light green to beautiful blazing red, fresh pears are a natural element to incorporate in your fall decorating. Here are some easy ideas.

FRUIT-FILLED VASE. In a small, water-filled glass, arrange fresh flowers. Center the glass inside a large clear vase. Place small pears in the large vase to cover the glass.

PEAR CANDLE DISPLAY. Cut a brown abaca mat to fit your table. (Ours measured 7 in. x 22 in.) Place the mat in the center of your table. Cut a wide ribbon 1-1/2 inches longer than the mat. Center the ribbon down the length of the mat; tuck ends under the mat.

Look for nine pears in assorted sizes. Cut the tops off of three pears (select ones that will stand upright). Use a melon baller to scoop out the inside, making an opening for a tea light candle in each; place the candle inside.

Arrange the pears, hydrangea blossoms, hypericum berries and eucalyptus on the abaca mat.

PEAR PLACE CARD. On coordinating card stock, cut out circles and leaf shapes. Write a name on each leaf. Rub the edges of the circles and leaves with brown chalk. Align the outer edges of each leaf and circle; punch a hole through both pieces. Thread brown cord through the hole and tie to the stem of a small pear. Set on a plate at each place setting.

It's been said that man can't live on bread alone. But a single bite of the moist and flavorful loaves, rolls and biscuits featured here could prove otherwise!

Adding these artisan favorites to your Thanksgiving feast couldn't be easier. But best of all, nothing gathers friends and family faster than the heavenly aroma of a loaf baking to golden perfection.

Whether it's the soft, chewy texture of Oat Rolls, the robust flavor of Onion Focaccia, the perfectly seasoned taste of Surprise Herb Rolls or the deliciously dense quality of Rosemary Walnut Bread, including any of these freshly baked delights in your feast will fill your kitchen with endless thanks.

FRESH FROM THE OVEN!
(PICTURED AT RIGHT)

Oat Rolls (p. 122)
Surprise Herb Rolls (p. 122)
Onion Focaccia (p. 124)
Rosemary Walnut Bread (p. 124)

a bounty
OF BREAD

oat rolls

(PICTURED ON PAGE 121)

Hearty oats lend appealing texture to moist rolls that have become a standard at our Thanksgiving meal.
LaDale Trimble | SONOMA, CA

1 cup milk

1 cup quick-cooking oats

1/2 cup shortening

1 teaspoon salt

1 package (1/4 ounce) active dry yeast

1/4 cup warm water (110° to 115°)

1/4 cup sugar

1 egg

1 egg yolk

2-1/2 to 2-3/4 cups all-purpose flour

TOPPING:

1/4 cup quick-cooking oats

1/4 teaspoon salt

1 egg white, lightly beaten

In a small saucepan, heat milk until bubbles form around sides of saucepan. Remove from the heat. In a large bowl, pour milk over oats. Add shortening and salt. Let stand until mixture cools to 110°-115°, stirring occasionally.

In a large bowl, dissolve yeast in warm water. Add the oat mixture, sugar, egg, egg yolk and 2 cups flour. Beat until smooth. Stir in enough remaining flour to form a soft dough (dough will be sticky).

Turn onto a floured surface; knead until smooth and elastic, about 6-8 minutes. Place in a greased bowl, turning once to grease the top. Cover and let rise in a warm place until doubled, about 1 hour.

Punch dough down. Turn onto a lightly floured surface; divide into 24 pieces. Shape each into a roll. Place in greased muffin cups. Cover and let rise until doubled, about 30 minutes.

In a small bowl, combine oats and salt. Brush egg white over rolls. Sprinkle with oat mixture. Bake at 375° for 12-15 minutes or until golden brown. Cool for 1 minute before removing from pans to wire racks. Serve warm. **YIELD:** 2 dozen.

surprise herb rolls

(PICTURED ON PAGE 121)

Once during the holidays, my mama and I decided to create a one-of-a-kind dinner roll using only the ingredients we had on hand. These tender bites with a seasoned sour cream filling were the fabulous result.
Hannah Heinritz | MENOMONEE FALLS, WI

1/2 cup sour cream

1/8 teaspoon dried thyme

1/8 teaspoon dried rosemary, crushed

1/8 teaspoon dried basil

1/8 teaspoon dried marjoram

1/8 teaspoon dried oregano

1/8 teaspoon dried parsley flakes

Dash rubbed sage

1 loaf (1 pound) frozen bread dough, thawed

2 tablespoons butter, melted

3 tablespoons grated Parmesan cheese

In a small bowl, combine the first eight ingredients; set aside. Cut bread dough into 12 slices. On a floured surface, roll each slice into a 4-in. circle. Place two teaspoonfuls of sour cream mixture in center of dough. Fold sides of dough over filling; pinch to seal. Place seam side down in greased muffin cups. Cover and let rise until doubled, about 45 minutes.

Brush tops with butter; sprinkle with cheese. Bake at 350° for 18-20 minutes or until golden brown. **YIELD:** 1 dozen.

buttery herb loaves

(PICTURED AT RIGHT)

A rich, buttery flavor—complemented by the perfect blend of herbs—makes slices of this loaf irresistible. People always comment on the pretty swirled appearance.

Lillian Hatcher | *PLAINFIELD, IL*

4 to 5 cups bread flour

1 package (1/4 ounce) active dry yeast

1/4 cup sugar

1 teaspoon salt

1-1/4 cups milk

1/3 cup butter, cubed

2 eggs

FILLING:

1/2 cup butter, softened

1 garlic clove, minced

1/2 teaspoon dried minced onion

1/2 teaspoon dried basil

1/2 teaspoon caraway seeds

1/4 teaspoon dried oregano

1/8 teaspoon cayenne pepper

In a large bowl, combine 2 cups flour, yeast, sugar and salt. In a small saucepan, heat milk and butter to 120°-130°. Add to dry ingredients; beat just until moistened. Add eggs; beat until smooth. Stir in enough remaining flour to form a soft dough.

Turn onto a floured surface; knead until smooth and elastic, about 6-8 minutes. Place in a greased bowl, turning once to grease top. Cover and let rise in a warm place until doubled, about 1 hour.

In a small bowl, combine filling ingredients; set aside. Punch down dough; divide in half. Turn onto a lightly floured surface. Roll each portion into a 15-in. x 9-in. rectangle. Spread filling over each to within 1/2 in. of edges. Roll up jelly-roll style, starting with a short side; pinch seams to seal and tuck ends under. Place seam side down in two greased 9-in. x 5-in. loaf pans. Cover and let rise in a warm place until doubled, about 30 minutes.

Bake at 350° for 20-25 minutes or until golden brown. Cool for 10 minutes before removing from pans to wire racks to cool completely. **YIELD:** 2 loaves (16 slices each).

onion focaccia

(PICTURED ON PAGE 121)

*Mouthwatering onion and garlic flavors are packed into every bite of this specialty bread.
Leftover slices make wonderful turkey sandwiches the next day.*

Jennifer Meacham | PORTLAND, OR

3-1/2 to 4 cups all-purpose flour

1 package (1/4 ounce) active dry yeast

2 teaspoons sugar

1/2 teaspoon salt

3/4 cup water

3/4 cup chicken broth

1/4 cup plus 2 tablespoons butter, divided

2 teaspoons dried minced onion

1 medium red onion, sliced

2 garlic cloves, minced

1/4 teaspoon pepper

2 teaspoons canola oil

In a large bowl, combine 2 cups flour, yeast, sugar and salt. In a small saucepan, heat the water, broth, 1/4 cup butter and dried minced onion to 120°-130°. Add to dry ingredients; beat just until moistened. Stir in enough remaining flour to form a soft dough.

Turn onto a floured surface; knead until smooth and elastic, about 6-8 minutes. Place in a greased bowl, turning once to grease top. Cover and let rise in a warm place until doubled, about 1 hour.

Punch dough down. Cover and let rest for 10 minutes. Meanwhile, in a large skillet, saute the red onion, garlic and pepper in remaining butter until onion is tender. Shape dough into a 12-in. circle; place on a greased baking sheet. Brush with oil. Top with onion mixture, pressing down lightly.

Bake at 375° for 30-35 minutes or until golden brown. Cut into wedges; serve warm. **YIELD:** 1 loaf (12 wedges).

rosemary walnut bread

(PICTURED ON PAGE 120)

*When my friend moved into her new apartment, she shared a family tradition of blessing the new home
with this dense, flavorful loaf. It's sure to add blessings to your own home at Thanksgiving.*

Robin Haas | CRANSTON, RI

1-1/4 teaspoons active dry yeast

1/2 cup warm water (110° to 115°)

1/4 cup whole wheat flour

1-1/2 to 2 cups all-purpose flour

1/3 cup finely chopped walnuts

2 tablespoons honey

1 tablespoon olive oil

1-1/2 teaspoons dried rosemary, crushed

1/2 teaspoon salt

In a large bowl, dissolve yeast in warm water. Stir in whole wheat flour and 1/4 cup white flour. Cover and let stand for 45 minutes. Add the walnuts, honey, oil, rosemary, salt and 3/4 cup white flour. Beat until smooth. Stir in enough remaining flour to form a soft dough.

Turn onto a floured surface; knead until smooth and elastic, about 6-8 minutes. Place in a greased bowl, turning once to grease the top. Cover and let rise in a warm place until doubled, about 1 hour.

Punch dough down. Turn onto a lightly floured surface; divide dough into thirds. Shape each into a 12-in. rope. Place ropes on a greased baking sheet and braid; pinch ends to seal and tuck under. Cover and let rise until doubled, about 1 hour.

Bake at 375° for 20-25 minutes or until golden brown. Remove from pans to wire racks to cool. **YIELD:** 1 loaf (9 slices).

cornmeal biscuits

(PICTURED AT RIGHT)

This is an old, Southern biscuit recipe that I have used often. The cornmeal adds a unique texture that people love. The secret to making a perfect batch is to not mix or handle the dough too much.

Maxine Reese | CANDLER, NC

1-1/2 cups all-purpose flour

1/2 cup cornmeal

1 tablespoon sugar

2 teaspoons baking powder

1/2 teaspoon baking soda

1/2 teaspoon salt

1/4 cup shortening

3/4 cup sour cream

1 egg

4 teaspoons butter, melted

In a large bowl, combine the first six ingredients. Cut in shortening until mixture resembles coarse crumbs. In a small bowl, combine sour cream and egg; add to dry ingredients just until moistened. Turn onto a lightly floured surface; knead 8-10 times.

Pat or roll out to 1/2-in. thickness; cut with a floured 2-1/2-in. biscuit cutter. Place 2 in. apart on a greased baking sheet. Brush with butter. Bake at 425° for 8-12 minutes or until golden brown. Serve warm. **YIELD:** 13 biscuits.

bacon-onion oatmeal buns

Oats create a unique texture while diced bacon and chopped onion add savory flavor to homemade sandwich buns. Of course, you can also enjoy them alone with butter.

Arline Hofland | DEER LODGE, MT

1/2 pound bacon strips, diced

2 large onions, finely chopped

1 cup water

1 cup milk

1 cup quick-cooking oats

1/4 cup molasses

3 tablespoons canola oil

2 teaspoons salt

2 tablespoons active dry yeast

1/2 cup packed brown sugar, divided

1/3 cup warm water (110° to 115°)

1 egg

2 cups whole wheat flour

4 to 4-1/2 cups bread flour

In a large skillet, cook bacon over medium heat until crisp. Using a slotted spoon, remove to paper towels to drain. Saute onions in drippings; drain and set aside.

Meanwhile, in a small saucepan, bring water and milk just to a boil. In a large bowl, pour boiling liquid over oats. Add molasses, oil and salt. Let stand until mixture cools to 110°-115°, stirring occasionally.

In a large bowl, dissolve yeast and 1 tablespoon brown sugar in warm water. Add the bacon, onions, oatmeal mixture, egg, whole wheat flour, 3-1/2 cups bread flour and remaining brown sugar. Beat until smooth. Stir in enough remaining flour to form a soft dough (dough will be sticky).

Turn onto a floured surface; knead until smooth and elastic, about 6-8 minutes. Place in a greased bowl, turning once to grease the top. Cover and let rise in a warm place until doubled, about 1 hour.

Punch dough down. Turn onto a lightly floured surface; divide into 36 pieces. Shape each into a ball. Place 2 in. apart on greased baking sheets. Cover and let rise until doubled, about 30 minutes. Bake at 375° for 12-15 minutes or until golden brown. Cool for 1 minute before removing from pans to wire racks. **YIELD:** 3 dozen.

basil tomato bread

This deliciously different bread has a wonderful aroma and full flavor. Basil and Swiss cheese make it unique from other tomato-flavored breads. I use thick slices when preparing grilled cheese sandwiches.

Linda Nealley | NEWBURGH, ME

1/2 cup shortening

3/4 cup sugar

1 egg

2 cups all-purpose flour

2-1/2 teaspoons baking powder

2 teaspoons dried basil

1 teaspoon salt

1 cup milk

1/2 cup shredded Swiss cheese

1/4 cup oil-packed sun-dried tomatoes, chopped

In a large bowl, cream shortening and sugar until light and fluffy. Add egg; mix well. Combine the flour, baking powder, basil and salt; add to creamed mixture alternately with milk. Fold in cheese and tomatoes.

Transfer to a greased 9-in. x 5-in. loaf pan. Bake at 325° for 50-60 minutes or until a toothpick inserted near the center comes out clean. Cool for 10 minutes before removing from pan to a wire rack. **YIELD:** 1 loaf (16 slices).

pumpkin seed flat bread

(PICTURED AT RIGHT)

Here's a seasonal addition to your harvesttime feast. From its pretty orange color to the irresistible crunch of toasted pumpkin seeds, this flat bread is pleasing to the eye and taste buds. Using sunflower kernels instead of pumpkin seeds is a yummy change.

Terry Braswell | PEACHTREE CITY, GA

1 teaspoon active dry yeast

1 cup warm water (110° to 115°)

6 tablespoons butter, cubed

1/3 cup cornmeal

1 tablespoon sugar

1 tablespoon chili powder

1 teaspoon salt

3 to 3-1/2 cups all-purpose flour

1 egg

2 tablespoons water

1/4 cup salted pumpkin seeds or pepitas

1/2 teaspoon kosher salt

In a large bowl, dissolve yeast in warm water. Add the butter, cornmeal, sugar, chili powder, salt and 1-1/2 cups flour. Beat until smooth. Stir in enough remaining flour to form a soft dough.

Turn onto a floured surface; knead until smooth and elastic, about 6-8 minutes. Place in a greased bowl, turning once to grease the top. Cover and let rise in a warm place until doubled, about 45 minutes.

Punch dough down. Turn onto a lightly floured surface; divide in half. Roll each half into a 14-in. oval. Combine egg and water; brush over dough. Using a pastry wheel, cut each oval into 12 wedges or strips. Sprinkle with pumpkin seeds and kosher salt. Separate wedges and place on greased baking sheets.

Bake at 400° for 10-15 minutes or until golden brown. Remove from pans to wire racks to cool. **YIELD:** 2 loaves (12 wedges each).

bran rolls

A batch of these hearty rolls is among my favorite to bake for friends. Topped with a pad of butter while still warm, they are like a little piece of heaven. Their melt-in-your-mouth flavor makes you forget they're good for you, too!

Lucile Cline | *WICHITA, KS*

3/4 cup All-Bran

1/2 cup boiling water

2 packages (1/4 ounce each) active dry yeast

1/2 cup warm water (110° to 115°)

1/2 cup butter, softened

1/2 cup sugar

1-1/2 teaspoons salt

1 egg, beaten

3-1/2 to 3-3/4 cups all-purpose flour

1 tablespoon butter, melted

In a small bowl, combine bran and boiling water; set aside. In another bowl, dissolve yeast in warm water. In a large bowl, cream the butter, sugar and salt. Add egg and yeast mixture; mix well. Add bran mixture and 2 cups flour; beat on medium speed for 3 minutes. Stir in enough remaining flour to form a soft dough.

Turn onto a lightly floured surface; knead until smooth and elastic, about 6-8 minutes. Place in a greased bowl, turning once to grease top. Cover and let rise in a warm place until doubled, about 1 hour.

Punch dough down. Turn onto a lightly floured surface. Divide dough in half; divide each half into 12 pieces. Shape each into a ball; place balls into a greased 13-in. x 9-in. baking pan. Brush with melted butter. Cover and let rise until doubled, about 1 hour.

Bake at 375° for 20-25 minutes or until golden brown. Remove from pan to wire racks. **YIELD:** 2 dozen.

egg bread braids

With its pretty braided shape, lovely golden color and tender texture, this traditional egg bread will become a recipe-box treasure. Best of all, the impressive loaf is simple enough for even a novice baker.

Robin Price | *ARGILLITE, KY*

1 package (2-1/4 ounces) active dry yeast

1-1/4 cups warm water (110° to 115°)

2 egg yolks

1 tablespoon canola oil

2 teaspoons sugar

2 teaspoons salt

3-1/2 to 4 cups all-purpose flour

1 egg white

1 teaspoon water

In a large bowl, dissolve yeast in warm water. Add the egg yolks, oil, sugar, salt and 3 cups flour. Beat until smooth. Stir in enough remaining flour to form a firm dough.

Turn onto a floured surface; knead until smooth and elastic, about 6-8 minutes. Place in a greased bowl, turning once to grease the top. Cover and let rise in a warm place until doubled, about 1 hour.

Punch dough down. Turn onto a lightly floured surface; divide dough into six pieces. Shape each into a 16-in. rope. Place three ropes on a greased baking sheet and braid; pinch ends to seal and tuck under. Repeat with remaining dough. Combine egg white and water; brush over dough. Cover and let rise until doubled, about 40 minutes.

Brush with remaining egg white mixture. Bake at 375° for 20-25 minutes or until golden brown. Remove from pan to wire rack. Serve warm. **YIELD:** 2 loaves (10 servings each).

swiss beer bread

(PICTURED AT RIGHT)

Mellow Swiss cheese adds wonderful flavor to this moist batter bread that's delicious alongside soup and salad...or all by itself. The aroma of it baking draws people to the kitchen in a hurry.

Debi Wallace | CHESTERTOWN, NY

4 ounces Jarlsberg or Swiss cheese

3 cups all-purpose flour

3 tablespoons sugar

3 teaspoons baking powder

1-1/2 teaspoons salt

1/2 teaspoon pepper

1 can (12 ounces) light beer or nonalcoholic beer

2 tablespoons butter, melted

Divide cheese in half. Cut half of cheese into 1/4-inch cubes; shred remaining cheese. In a large bowl, combine the flour, sugar, baking powder, salt and pepper. Stir beer into dry ingredients just until moistened. Fold in cheeses.

Transfer to a greased 8-in. x 4-in. loaf pan. Drizzle with butter. Bake at 375° for 50-60 minutes or until a toothpick inserted near the center comes out clean. Cool for 10 minutes before removing from pan to a wire rack. **YIELD:** 1 loaf (12 slices).

STORING HOMEMADE BREAD

Think you don't have time to make home-baked breads? Breads actually keep very well so you can make them when time allows.

To store, place cooled breads in an airtight container or resealable plastic bag; keep at room temperature for 2 to 3 days. Breads containing perishable items should be refrigerated.

For longer storage, breads can be frozen for up to 3 months. Thaw at room temperature before serving.

When the weather turns cooler, nothing warms the spirit quite like a generous slice of spiced pumpkin pie. And let's face it, what would Thanksgiving be without this pleasing pie?

But this autumn, why not think outside of the pie plate and offer your friends and relatives the wonderful flavor of pumpkin in a variety of delicious desserts?

With a subtle orange-flavored cake, creamy pumpkin filling and caramel drizzle, Orange Pumpkin Cake is a festive finale to any special dinner.

BEYOND PUMPKIN PIE
(PICTURED AT RIGHT)

Orange Pumpkin Cake (p. 132)

fall into
PUMPKIN DESSERTS

orange pumpkin cake

(PICTURED ON PAGE 131)

A subtle orange flavor really brings out the pumpkin flavor in this elegant layered cake.
Our holiday dinners aren't complete until pieces of this cake are passed around.

Jo Raines | SANDYVILLE, WV

3/4 cup shortening

2-1/4 cups packed brown sugar

3 eggs

1-1/2 cups canned pumpkin

1/2 cup frozen orange juice concentrate

2-1/2 cups all-purpose flour

1-1/2 teaspoons baking powder

1-1/2 teaspoons ground cinnamon

3/4 teaspoon baking soda

3/4 teaspoon ground nutmeg

3/4 teaspoon ground allspice

1/3 cup milk

FILLING:

1 package (8 ounces) cream cheese, softened

1 cup confectioners' sugar

1/2 teaspoon pumpkin pie spice

1 carton (8 ounces) frozen whipped topping, thawed

1/2 cup canned pumpkin

1/4 cup chopped pecans

1/4 cup caramel ice cream topping

In a large bowl, cream shortening and brown sugar until light and fluffy. Add eggs, one at a time, beating well after each addition. Stir in pumpkin and orange juice concentrate. In another bowl, combine flour, baking powder, cinnamon, baking soda, nutmeg and allspice; add to the creamed mixture alternately with the milk, beating well after each addition.

Pour into two greased and floured 9-in. round baking pans. Bake at 350° for 28-32 minutes or until a toothpick inserted near the center comes out clean. Cool for 10 minutes before removing from pans to wire racks to cool completely.

For filling, in a large bowl, beat cream cheese until light and fluffy. Add confectioners' sugar and pie spice; beat until smooth. Fold in whipped topping and pumpkin.

Cut each cake horizontally into two layers. Place bottom layer on a serving plate; spread with a fourth of the filling. Repeat layers three times. Sprinkle with pecans; drizzle with caramel topping. Store in the refrigerator. **YIELD:** 12 servings.

CANDIED PUMPKIN SEEDS

Instead of making the usual savory pumpkin seed snack, try this sweet version.

In a small bowl, combine 1 cup fresh pumpkin seeds, 1/4 cup packed brown sugar, 1/2 teaspoon pumpkin pie spice and 1/4 teaspoon salt. Spread into a greased foil-lined 15-in. x 10-in. x 1-in. baking pan.

Bake, uncovered, at 250° for 45-50 minutes or until seeds are well-glazed, stirring occasionally. Cool completely; break into pieces. Store in an airtight container.

bourbon pumpkin tart with walnut streusel

(PICTURED AT RIGHT)

Because my husband loves pumpkin pie, I've looked high and low for that "perfect" recipe. But as soon as he tasted this tart, he told me to stop searching, declaring this the best he's ever tried!

Brenda Ryan | MARSHALL, MO

2 cups all-purpose flour

1/3 cup sugar

1 teaspoon grated orange peel

1/2 teaspoon salt

2/3 cup cold butter

1 egg, lightly beaten

1/4 cup heavy whipping cream

FILLING:

1 can (15 ounces) solid-pack pumpkin

3 eggs

1/2 cup sugar

1/2 cup heavy whipping cream

1/4 cup packed brown sugar

1/4 cup bourbon

2 tablespoons all-purpose flour

1 teaspoon ground cinnamon

1 teaspoon ground ginger

1/4 teaspoon salt

1/4 teaspoon ground cloves

TOPPING:

3/4 cup all-purpose flour

1/3 cup sugar

1/3 cup packed brown sugar

1/2 teaspoon salt

1/2 teaspoon ground cinnamon

1/2 cup cold butter

3/4 cup coarsely chopped walnuts, toasted

1/4 cup chopped candied or crystallized ginger

In a large bowl, combine the flour, sugar, orange peel and salt. Cut in butter until crumbly. Add egg. Gradually add cream, tossing with a fork until a ball forms. Cover and refrigerate for at least 30 minutes or until easy to handle.

On a lightly floured surface, roll out pastry into a 13-in. circle. Press onto the bottom and up the sides of an ungreased 11-in. fluted tart pan with removable bottom.

In a large bowl, combine the filling ingredients. Pour into crust. For topping, combine the flour, sugar, brown sugar, salt and cinnamon. Cut in butter until crumbly. Stir in walnuts and ginger. Sprinkle over filling.

Bake at 350° for 45-55 minutes or until a knife inserted near the center comes out clean. Cool on a wire rack. Refrigerate leftovers.
YIELD: 14 servings.

pumpkin gingerbread with hard sauce

Cakes are a terrific dessert to take to potlucks because they travel well and feed a lot of people. The slightly sweet hard sauce can also be served with quick breads and scones.

Iola Egle | BELLA VISTA, AR

1 cup butter, softened

1 cup sugar

1/2 cup packed brown sugar

4 eggs

1 can (15 ounces) solid-pack pumpkin

1/2 cup molasses

3-1/2 cups all-purpose flour

3 teaspoons baking powder

1/2 teaspoon baking soda

2-1/2 teaspoons ground ginger

1/2 teaspoon salt

1/2 teaspoon pumpkin pie spice

1 cup shredded peeled apple

Confectioners' sugar

SAUCE:

1/2 cup butter, softened

2 cups confectioners' sugar

1 teaspoon vanilla extract

In a large bowl, cream butter and sugars until light and fluffy. Add eggs, one at a time, beating well after each addition. Stir in the pumpkin and molasses. Combine flour, baking powder, baking soda, ginger, salt and pie spice; add to the creamed mixture. Beat just until combined. Fold in apple.

Transfer to a greased and floured 10-in. fluted tube pan. Bake at 350° for 55-60 minutes or until a toothpick inserted near center comes out clean. Cool for 10 minutes before removing from pan to a wire rack to cool completely. Dust with confectioner's sugar.

In a large bowl, beat the butter, confectioners' sugar and vanilla until smooth. Serve with gingerbread. **YIELD:** 12 servings.

pumpkin chiffon pie

This fluffy and light treat from my mother is a nice variation of traditional pumpkin pie.

Jane Bradford | DECATUR, AL

1 envelope unflavored gelatin

1/3 cup orange juice

3/4 cup packed brown sugar

1/2 cup milk

1/2 teaspoon pumpkin pie spice

3 eggs, separated

1-1/4 cups canned pumpkin

3 tablespoons sugar

1/4 teaspoon vanilla extract

1 pastry shell (9 inches), baked

Whipped topping

In a small saucepan, sprinkle gelatin over orange juice; let stand for 1 minute. Heat over low heat, stirring until gelatin is completely dissolved. Stir in the brown sugar, milk and pie spice. Cook and stir over medium heat until brown sugar is dissolved. Remove from the heat.

Stir a small amount of hot filling into egg yolks; return all to the pan, stirring constantly. Cook and stir over low heat for 3 minutes or until mixture is slightly thickened and a thermometer reaches 160° (do not boil). Remove from the heat; whisk in the pumpkin. Cover and refrigerate for 1 hour, stirring occasionally.

In a small heavy saucepan, combine egg whites and sugar over low heat. With a portable mixer, beat on low speed over low heat until mixture reaches 160°. Remove from the heat. Add vanilla; beat on high until stiff peaks form. Fold into pumpkin mixture. Spoon into pie shell. Cover and refrigerate for 4 hours or until set. Serve with whipped topping. **YIELD:** 6-8 servings.

tapioca pudding in pumpkins

(PICTURED AT RIGHT)

Dinner guests will love this unique, delicious dessert. For those who really love pumpkin, scoop some out along with the tapioca.

Lesli Dustin | SHELLEY, ID

6 small pie pumpkins (4- to 6-inch diameter)

1 teaspoon ground cinnamon, divided

1 cup sugar

6 tablespoons quick-cooking tapioca

1/2 teaspoon salt

4 cups milk

4 eggs, lightly beaten

2 teaspoons vanilla extract

Wash each pumpkin; cut a 2-in. circle around stem. Remove top and discard. Remove loose fibers and seeds from the inside and discard or save seeds for roasting. Sprinkle the insides of pumpkins with 1/2 teaspoon cinnamon. Place in a shallow roasting pan; add 1 in. of water to the pan. Cover and bake at 350° for 45 minutes.

Meanwhile, in a large saucepan, combine the sugar, tapioca, salt and milk. Let stand for 5 minutes. Bring to a boil, stirring constantly. Remove from the heat. Stir a small amount of hot mixture into eggs; return all to the pan, stirring constantly. Bring to a gentle boil; cook and stir 2 minutes longer.

Remove from the heat. Stir in vanilla. Pour into the pumpkins. Cover and bake 15-30 minutes longer or until pumpkins are tender. Sprinkle with the roasted pumpkin seeds if desired and remaining cinnamon. **YIELD:** 6 servings.

PIE PUMPKINS

Pie pumpkins are the most flavorful variety for use in baking. Pick when fully ripened and ready to harvest—the color will be deep orange, and the stem will easily break loose.

Wash, peel and remove seeds. Cut pumpkin into chunks and steam until soft. Puree using a food mill or processor. Cool and pack into freezer bags or containers in the amounts needed for recipes. Use cup-for-cup in place of canned pumpkin.

maple pumpkin cheesecake

For our first Thanksgiving with my husband's family, I wanted to bring a special dish that was sure to impress. I decided I couldn't go wrong with a delectable dessert that combines cheesecake and pumpkin pie. It was a huge success!

Jodi Gobrecht | BUCYRUS, OH

1-1/4 cups graham cracker crumbs

1/4 cup sugar

1/4 cup butter, melted

3 packages (8 ounces each) cream cheese, softened

1 can (14 ounces) sweetened condensed milk

1 can (15 ounces) solid-pack pumpkin

1/4 cup maple syrup

1-1/2 teaspoons ground cinnamon

1 teaspoon ground nutmeg

1/2 teaspoon salt

3 eggs, lightly beaten

TOPPING:

2 cups (16 ounces) sour cream

1/3 cup sugar

1 teaspoon vanilla extract

In a small bowl, combine the cracker crumbs, sugar and butter. Press onto the bottom of a greased 9-in. springform pan. Place on a baking sheet. Bake at 325° for 12 minutes. Cool on a wire rack.

In a large bowl, beat cream cheese and milk until smooth. Beat in the pumpkin, syrup, cinnamon, nutmeg and salt. Add eggs; beat on low speed just until combined.

Pour into crust. Place pan on baking sheet. Bake at 325° for 70-75 minutes or until center is almost set. Combine the topping ingredients; spread over cheesecake. Bake 5 minutes longer.

Cool on a wire rack for 10 minutes. Carefully run a knife around edge of pan to loosen; cool 1 hour longer. Refrigerate overnight. Remove sides of pan. Refrigerate leftovers. **YIELD:** 12-14 servings.

COOLING A CHEESECAKE

To prevent cracks during cooling, it's important to loosen the cheesecake from the sides of the pan after baking. First cool the cheesecake on a wire rack for 10 minutes. Then carefully run a table knife or small metal spatula between the cheesecake and the inside of the pan. Cool 1 hour longer. Refrigerate overnight before removing the sides of the pan.

pumpkin wontons with butterscotch sauce

(PICTURED AT RIGHT)

As a change from the usual pumpkin pie or cake, our home economists created these deliciously different wontons. The butterscotch sauce would also taste great over ice cream.

1 cup canned pumpkin

2 ounces cream cheese, softened

2 tablespoons brown sugar

2 teaspoons grated fresh gingerroot

1/4 teaspoon ground cinnamon

1/4 teaspoon vanilla extract

1/8 teaspoon ground cloves

48 wonton wrappers

Oil for frying

SAUCE:

1 cup packed brown sugar

2/3 cup light corn syrup

1/4 cup butter, cubed

2/3 cup evaporated milk

1 teaspoon vanilla extract

1/8 teaspoon baking soda

For filling, in a large bowl, beat the first seven ingredients until blended. Place a tablespoon of filling in the center of each wonton wrapper. (Keep remaining wrappers covered with a damp paper towel until ready to use.) Moisten edges with water; top with another wonton wrapper. Pinch edges with a fork to seal. Repeat with remaining wrappers and filling.

In an electric skillet, heat 1 in. of oil to 375°. Fry wontons, a few at a time, for 30-60 seconds on each side or until golden brown. Drain on paper towels.

For sauce, in a small saucepan, combine the brown sugar, corn syrup and butter. Bring to a boil, stirring constantly; boil for 1 minute, without stirring. Remove from the heat. Let stand for 5 minutes. Stir in remaining ingredients. Serve with the wontons. **YIELD:** 12 servings (2 cups sauce).

pumpkin spice layer cake

I made up this recipe when my son requested pumpkin cake for Thanksgiving. It was a hit!

Jeanne Cerrone | PEORIA, AZ

1/2 cup butter-flavored shortening

1-1/3 cups sugar

1/2 cup packed brown sugar

2 eggs

1 can (15 ounces) solid-pack pumpkin

2 cups all-purpose flour

2 teaspoons baking powder

1-1/2 teaspoons ground allspice

1 teaspoon ground cinnamon

1/2 teaspoon baking soda

1/2 teaspoon ground ginger

1/2 teaspoon ground nutmeg

FROSTING:

2 packages (3 ounces each) cream cheese, softened

1/2 cup butter, softened

2 teaspoons vanilla extract

1/4 teaspoon salt

5 to 6 cups confectioners' sugar

In a large bowl, cream the shortening, sugar and brown sugar until crumbly, about 2 minutes. Beat in eggs and pumpkin. Combine the flour, baking powder, allspice, cinnamon, baking soda, ginger and nutmeg. Gradually beat into pumpkin mixture; mix well.

Spoon into two greased and floured 9-in. round baking pans. Bake at 350° for 30-35 minutes or until a toothpick inserted near center comes out clean. Cool for 10 minutes before removing from the pans to wire racks to cool completely.

In a large bowl, beat the cream cheese, butter, vanilla and salt until smooth. Gradually beat in confectioners' sugar. Spread the frosting between the layers and over top and sides of cake. Store in the refrigerator. **YIELD:** 10-12 servings.

frosted pumpkin bars

Classic pumpkin bars are a staple for fall get-togethers and always disappear at potlucks and parties.

Sandra McKenzie | BRAHAM, MN

2 cups all-purpose flour

1-1/2 cups sugar

2 teaspoons baking powder

2 teaspoons ground cinnamon

1 teaspoon baking soda

1/4 teaspoon salt

1/4 teaspoon ground cloves

4 eggs

1 can (15 ounces) solid-pack pumpkin

1 cup canola oil

CREAM CHEESE FROSTING:

1/2 cup butter, softened

2 packages (3 ounces each) cream cheese, softened

2 teaspoons vanilla extract

4 cups confectioners' sugar

30 pumpkin-shaped candies

In a large bowl, combine the first seven ingredients. In another bowl, combine the eggs, pumpkin and oil; stir into dry ingredients. Spread into a greased 15-in. x 10-in. x 1-in. baking pan. Bake at 350° for 18-22 minutes or until a toothpick inserted near the center comes out clean. Cool on a wire rack.

For frosting, in a large bowl, beat the butter, cream cheese and vanilla until smooth. Gradually add confectioners' sugar; mix well. Spread over top. Cut into 30 bars; top each bar with a pumpkin candy. **YIELD:** 2-1/2 dozen.

pumpkin tiramisu

(PICTURED AT RIGHT)

Tiramisu is a classic dessert that everyone enjoys. For fabulous flavor that smacks of fall, try this version, which features pumpkin pie filling and spices.

Holly Billings | SPRINGFIELD, MO

1-1/2 cups heavy whipping cream

2 packages (8 ounces each) cream cheese, softened

1 can (15 ounces) solid-pack pumpkin

3/4 cup milk

1/2 cup packed brown sugar

4 teaspoons pumpkin pie spice, divided

2 teaspoons vanilla extract, divided

1 cup strong brewed coffee, room temperature

2 packages (3 ounces each) ladyfingers, split

1 container (8 ounces) frozen whipped topping, thawed

Additional pumpkin pie spice

In a large bowl, beat cream until stiff peaks form; set aside. In another bowl, beat the cream cheese, pumpkin, milk, brown sugar, 1 teaspoon pie spice and 1 teaspoon vanilla until blended. Fold in whipped cream.

In a small bowl, combine coffee and remaining pie spice and vanilla; brush over ladyfingers. In a 3-qt. trifle dish, layer a fourth of the ladyfingers, pumpkin mixture and whipped topping. Repeat layers two times. Sprinkle with additional pie spice. Cover and refrigerate for 4 hours or until chilled. **YIELD:** 16 servings.

EASTER
gatherings

Our inviting Easter dinner showcases Glazed Pork Crown Roast and Parsnip-Asparagus au Gratin. Spring is a time to focus on fresh flavors. So prepare your family a lively assortment of lighter chicken dishes (including Curry-Glazed Golden Chicken and Chicken with Basil Artichoke Sauce) and delightful desserts (such as Creamy Orange Flans and Raspberry Almond Cake).

A rainbow of decorated eggs... dainty yellow daffodils...pretty wicker baskets...everything about Easter signals the arrival of spring!

Such a lighthearted occasion calls for dishes that really showcase this lively season.

For an eye-catching yet easy entree, Glazed Pork Crown Roast is sure to impress dinner guests (especially when filled with an attractive kumquat garnish).

For two refreshing sides, you can't go wrong with make-ahead Lemony Fennel Olives and Parsnip-Asparagus au Gratin.

FRESH FLAVORS

(PICTURED AT RIGHT)

Glazed Pork Crown Roast (p. 146)
Lemony Fennel Olives (p. 146)
Parsnip-Asparagus au Gratin (p. 150)

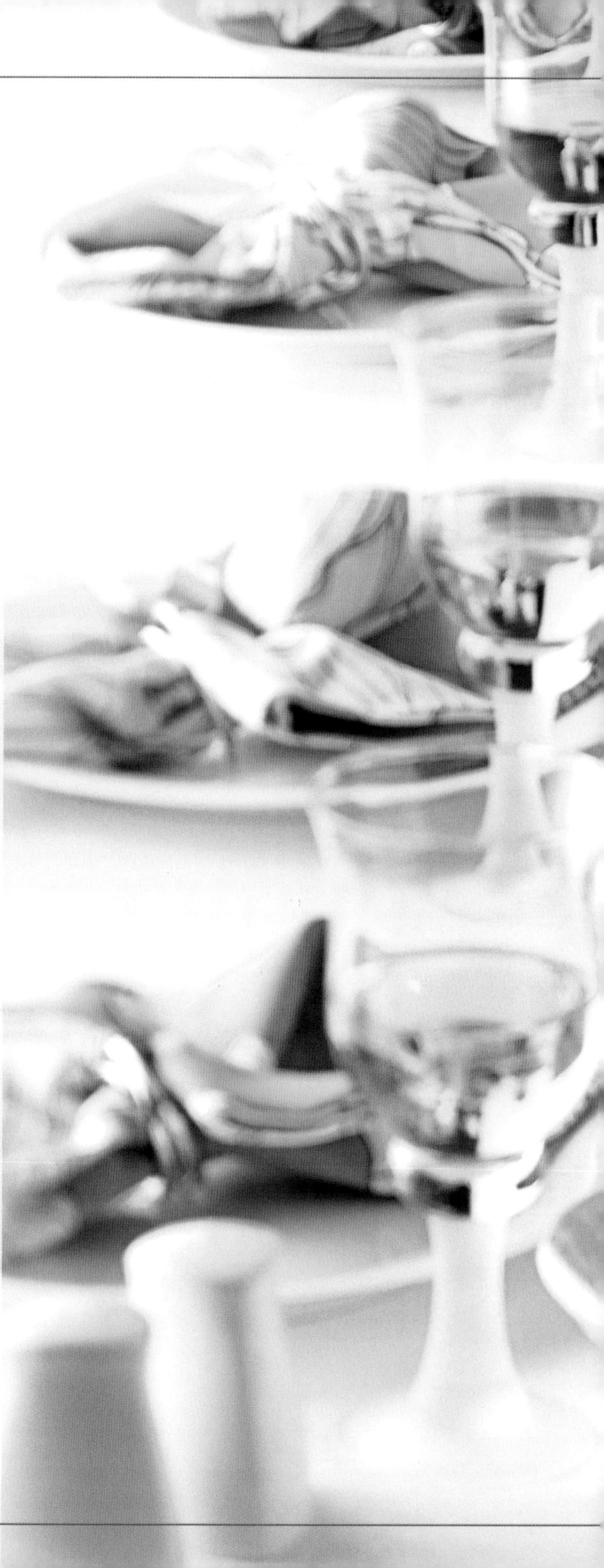

inviting
EASTER MEAL

Easter Dinner
Agenda

A Few Weeks Before:
- Prepare two grocery lists—one for nonperishable items to purchase now and one for perishable items to purchase a few days before Easter.
- Order the pork crown roast.
- Bake Onion Crescents; cool. Transfer to a heavy-duty resealable plastic bag; seal and freeze.

One Week Before:
- If desired, grow the grass seed for the Dainty Daffodil Centerpiece and Flowering Party Favors. (See page 151.)

Two Days Before:
- Buy remaining grocery items, including the pork crown roast.

The Day Before:
- Set the table.
- Make Lemony Fennel Olives; cover and refrigerate.
- For the Caramelized Onion Tart, roast the garlic and bake the crust. When cool, cover and store at room temperature. Saute the onions; place in an airtight container and chill.
- Make the Spring Pea Soup, but don't heat through after pureeing. Cover and refrigerate.
- For Sweet Onion Rice Bake, cook the rice and chop the onions; cover and chill in separate airtight containers.
- Chop the onions; peel and trim the parsnips and asparagus for Parsnip-Asparagus au Gratin. Refrigerate in resealable plastic bags.
- For Lemon Mousse Cornucopias, bake the cornucopias; let cool and store in an airtight container at room temperature. Make the lemon mixture up to the point of whipping the cream; cover and chill.

Easter Day:
- In the morning, thaw the Onion Crescents at room temperature.
- Make Glazed Pork Crown Roast.
- One hour before guests arrive, remove the Lemony Fennel Olives from the refrigerator. Assemble the Caramelized Onion Tart and bake as directed.
- Put together the Sweet Onion Rice Bake and bake.
- Prepare Parsnip-Asparagus au Gratin.
- When the crown roast is standing, reheat the Spring Pea Soup.
- If desired, wrap the crescent rolls in foil and reheat in a 350° oven for 10 minutes. Serve with butter.
- Whip the cream for Lemon Mousse Cornucopias; stir into the lemon mixture and pipe into cornucopias. Garnish and serve.

caramelized onion tart

(PICTURED AT RIGHT)

I've been delighted with the Georgia-grown Vidalia onions ever since I moved here more than 35 years ago. Paired with basil and goat cheese, this appetizer pizza is always well received.

Carol Jordan | *LAWRENCEVILLE, GA*

1 whole garlic bulb

3 tablespoons olive oil, divided

2 pounds sweet onions, sliced

1 tablespoon balsamic vinegar

1-1/2 cups all-purpose flour

3/4 cup cold butter, cubed

1/4 teaspoon salt

FILLING:

10 ounces fresh goat cheese

3 eggs

1 teaspoon minced fresh parsley

1/2 teaspoon salt

1/4 teaspoon coarsely ground pepper

3/4 cup shredded Parmesan cheese, divided

1 cup minced fresh basil

Remove papery outer skin from garlic (do not peel or separate cloves). Cut top off of garlic bulb. Brush with 1 tablespoon oil. Wrap bulb in heavy-duty foil. Bake at 425° for 30-35 minutes or until softened.

Meanwhile, in a large skillet, cook the onions and vinegar in the remaining oil over medium heat for 15-20 minutes or until the onions are golden brown, stirring frequently. Set aside.

Cool the garlic for 10-15 minutes. Squeeze softened garlic into a food processor; add the flour, butter and salt. Cover and process until mixture resembles coarse crumbs. Press onto the bottom and up the sides of an ungreased 11-in. fluted tart pan with a removable bottom. Bake at 350° for 15 minutes.

In a food processor, combine the goat cheese, eggs, parsley, salt and pepper; cover and process until blended. Sprinkle 1/2 cup Parmesan cheese into crust; top with basil. Spread the goat cheese mixture into crust.

Arrange onions over top; sprinkle with remaining Parmesan cheese. Bake for 25-30 minutes or until set. **YIELD:** 16 servings.

glazed pork crown roast

(PICTURED ON PAGE 143)

If you need an elegant entree to serve a crowd, you can't go wrong with crown roast of pork. An easy glaze enhances every bite. When you share the recipe, guests will be pleasantly surprised by the short list of ingredients.

Rita Kitsteiner | *TUCSON, AZ*

1 jar (10 ounces) seedless blackberry spreadable fruit

1 cup orange juice

1/2 cup brandy

1 envelope onion soup mix

6 garlic cloves, minced

1/2 teaspoon ground ginger

1 pork crown roast (16 ribs and about 8 pounds)

In a small saucepan, combine the first six ingredients. Cook and stir over medium heat until jam is melted; brush over roast.

Place roast on a rack in a large shallow roasting pan. Cover rib ends with foil; loosely cover entire roast with foil. Bake at 350° for 2 hours. Uncover and bake 1 to 1-1/2 hours longer or until a meat thermometer reads 160°, basting occasionally with pan juices.

Transfer to a serving platter; let stand for 10-15 minutes. Remove foil from rib ends. Cut between ribs to serve. **YIELD:** 16 servings.

lemony fennel olives

(PICTURED ON PAGE 143)

When spring arrives, I like to prepare recipes with fresh flavor. This make-ahead dish can be served as an appetizer alongside crackers or as a condiment for a meat entree.

Lorraine Caland | *THUNDER BAY, ON*

1 small fennel bulb

2 cups pitted ripe olives

1 small lemon, cut into wedges

1/2 teaspoon whole peppercorns

1/2 cup olive oil

1/2 cup lemon juice

Trim fennel bulb and cut into wedges. Snip feathery fronds; reserve 2 teaspoons. In a small saucepan, bring salted water to a boil. Add fennel. Boil, uncovered, for 1 minute or until crisp-tender. Drain and rinse in cold water.

In a large bowl, combine the fennel, olives, lemon wedges, peppercorns and reserved fennel fronds. Whisk the oil and lemon juice; pour over the olive mixture. Toss to coat. Cover and refrigerate overnight.

Remove from the refrigerator 1 hour before serving. Transfer to a serving bowl; serve with a slotted spoon. **YIELD:** 16 servings.

spring pea soup

(PICTURED AT RIGHT)

I've had this tried-and-true recipe for years. The pleasing pea soup is easy to prepare and has wonderful texture and flavor. Purple chive blossoms make for a pretty garnish.

Denise Patterson | *BAINBRIDGE, OH*

4 cups cubed peeled potatoes

1/4 cup butter, cubed

12 cups chicken broth

4 cups fresh or frozen peas

1/4 cup minced chives

In a Dutch oven, saute potatoes in butter until lightly browned. Stir in broth. Bring to a boil. Reduce heat; cover and simmer for 12 minutes. Stir in peas; cook 5-8 minutes longer or until potatoes and peas are tender. Cool slightly. In a blender, process soup in batches until smooth. Return all to pan and heat through. Sprinkle with chives. **YIELD:** 16 servings (4 quarts).

onion crescents

This recipe is so easy to make, yet offers homemade taste and fills your home with the wonderful aroma of baked bread. The mild onion flavor of the tender rolls complements many main courses. They're so good...you may want to make more than one batch.

Mary Maxeiner | *LAKEWOOD, CO*

1/2 cup butter, softened

1/2 cup sugar

2 eggs

1 package (1/4 ounce) active dry yeast

1 cup warm milk (110° to 115°)

1/2 cup dried minced onion

1/2 teaspoon salt

3-1/2 to 4-1/2 cups all-purpose flour

2 tablespoons butter, melted

In a large bowl, cream the butter and sugar. Add the eggs, one at a time, beating well after each addition. Dissolve the yeast in warm milk; add to the creamed mixture.

Add the onion, salt and 2 cups flour. Beat until blended. Stir in enough remaining flour to form a soft dough.

Turn onto a floured surface; knead until smooth and elastic, about 6-8 minutes. Place in a greased bowl, turning once to grease top. Cover and let rise in a warm place until doubled, about 1 hour.

Punch the dough down. Turn onto a lightly floured surface; divide in half. Roll each into a 12-in. circle; cut each circle into 12 wedges. Roll up the wedges from the wide end and place point side down 2 in. apart on greased baking sheets. Curve the ends to form a crescent shape.

Cover and let rise until doubled, about 30 minutes. Bake at 400° for 8-12 minutes or until golden brown. Brush with melted butter; remove to wire racks. **YIELD:** 2 dozen.

SHAPING CRESCENT ROLLS

Roll a portion of the dough into a 12-in. circle. Cut into 12 wedges and roll up, beginning at the wide end. Place pointed side down 2 in. apart on greased baking sheets. Curve ends to form crescent shape.

lemon mousse cornucopias

(PICTURED AT RIGHT)

I turn refrigerated pie pastry into cute cornucopias that hold a sweet-tart lemon mousse. They're a refreshing dessert for Easter.

Carol Bess White | PORTLAND, OR

20 ice cream sugar cones

2 packages (15 ounces each) refrigerated pie pastry

2 eggs, beaten

2 tablespoons coarse sugar

2 envelopes unflavored gelatin

1 cup lemon juice

1/2 cup cold water

2 teaspoons grated lemon peel

2 packages (8 ounces each) cream cheese, softened

2 cups confectioners' sugar

2 cups heavy whipping cream

Fresh mint leaves and lemon peel strips, optional

Cover sugar cones with foil; lightly spray with cooking spray. Cut the pastry into 1-in.-wide strips; wrap the strips around the prepared cones, sealing seams. Brush with egg; sprinkle with coarse sugar. Bake at 425° for 10-12 minutes or until golden brown. Cool for 10 minutes before removing pastry from cones to a wire rack to cool completely.

Meanwhile, in a small saucepan, sprinkle gelatin over lemon juice and water; let stand for 1 minute or until softened. Heat over low heat, stirring until gelatin is completely dissolved; stir in lemon peel.

In a large bowl, beat cream cheese and confectioners' sugar until smooth; add gelatin mixture. Refrigerate for at least 15 minutes or until thickened.

In a small bowl, beat cream until stiff peaks form; fold into lemon mixture. Pipe into pastry cones; garnish with mint leaves and lemon peel strips if desired. **YIELD:** 20 servings.

parsnip-asparagus au gratin

(PICTURED ON PAGE 143)

*Our home economists pair parsnips with spring asparagus to create a terrific spring side dish.
The cheesy and buttery crumb topping will entice everyone to eat their veggies!*

10 medium parsnips, peeled and cut into 1-inch slices

1/2 teaspoon salt

1/8 teaspoon pepper

1/2 cup butter, divided

2 pound fresh asparagus, trimmed and cut into 2-inch pieces

2 medium onions, chopped

4 garlic cloves, minced

2 cups soft bread crumbs

1/2 cup grated Parmesan cheese

In a large bowl, combine the parsnips, salt and pepper. In a microwave, melt 2 tablespoons butter. Drizzle over parsnips; toss to coat. Transfer to a greased 15-in. x 10-in. x 1-in. baking pan. Bake at 400° for 20 minutes.

Meanwhile, in a microwave, melt 2 tablespoons butter. Combine asparagus and melted butter; add to parsnips. Bake 20-25 minutes longer or until vegetables are tender.

In a large saucepan, saute onions in remaining butter until tender. Add garlic; saute 1 minute longer. Add bread crumbs; cook and stir until lightly toasted. Stir in cheese. Transfer parsnip mixture to a serving platter; sprinkle with crumb mixture. **YIELD:** 16 servings.

sweet onion rice bake

*You'd be hard-pressed to find me serving a different rice dish at Easter. Guests have come to expect
this rich and creamy, comforting casserole every year...and I'm happy to oblige.*

Carol Weber | *CEDAR BLUFFS, NE*

1-1/2 cups uncooked basmati rice

3 pounds sweet onions, chopped

1/2 cup butter

2 cups (8 ounces) shredded Swiss cheese

1 cup heavy whipping cream

2 tablespoons minced fresh parsley

1 teaspoon salt

1/4 teaspoon white pepper

1/4 teaspoon paprika

Cook rice according to package directions. Meanwhile, in a large skillet, cook onions in butter over medium heat for 15-20 minutes or until onions are golden brown, stirring frequently.

In a large bowl, combine the cheese, cream, parsley, salt, pepper, rice and onions. Transfer to a greased 13-in. x 9-in. baking dish; sprinkle with paprika. Bake at 325° for 45-50 minutes or until golden brown. **YIELD:** 18 servings.

dainty daffodil centerpiece

(PICTURED AT RIGHT)

Start the grass seed for this springtime centerpiece at least one week before Easter.

White round serving dish (about 14-in. diameter x 3-in. high)

Tete-a-tete daffodil plant for the center of the centerpiece and three or four additional plants for extra blossoms (choose plants that are about 3 inches tall)

Rye grass seed

Potting soil

Place the daffodil plant in the center of white container. Fill the remainder of the container with potting soil.

Add grass seed to the soil. The grass will germinate and grow to be a couple of inches high in a week. It will continue to grow and fill in the space around the plant. (If the grass gets too long, cut it back with a scissors.)

Before displaying, cut blossoms from the extra plants and insert a toothpick into the stem. Place the blossoms in the grass where desired. (These blossoms will stay fresh for a couple of days.)

EDITOR'S NOTE: The daffodil plant in the centerpiece could be left in its plastic flowerpot. That way, it could be swapped out if the blossoms aren't fully opened on the day it is needed.

FLOWERING PARTY FAVORS

Give guests mini versions of the daffodil centerpiece by making these coordinating party favors. Be sure to begin this project about a week in advance.

Start by spray painting a 3-in. clay pot and matching saucer white; let dry. Plant a tete-a-tete daffodil bulb (about 3 in. tall) in the pot. Fill the pot with potting soil. Add rye grass seed to the soil.

The grass will germinate and grow to be a couple of inches high in a week. It will continue to grow and fill in the space around the daffodil. (If the grass gets too long, cut it back with a scissors.)

When spring has sprung in your neck of the woods, it's time to put away your recipes for heavy winter fare and to start serving lighter cuisine.

One way you can lighten up is by planning menus around chicken. After all, there are endless ways to prepare this popular poultry.

For roasters, reach for a classic dish like Chicken with Fennel Stuffing. It's simple enough for everyday, yet also elegant for guests.

Or turn basic boneless, skinless breasts into something special by making Chicken with Basil Artichoke Sauce or Lemony Chicken Asparagus with Bow Ties.

CHOICE CHICKEN
(PICTURED AT RIGHT)

Lemony Chicken Asparagus with Bow Ties (p. 156)
Chicken with Basil Artichoke Sauce (p. 154)
Chicken with Fennel Stuffing (p. 154)

spring chicken
DINNERS

chicken with fennel stuffing

(PICTURED ON PAGE 152)

*Our Test Kitchen home economists stuff a beautiful golden bird
with fantastic fennel stuffing for an easy, yet impressive main course.*

1 fennel bulb, chopped

1 large onion, chopped

4 tablespoons butter, divided

5 cups unseasoned stuffing cubes

1-1/2 cups chicken broth

1 tablespoon minced fresh thyme

1 teaspoon rubbed sage

1 teaspoon salt, divided

3/4 teaspoon pepper, divided

1 roasting chicken (7 to 8 pounds)

In a large skillet, saute fennel and onion in 2 tablespoons butter until tender. Place in a large bowl. Stir in the stuffing cubes, broth, thyme, sage, 3/4 teaspoon salt and 1/2 teaspoon pepper. Just before baking, loosely stuff chicken with 3 cups of stuffing. Place remaining stuffing in a greased 1-qt. baking dish; refrigerate until ready to bake.

Place the chicken breast side up on a rack in a roasting pan. Melt remaining butter; brush over chicken. Sprinkle with remaining salt and pepper. Bake, uncovered, at 350° for 2-3/4 to 3-1/4 hours or until a meat thermometer reads 180° for chicken and 165° for stuffing.

Bake additional stuffing, covered, for 20 minutes. Uncover; bake 15-20 minutes longer or until lightly browned. Cover the chicken and let stand for 10 minutes before removing stuffing and carving chicken. **YIELD:** 6 servings (6 cups stuffing).

chicken with basil artichoke sauce

(PICTURED ON PAGE 153)

*Lemon-flavored chicken and a basil-artichoke sauce make this
an elegant entree for Easter. It's delicious served over hot cooked pasta or rice.*

Andrea Metzler | MOSCOW, ID

4 boneless skinless chicken breast halves (4 ounces each)

1/4 teaspoon salt

1/4 teaspoon pepper

1 tablespoon canola oil

2 tablespoons lemon juice

SAUCE:

3-1/2 teaspoons cornstarch

1-1/2 cups milk

1 can (14 ounces) water-packed artichoke hearts, rinsed, drained and quartered

3 tablespoons grated Parmesan cheese

2 tablespoons minced fresh basil

2 tablespoons white wine or chicken broth

2 teaspoons lemon juice

1/4 teaspoon salt

1/4 teaspoon pepper

Rub chicken with salt and pepper. In a large skillet, brown chicken in oil on both sides. Transfer to a greased 13-in. x 9-in. baking dish. Drizzle with lemon juice. Bake, uncovered, at 375° for 20-25 minutes or until chicken juices run clear.

Meanwhile, in a small heavy saucepan, whisk cornstarch and milk until smooth. Bring to a boil; cook and stir for 2 minutes or until thickened. Stir in the remaining ingredients; heat through. Serve sauce with chicken. **YIELD:** 4 servings.

tarragon chicken with grapes & linguine

(PICTURED AT RIGHT)

Grapes are definitely a different addition to a chicken dish. But they provide a burst of fruity flavor, especially when paired with a savory tarragon sauce.

Gail Long | *O'FALLON, IL*

8 ounces uncooked linguine

4 boneless skinless chicken breast halves (6 ounces each)

1/4 teaspoon salt

1/4 teaspoon pepper

2 tablespoons olive oil

2 tablespoons butter

1/2 cup white wine or chicken broth

1/2 cup heavy whipping cream

1 cup green grapes, halved

2 tablespoons minced fresh tarragon

Cook linguine according to package directions. Meanwhile, sprinkle chicken with salt and pepper. In a large skillet over medium heat, cook chicken in oil and butter for 5-8 minutes on each side or until juices run clear. Remove and keep warm.

Add wine to skillet; stir to loosen brown bits. Bring to a boil; cook until liquid is reduced by half. Stir in cream; cook and stir until thickened. Add the grapes, tarragon and chicken; heat through. Drain linguine. Serve with chicken mixture. **YIELD:** 4 servings.

FLATTEN FOR FAST COOKING

Chicken breasts will cook more quickly if they're first flattened to about 1/4-inch thickness. The easiest way to do this is to place the poultry in a resealable plastic bag. Close the bag; pound the chicken with the bottom of a small skillet or the smooth side of a meat mallet. To ensure even cooking, pound all breasts to the same thickness.

lemony chicken asparagus with bow ties

(PICTURED ON PAGE 152)

*With plenty of lemon flavor and fresh asparagus, this chicken entree
really shouts, "Spring!" Guests are always intrigued by the lovely lemon cream.*

Helen McGibbon | *DOWNERS GROVE, IL*

8 ounces uncooked bow tie pasta

3/4 pound boneless skinless chicken breasts,
cut into 1/4-inch strips

2 tablespoons butter

1 pound fresh asparagus, trimmed and cut into
1/2-inch pieces

1/4 cup chicken broth

2 tablespoons lemon juice

1/4 cup heavy whipping cream

3 green onions, sliced

2 tablespoons minced fresh parsley

1 teaspoon grated lemon peel

1/2 teaspoon salt

1/4 teaspoon pepper

Cook the pasta according to package directions. In a large skillet, saute the chicken in butter until juices run clear. Remove with a slotted spoon. Reduce heat to medium; add the asparagus, broth and lemon juice. Cover and cook for 4-5 minutes or until the asparagus is crisp-tender.

Stir in the cream, onions, parsley, lemon peel, salt and pepper. Return chicken to the pan; heat through. Drain pasta; add to the skillet. **YIELD:** 4 servings.

barbecue chicken sandwiches

*I love to use my slow cooker. In fact, I have three of them in various sizes!
These saucy chicken sandwiches are real crowd pleasers.*

Lynn Ireland | *LEBANON, WI*

3 pounds boneless skinless chicken thighs

1 cup ketchup

1 small onion, chopped

1/4 cup water

1/4 cup cider vinegar

2 tablespoons Worcestershire sauce

1 tablespoon brown sugar

1 garlic clove, minced

1 bay leaf

2 teaspoons paprika

1 teaspoon dried oregano

1 teaspoon chili powder

1/2 teaspoon salt

1/2 teaspoon pepper

10 kaiser rolls, split

Place chicken in a 5-qt. slow cooker. Combine the ketchup, onion, water, vinegar, Worcestershire sauce, brown sugar, garlic, bay leaf and seasonings. Pour over chicken. Cover and cook on low for 5 hours or until meat is tender.

Discard bay leaf. Remove chicken; shred with two forks and return to slow cooker. Heat through. Serve on rolls. **YIELD:** 10 servings.

grilled chicken with black bean salsa

(PICTURED AT RIGHT)

Mango salsa gives this dish a Southwestern taste without too much heat. I like to slice the chicken and serve it over a long grain and wild rice mix.

Terri Clouse | CONNOQUENESSING, PA

1 cup lime juice

2 tablespoons olive oil

2 teaspoons ground cumin

1 teaspoon salt

1 teaspoon dried oregano

1/2 teaspoon pepper

5 boneless skinless chicken breast halves (4 ounces each)

BLACK BEAN SALSA:

1 can (15 ounces) black beans, rinsed and drained

1 mango, peeled and cubed

1/4 cup minced fresh cilantro

3 tablespoons lime juice

1 tablespoon olive oil

2 teaspoons brown sugar

1 teaspoon diced seeded jalapeno pepper

For marinade, in a small bowl, combine the first six ingredients. Pour 2/3 cup into a large resealable plastic bag; add the chicken. Seal bag and turn to coat; refrigerate for 1-2 hours. Cover and refrigerate remaining marinade for basting.

In a small bowl, combine the salsa ingredients. Cover and refrigerate until serving.

Drain and discard marinade. Grill chicken, covered, over medium heat for 5 minutes. Turn and baste with reserved marinade. Grill 7-10 minutes longer or until juices run clear, basting occasionally. Serve with salsa. **YIELD:** 5 servings.

EDITOR'S NOTE: When cutting hot peppers, disposable gloves are recommended. Avoid touching your face.

indian chicken dish

*I enjoy cooking for my family and try to incorporate new,
healthy foods into our menus. This authentic Indian dish is a favorite.*

Aruna Kancharla | BENTONVILLE, AR

10 garlic cloves, peeled

6 whole cloves

4-1/2 teaspoons chopped fresh gingerroot

1 tablespoon unblanched almonds

1 tablespoon salted cashews

1 teaspoon ground cinnamon

4 cardamom seeds

6 small red onions, chopped

4 jalapeno peppers, seeded and finely chopped

1/4 cup canola oil

3 tablespoons water

1-1/2 pounds boneless skinless chicken breasts,
cut into 1/2-inch cubes

1 cup coconut milk

1 cup (8 ounces) plain yogurt

1 teaspoon ground turmeric

Fresh cilantro leaves

Hot cooked basmati rice, optional

In a food processor, combine the first seven ingredients; cover and process until blended and set aside.

In a large skillet, saute onions and jalapenos in oil until tender. Stir in water and the garlic mixture. Add the chicken, milk, yogurt and turmeric. Bring to a boil. Reduce heat; simmer, uncovered, for 8-10 minutes or until chicken juices run clear. Sprinkle with cilantro. Serve with rice if desired. **YIELD:** 6 servings.

EDITOR'S NOTE: When cutting hot peppers, disposable gloves are recommended. Avoid touching your face.

onion-topped chicken with berry sauce

*I created this recipe by mistake...but now it's part of my regular dinner menus.
A strawberry and spinach salad would be a tasty accompaniment.*

Katie Sloan | CHARLOTTE, NC

4 bone-in chicken breast halves (8 ounces each)

1/2 teaspoon salt

2 tablespoons butter

1 medium onion, thinly sliced

1 celery rib, thinly sliced

1/2 small green pepper, thinly sliced

1 cup chicken broth

1 cup seedless strawberry jam

1/3 cup orange juice

2 tablespoons balsamic vinegar

2 tablespoons minced fresh parsley

1 tablespoon minced fresh thyme or 1 teaspoon dried thyme

Sprinkle chicken with salt. In a large skillet, brown chicken in butter on all sides. Remove and keep warm.

In the same pan, saute the onion, celery and green pepper in drippings until tender. Add the broth, jam, orange juice, vinegar, parsley and thyme. Cook and stir until jam is melted.

Return chicken to the pan. Cover and cook for 30-35 minutes or until the chicken juices run clear. Serve chicken with the sauce. **YIELD:** 4 servings.

curry-glazed golden chicken

(PICTURED AT RIGHT)

After tasting the unique combination of coconut, ketchup and applesauce, your family will want seconds of this glazed chicken. We make it frequently for special occasions.

Julia Detrick | *NILES, MI*

6 tablespoons all-purpose flour

1-1/2 teaspoons salt

1 teaspoon ground ginger

1 broiler/fryer chicken (about 4 pounds), cut up

6 tablespoons butter, melted

GLAZE:

3 bacon strips, finely diced

1/4 cup chopped onion

1 tablespoon all-purpose flour

1/2 cup beef broth

1 tablespoon flaked coconut

1 tablespoon lemon juice

1 tablespoon unsweetened applesauce

1 tablespoon ketchup

1-1/2 teaspoons sugar

1/2 teaspoon curry powder

In a large resealable plastic bag, combine the flour, salt and ginger. Add chicken, a few pieces at a time, and shake to coat. Pour butter into a 13-in. x 9-in. baking pan. Place chicken in pan skin side down; turn once to coat. Bake, uncovered, at 400° for 20 minutes.

Meanwhile, in a large skillet, saute bacon and onion until onion is tender. Stir in flour until blended; gradually add broth. Bring to a boil; cook and stir for 2 minutes or until thickened. Stir in remaining ingredients. Spoon over chicken.

Bake 20 minutes longer or until chicken is crisp and a meat thermometer reads 180°. **YIELD:** 6 servings.

coq au vin

*Coq au vin is a traditional French dish featuring a whole chicken
cooked in red wine. Classic cuisine never goes out of style!*

Doreen Kelly | HATBORO, PA

1/4 cup all-purpose flour

1/4 teaspoon salt

1/4 teaspoon pepper

1 roasting chicken (6 to 7 pounds), cut up and
skin removed

4 tablespoons olive oil, divided

1 pound small fresh mushrooms

1 cup chopped carrots

1 cup chopped celery

2 tablespoons chopped shallots

1-1/2 cups diced plum tomatoes

2/3 cup dry red wine or chicken broth

1/2 cup chicken broth

1 tablespoon minced fresh tarragon or
1 teaspoon dried tarragon

1 bay leaf

2 tablespoons minced chives

Hot cooked rice

In a large resealable plastic bag, combine the flour, salt and pepper. Add chicken, a few pieces at a time, and shake to coat.

In a Dutch oven, brown chicken in 3 tablespoons oil on all sides in batches. Remove and set aside. In the same skillet, saute the mushrooms, carrots, celery and shallots in remaining oil until tender.

Stir in the tomatoes, wine, broth, tarragon, bay leaf and reserved chicken. Bring to a boil. Reduce heat; cover and simmer for 50-60 minutes or until a meat thermometer reads 180°, stirring occasionally. Discard the bay leaf. Sprinkle with chives. Serve with rice. **YIELD:** 6 servings.

cashew chicken with bok choy

*With bok choy and red pepper, this light and lively entree from our home economists is not only colorful
but delicious as well. Your family will ask you to prepare it all year long.*

1 pound boneless skinless chicken breasts,
cut into strips

1 cup chopped celery

1 medium sweet red pepper, julienned

1/2 cup chopped onion

1 teaspoon minced garlic

1/4 cup stir-fry sauce

1 tablespoon canola oil

1 teaspoon cornstarch

1/4 cup chicken broth

1/4 cup sherry or additional chicken broth

1/4 teaspoon salt

1/8 teaspoon pepper

1 head bok choy, trimmed

1/2 cup salted cashews

Hot cooked rice

In a large skillet or wok, stir-fry the chicken, celery, red pepper, onion and garlic in stir-fry sauce and oil until chicken is no longer pink.

In a small bowl, combine the cornstarch, broth, sherry, salt and pepper until smooth. Stir into skillet. Bring to a boil. Cook and stir for 2 minutes or until thickened. Stir in bok choy. Reduce heat to medium; cover and cook for 5 minutes or until bok choy is tender. Sprinkle with cashews. Serve with rice. **YIELD:** 4 servings.

chicken with onions & figs

(PICTURED AT RIGHT)

Friends and family can't get enough of tender chicken thighs in a sweet onion and fig sauce. When prepared this way, the meat turns out moist every time.

Helen Conwell | *FAIRHOPE, AL*

3 large red onions, halved and sliced

3 tablespoons butter

10 dried figs, coarsely chopped

1/4 cup honey

2 tablespoons lemon juice

1 garlic clove, minced

1 teaspoon salt

16 boneless skinless chicken thighs (3 ounces each)

1 teaspoon paprika

In a large skillet, saute onions in butter until tender. Add the figs, honey, lemon juice, garlic and salt. Bring to a boil. Reduce heat; cover and simmer for 20 minutes or until mixture is thick, stirring occasionally.

Place the chicken in two greased 13-in. x 9-in. baking dishes. Spoon onion mixture over chicken. Sprinkle with paprika. Bake at 350° for 35-40 minutes or until juices run clear. Serve with the pan juices. **YIELD:** 8 servings.

CHICKEN TIPS

When purchasing chicken, make sure the package is cold and is free from tears or holes. Always buy before the "sell by" date and use or freeze within 1 to 2 days of purchase.

Never thaw frozen chicken at room temperature. Instead, defrost on a tray in the refrigerator.

After handling raw poultry, use hot, soapy water to thoroughly wash your hands and any utensils, cutting boards or surfaces that have come in contact with the uncooked poultry.

Cook chicken breasts to an internal temperature of 170°, whole birds to 180° and ground chicken to 165°. Cubes and strips are cooked when no longer pink and juices run clear.

If you're "dyeing" for new ways to impress your Easter guests, look no further than this stunning collection of spring desserts.

While baskets of colored eggs and chocolate bunnies are a welcome sight, nothing celebrates Easter like an elegant dessert. From delightful cakes and pleasing pies to velvety custards and delicate pastries, indulge your senses in these from-scratch delights.

Whether you're serving a crowd or hosting a small gathering, you'll find a special treat for every occasion. If entertaining only a few guests, individual Creamy Orange Flans make a vibrant finale to springtime meals. Every bite bursts with refreshing orange flavor that's hard to resist.

SPRING SENSATION
(PICTURED AT RIGHT)

Creamy Orange Flans (p. 164)

luscious
SPRING DESSERTS

creamy orange flans

(PICTURED ON PAGE 163)

*The smooth, velvety texture and vibrant orange flavor
makes these individual flans a delightful way to end a spring meal. Every bite is sheer heaven.*

Elke Rose | WAUKESHA, WI

3/4 cup sugar

1/4 cup orange juice

CUSTARD:

3-1/2 cups milk

6 eggs

1 cup sugar

1/2 teaspoon salt

1 teaspoon grated orange peel

1 teaspoon orange extract

In a small skillet, combine sugar and orange juice; cook over medium-low heat for 10-15 minutes or until mixture is golden brown, stirring occasionally. Quickly pour into six ungreased 6-ounce ramekins or custard cups, tilting to coat bottom of dish. Let stand for 10 minutes.

For custard, in a small saucepan, heat milk until bubbles form around sides of saucepan. Remove from the heat. In a small bowl, whisk the eggs, sugar and salt. Stir half of the warm milk into egg mixture; return all to pan and mix well. Stir in orange peel and extract. Slowly pour into prepared ramekins.

Place ramekins in a baking pan. Fill pan with boiling water to a depth of 3/4 in. Bake, uncovered, at 325° for 30-35 minutes or until centers are just set (mixture will jiggle). Remove ramekins from water bath; cool for 1 hour. Cover and refrigerate for at least 3 hours.

Carefully, run a knife around edge of dishes to loosen; invert each dish onto a rimmed serving dish. Serve immediately. **YIELD:** 6 servings.

pretty strawberry pizza

In this eye-fetching finale, a fresh strawberry topping covers a sweet and creamy filling.

Edna Hoffman | HEBRON, IN

1 cup butter, softened

1/4 cup packed brown sugar

1-1/2 cups all-purpose flour

1/2 cup finely chopped pecans

FILLING:

1 package (8 ounces) cream cheese, softened

1/4 cup confectioners' sugar

1 carton (8 ounces) frozen whipped topping, thawed

TOPPING:

1/2 cup sugar

2 tablespoons cornstarch

Dash of salt

1 cup water

1 package (3 ounces) strawberry gelatin

4 cups sliced fresh strawberries

In a small bowl, cream butter and brown sugar until light and fluffy. Stir in flour and pecans. Pat onto a 12-in. pizza pan. Bake at 400° for 10-12 minutes or until set. Cool on a wire rack.

In a large bowl, beat cream cheese and confectioners' sugar until smooth. Beat in whipped topping until blended. Spread over crust.

For topping, combine the sugar, cornstarch and salt in a small saucepan. Stir in water until smooth. Bring to a boil. Cook and stir for 1-2 minutes or until thickened. Remove from the heat; stir in gelatin until dissolved.

Cool to room temperature, stirring occasionally. Place strawberries in a large bowl; add gelatin mixture and gently toss to coat. Spoon over cream cheese layer. Refrigerate for at least 2 hours before serving. **YIELD:** 12 slices.

magnificent carrot cake

(PICTURED AT RIGHT)

If you're looking for something a little more traditional, nothing says Easter like a homemade carrot cake covered in cream cheese frosting. A touch of rum extract lends wonderful flavor to every bite of this baked-from-scratch indulgence.

Melanie Madeira | DALLAS, PA

2 cups sugar

3/4 cup buttermilk

3/4 cup canola oil

3 eggs

3 teaspoons rum extract

2 cups all-purpose flour

2 teaspoons baking soda

2 teaspoons ground cinnamon

1/2 teaspoon salt

1/2 teaspoon ground allspice

2 cups shredded carrots

1 can (8 ounces) crushed pineapple, drained

3/4 cup chopped walnuts

3/4 cup dried currants

GLAZE:

1/2 cup sugar

1/4 cup buttermilk

1/4 cup butter, cubed

1/2 teaspoon corn syrup

1/4 teaspoon baking soda

1/2 teaspoon vanilla extract

FROSTING:

2 packages (8 ounces each) cream cheese, softened

2/3 cup butter, softened

4 cups confectioners' sugar

4 teaspoons rum extract

In a large bowl, beat the sugar, buttermilk, oil, eggs and extract until well blended. In another bowl, combine the flour, baking soda, cinnamon, salt and allspice; gradually beat into sugar mixture until blended. Stir in the carrots, pineapple, walnuts and currants.

Transfer to two greased and floured 9-in. round baking pans. Bake at 350° for 30-35 minutes or until a toothpick inserted near the center comes out clean.

Meanwhile, for glaze, combine the sugar, buttermilk, butter, corn syrup and baking soda in a small saucepan. Bring to a boil; cook and stir for 4 minutes. Remove from the heat; stir in vanilla. Pour glaze over hot cakes; cool for 10 minutes before removing from pans to wire racks to cool completely.

For frosting, in a large bowl, beat cream cheese and butter until fluffy. Add confectioners' sugar and extract; beat until smooth.

Place one cake layer on a serving plate; spread with 1 cup frosting. Top with remaining cake layer. Frost top and sides of cake. Store in the refrigerator. **YIELD:** 16 servings.

orange dream angel food cake

A basic angel food cake becomes a heavenly indulgence thanks to a hint of orange flavor swirled into every bite.
The orange color makes slices of the cake look so pretty when arranged on individual dessert plates.

Lauren Osborne | HOLTWOOD, PA

12 egg whites

1 cup all-purpose flour

1-3/4 cups sugar, divided

1-1/2 teaspoons cream of tartar

1/2 teaspoon salt

1 teaspoon almond extract

1 teaspoon vanilla extract

1 teaspoon grated orange peel

1 teaspoon orange extract

6 drops red food coloring, optional

6 drops yellow food coloring, optional

Place egg whites in a large bowl; let stand at room temperature for 30 minutes. Sift flour and 3/4 cup sugar together twice; set aside.

Add the cream of tartar, salt and extracts to egg whites; beat on medium speed until soft peaks form. Gradually add remaining sugar, about 2 tablespoons at a time, beating on high until stiff glossy peaks form and sugar is dissolved. Gradually fold in flour mixture, about 1/2 cup at a time.

Gently spoon half of batter into an ungreased 10-in. tube pan. To the remaining batter stir in the orange peel, orange extract and food colorings if desired. Gently spoon orange batter over white batter. Cut through both layers with a knife to swirl the orange and remove air pockets.

Bake on the lowest oven rack at 375° for 30-35 minutes or until lightly browned and entire top appears dry. Immediately invert pan; cool completely, about 1 hour.

Run a knife around side and center tube of pan. Remove cake to a serving plate. **YIELD:** 16 servings.

COOLING FOAM CAKES

Foam cakes are done when the top springs back when touched with your finger and the cracks at the top of the cake look and feel dry. It's important to cool foam cakes upside down in the pan, otherwise they will collapse and flatten.

If using a tube pan with legs, invert the pan onto its legs until the cake is completely cool.

If using a tube pan without legs, invert the pan and place the neck over a funnel or narrow bottle until the cake is completely cool.

rhubarb cherry cobbler

(PICTURED AT RIGHT)

What could be more welcoming than a fruit cobbler fresh from the oven? Here's a simple way to enjoy a springtime twist on the comforting favorite using fresh rhubarb and cherry pie filling.

Jill Head | HILBERT, WI

1/4 cup sugar

2 tablespoons cornstarch

3/4 teaspoon ground allspice

2 cans (21 ounces each) cherry pie filling

3 cups diced fresh or frozen rhubarb, thawed

ALMOND TOPPING:

2 cups all-purpose flour

3 tablespoons plus 2 teaspoons sugar, divided

2 teaspoons baking powder

1/2 teaspoon salt

2 cups heavy whipping cream

1/2 teaspoon almond extract

1/4 cup sliced almonds

In a large bowl, combine the sugar, cornstarch and allspice. Fold in the pie filling and rhubarb.

Transfer to an ungreased 13-in. x 9-in. baking dish. Cover and bake at 400° for 15-20 minutes or until rhubarb is tender.

Meanwhile, in a large bowl, combine the flour, 3 tablespoons sugar, baking powder and salt; stir in the cream and extract just until a soft dough forms. Drop by spoonfuls over cherry mixture; sprinkle with almonds and remaining sugar.

Bake, uncovered, for 30-35 minutes or until topping is golden brown and filling is bubbly. Serve warm. **YIELD:** 12 servings.

EDITOR'S NOTE: If using frozen rhubarb, measure rhubarb while still frozen, then thaw completely. Drain in a colander, but do not press liquid out.

rhubarb orange cream pie

The unique flavor combination in this specialty pie makes it a favorite around my dinner table. The creamy custard-like filling, bits of fresh rhubarb and crunchy pecan topping add a variety of textures my guests rave about.

Terri Rocheleau | MAUCKPORT, IN

1 sheet refrigerated pie pastry

3 eggs, separated

1 cup sugar, divided

3 tablespoons orange juice concentrate

1/3 cup all-purpose flour

1/4 teaspoon salt

2-1/2 cups chopped fresh rhubarb

1/4 cup butter, melted

1/3 cup chopped pecans

Unroll pastry into a 9-in. pie plate; flute edges.

In a small bowl, beat egg whites on medium speed until soft peaks form. Gradually beat in 1/4 cup sugar, 1 tablespoon at a time, on high until stiff peaks form; set aside.

In a large bowl, combine egg yolks and orange juice concentrate; stir in the flour, salt and remaining sugar. Stir in rhubarb and butter. Fold in egg white mixture.

Pour into pastry shell; sprinkle with pecans. Bake at 375° for 15 minutes. Reduce heat to 325°. Bake 35-40 minutes longer or until center is set. Cool on a wire rack for 1 hour. Store in the refrigerator. **YIELD:** 8 servings.

strawberry-white chocolate layer cake

An irresistible strawberry buttercream frosting is spread between layers of tender strawberry-chocolate flavored cake. For a stunning presentation, garnish the cake with sliced fresh strawberries.

Becky Duncan | LEMING, TX

4 eggs, separated

1 cup butter, softened

1-3/4 cups sugar

1 teaspoon vanilla extract

1/2 teaspoon strawberry extract

1 cup buttermilk

1/2 cup water

2-1/2 cups cake flour

1 teaspoon baking soda

1 teaspoon salt

4 squares (1 ounce each) white baking chocolate, melted

FROSTING:

1 cup butter, softened

3 cups confectioners' sugar

2/3 cup seedless strawberry jam

Let eggs stand at room temperature for 30 minutes. Line three greased 9-in. round baking pans with waxed paper and grease paper; set aside.

In a large bowl, cream butter and sugar until light and fluffy. Add egg yolks, one at a time, beating well after each addition. Add the extracts. In a small bowl, combine buttermilk and water.

Combine the flour, baking soda and salt; add to the creamed mixture alternately with buttermilk mixture, beating well after each addition. Stir in chocolate. In a small bowl, beat egg whites until stiff peaks form; fold into batter. Pour into prepared pans.

Bake at 350° for 20-25 minutes or until a toothpick inserted near the center comes out clean. Cool for 10 minutes before removing from pans to wire racks; gently peel off waxed paper.

For frosting, in a large bowl, cream butter and confectioners' sugar until light and fluffy. Beat in jam. Spread between layers and over top of cake. Store in the refrigerator. **YIELD:** 12 servings.

chocolate raspberry napoleons

(PICTURED AT RIGHT)

Add a touch of whimsy to your Easter feast with this springtime version of a classic pastry. Fluffy chocolate mousse and bright raspberries are sandwiched between flaky sheets of phyllo, then sprinkled with powdered sugar for an elegant finish.

Jordan Sucher | BROOKLYN, NY

4 squares (1 ounce each) bittersweet chocolate, chopped

1 cup heavy whipping cream

8 sheets phyllo dough

6 tablespoons butter, melted

3 tablespoons sugar

2 cups fresh raspberries

Confectioners' sugar

Place chocolate in a small bowl. In a small saucepan, bring cream just to a boil. Pour over chocolate; whisk until smooth. Refrigerate until chilled.

Meanwhile, place one sheet of phyllo dough on a work surface (keep remaining dough covered with plastic wrap and a damp towel to prevent it from drying out). Brush with butter; sprinkle with sugar. Repeat layers seven times. Cut into eight rectangles. Place on an ungreased baking sheet.

Bake at 350° for 10-12 minutes or until golden brown. Cool on a wire rack.

In a small bowl, beat chocolate mixture until soft peaks form, about 15 seconds.

Gently split each pastry in half horizontally. Spread 3 tablespoons chocolate mixture over bottom halves; layer with raspberries and remaining chocolate mixture. Replace tops. Sprinkle with confectioners' sugar. Serve immediately. **YIELD:** 8 servings.

PHYLLO DOUGH POINTERS

Phyllo (pronounced FEE-lo) is a tissue-thin dough generally sold in the freezer section of grocery stores. Typically used for desserts, appetizers and main dishes, phyllo dough is liberally basted with melted butter between each sheet so that it bakes up crisp and flaky.

SPECIAL
celebrations

Italian-themed dinners, March Madness get-togethers, July Fourth affairs, pool-side parties and Halloween bashes are just a few reasons to celebrate throughout the year. And our eye-catching cakes turn any occasion into something special! For no-fuss dining, stock your freezer with a selection of flavorful fare. Or perk up your menu by preparing foods featuring robust coffee!

Italian cuisine is comfort food at its finest. Now you can bring a little taste of Italy to your table with all of the mouthwatering recipes featured here.

Start the dinner with a Classic Antipasto, featuring a selection of savory meats, cheeses, olives and more.

With beans and meatballs, hearty Zuppa di Fagioli will warm the hearts of dinner guests.

Friends and family will give their complimenti alla cuoca (compliments to the cook) when you set out hearty entrees such as traditional Osso Buco and Shrimp Filetto di Pomodoro.

A platter of Arancini di Riso (rice balls) rounds out the meal.

BUON APPETITO!

(PICTURED AT RIGHT)

Shrimp Filetto di Pomodoro (p. 176)
Arancini di Riso (p. 174)
Zuppa di Fagioli (p. 178)
Osso Buco (p. 180)
Classic Antipasto (p. 181)

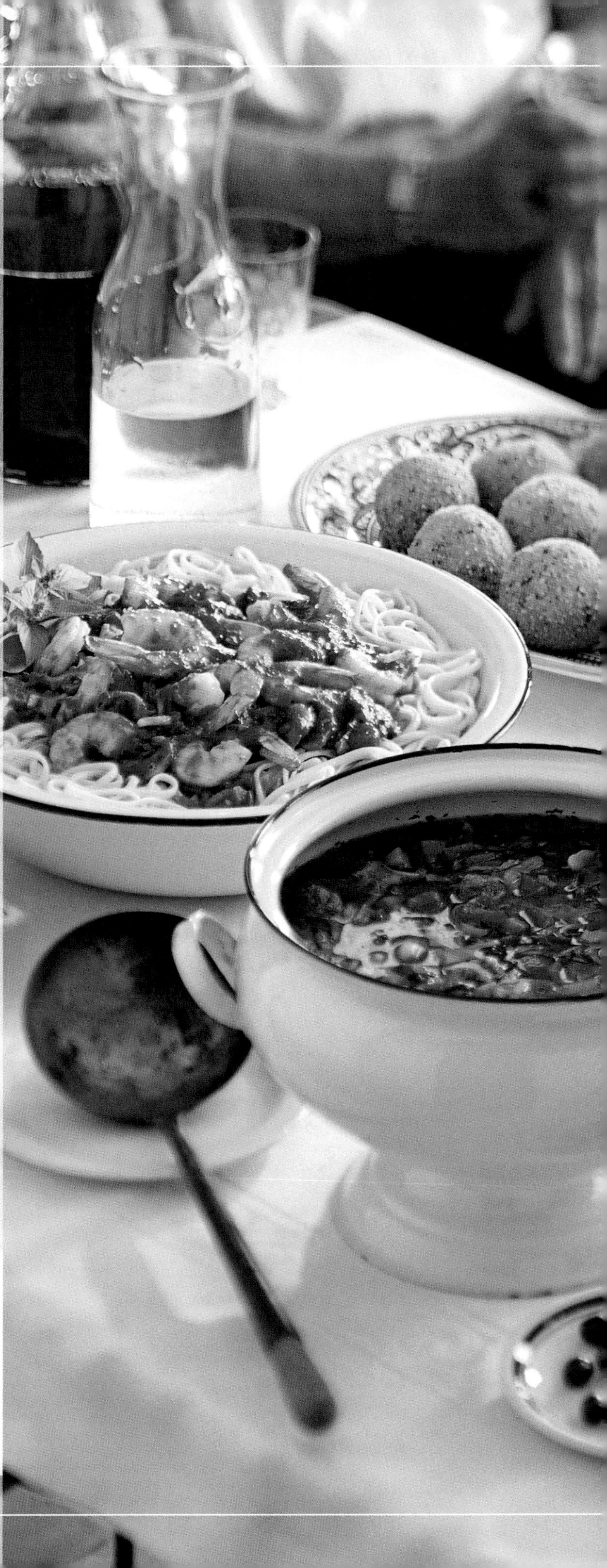

make it
ITALIAN!

arancini di riso

(PICTURED AT FAR RIGHT AND ON PAGE 172)

In Italy, rice balls are often served as a side dish, like bread. This version features a ground beef and green pea filling, making them a great addition to a main course. Serve them with your favorite marinara sauce if desired.

Enza Margiotta | *SICILY, ITALY*

2 cups uncooked arborio rice

1 egg yolk

1/2 cup grated Parmesan cheese

1/4 cup butter, melted

1/3 pound ground beef

1 medium onion, chopped

1/2 cup Italian tomato sauce

1/2 cup frozen peas, thawed

1/4 teaspoon salt

1/4 teaspoon pepper

2 egg whites

1-1/2 cups seasoned bread crumbs

Oil for deep-fat frying

Cook rice according to package directions. Cool slightly. Stir in the egg yolk, cheese and butter. Cover and refrigerate until cooled.

Meanwhile, in a large skillet, cook beef and onion over medium heat until meat is no longer pink; drain. Stir in the tomato sauce, peas, salt and pepper.

Shape the rice mixture into 11 patties. Place one heaping tablespoonful of meat filling in center of each patty. Shape rice around filling, forming a ball.

Place egg whites and bread crumbs in separate shallow bowls. Dip rice balls in egg whites, then roll in the bread crumbs. In an electric skillet or deep-fat fryer, heat oil to 375°. Fry rice balls, a few at a time, for 1-2 minutes on each side or until golden brown. Drain on paper towels. **YIELD:** 11 servings.

MUDRICA MEANS TOASTED BREAD CRUMBS

Instead of sprinkling grated Parmesan cheese over Homemade Ravioli in the photo pictured at right, we used toasted bread crumbs or "Mudrica."

In Italy, Pasta con Mudrica (spaghetti tossed with olive oil and bread crumbs) is often served on March 19th, the Feast of St. Joseph. The bread crumbs are meant to resemble sawdust, representing St. Joseph's work as a carpenter.

Ann Gagliano from West Allis, Wisconsin shares her version of Mudrica. Cook 1 cup soft bread crumbs in a large heavy skillet over low heat for 7-9 minutes or until golden brown, stirring frequently. Stir in 2 tablespoons sugar and 1/4 teaspoon ground cinnamon. Remove from the heat. Store in an airtight container at room temperature. Sprinkle on a variety of Italian entrees.

homemade ravioli

(PICTURED AT RIGHT)

I love to bake and cook, especially Italian dishes. In fact, my idea of a perfect day consists of cooking my family's favorite foods then watching them dig in!

Lori Daniels | HARTLAND, MI

6 to 6-1/2 cups all-purpose flour

6 eggs

3/4 cup water

2 teaspoons olive oil

SAUCE:

1 can (28 ounces) crushed tomatoes

1-1/2 cups tomato puree

1/2 cup grated Parmesan cheese

1/3 cup water

1/3 cup tomato paste

3 tablespoons sugar

2 tablespoons minced fresh basil

1 tablespoon minced fresh parsley

1 tablespoon minced fresh oregano

1 garlic clove, minced

1/2 teaspoon salt

1/4 teaspoon pepper

FILLING:

1 carton (15 ounces) ricotta cheese

2 cups (8 ounces) shredded part-skim mozzarella cheese

1/3 cup grated Parmesan cheese

1 egg, lightly beaten

2 teaspoons minced fresh basil

1 teaspoon minced fresh parsley

1 teaspoon minced fresh oregano

1/4 teaspoon garlic powder

1/8 teaspoon salt

1/8 teaspoon pepper

Place 6 cups flour in a large bowl. Make a well in the center. Beat the eggs, water and oil; pour into well. Stir together, forming a ball. Turn onto a floured surface; knead until smooth and elastic, about 8-10 minutes, adding remaining flour if necessary to keep dough from sticking. Cover and let rest for 30 minutes.

Meanwhile, in a Dutch oven, combine the sauce ingredients. Bring to a boil. Reduce heat; cover and simmer for 1 hour, stirring occasionally.

In a large bowl, combine the filling ingredients. Cover and refrigerate until ready to use.

Divide dough into fourths; roll one portion to 1/16-in. thickness. (Keep the pasta covered until ready to use.) Working quickly, place rounded teaspoonfuls of filling 1 in. apart over half of pasta sheet. Brush around filling with water to moisten. Fold sheet over; press down to seal. Cut into squares with a pastry wheel. Repeat with remaining dough and filling.

Bring a soup kettle of salted water to a boil. Add ravioli. Reduce heat to a gentle simmer; cook for 1-2 minutes or until ravioli float to the top and are tender. Drain. Spoon sauce over ravioli. **YIELD:** 6 servings.

shrimp filetto di pomodoro

(PICTURED ON PAGE 172)

This sensational seafood and pasta dinner is great for special occasions.
Scallops can be used in place of the shrimp if desired.

Cherie Chism | *HOLLIDAYSBURG, PA*

1/2 pound bacon strips, diced

1 medium onion, sliced

1/2 pound sliced fresh mushrooms

4 garlic cloves, minced

1 tablespoon butter

2 cans (one 28 ounces, one 15 ounces) crushed tomatoes

1/4 cup minced fresh basil

1 tablespoon sugar

1/4 teaspoon salt

1/4 teaspoon pepper

1 package (16 ounces) linguine

2 pounds uncooked large shrimp, peeled and deveined

Grated Parmesan cheese, optional

In a large skillet, cook bacon over medium heat until crisp. Using a slotted spoon, remove to paper towels; drain, reserving 2 tablespoons drippings. Saute the onion, mushrooms and garlic in drippings and butter until tender. Add the tomatoes, basil, sugar, salt and pepper. Bring to a boil over medium heat. Reduce the heat; simmer, uncovered, for 15 minutes.

Meanwhile, cook linguine according to package directions. Add shrimp and reserved bacon to the tomato mixture; cook, uncovered, for 5-6 minutes or until shrimp turn pink. Drain linguine; place in a large bowl. Top with shrimp mixture. Garnish with cheese if desired. **YIELD:** 10 servings.

PEELING & DEVEINING SHRIMP

Remove the shell from the shrimp, starting on the underside by the head. Pull the shell up around the top to the other side. Pull off the shell by the tail.

To remove the black vein running down the back of the shrimp, use a paring knife to make a slit along the back from the head to the tail.

Rinse the shrimp under cold water to remove the vein.

Save prep time when dinner arrives by peeling and cleaning the shrimp earlier in the day. Refrigerate in a covered container.

eggplant rollatini

(PICTURED AT RIGHT)

These authentic eggplant roll-ups may take some time to prepare, but the end result is restaurant-quality.

Nancy Sousley | *LAFAYETTE, IN*

1 large eggplant

1 tablespoon salt

SAUCE:

1 small onion, chopped

2 garlic cloves, minced

1/4 cup olive oil

1 can (15 ounces) tomato sauce

1 can (14-1/2 ounces) diced tomatoes

1/2 cup chicken broth

1/4 cup tomato paste

2 tablespoons minced fresh parsley

2 teaspoons sugar

1/2 teaspoon salt

1/2 teaspoon dried basil

1/4 teaspoon pepper

1/8 teaspoon crushed red pepper flakes

FILLING:

1 carton (15 ounces) ricotta cheese

1 cup (4 ounces) shredded part-skim mozzarella cheese

1/2 cup grated Parmesan cheese

1/4 cup minced fresh parsley

1 egg, lightly beaten

1/8 teaspoon pepper

COATING:

3 eggs, beaten

1 cup seasoned bread crumbs

1 cup grated Parmesan cheese, divided

2 garlic cloves, minced

2 tablespoons minced fresh parsley

Dash each salt and pepper

Oil for frying

Peel and slice eggplant lengthwise into fifteen 1/8-in. thick slices. Place in a colander over a plate; sprinkle with salt and toss. Let stand for 30 minutes.

Meanwhile, for sauce, in a large saucepan, saute onion and garlic in oil. Add remaining ingredients. Bring to a boil. Reduce heat; simmer, uncovered, for 20-25 minutes or until flavors are blended, stirring occasionally. Rinse and drain eggplant.

In a large bowl, combine the filling ingredients; set aside.

Place eggs in a shallow bowl. In another shallow bowl, combine the bread crumbs, 1/2 cup Parmesan cheese, garlic, parsley, salt and pepper. Dip eggplant in eggs, then bread crumb mixture.

In an electric skillet, heat 1/2 in. of oil to 375°. Fry eggplant in batches for 2-3 minutes on each side or until golden brown. Drain on paper towels.

Spoon 1 cup sauce into an ungreased 13-in. x 9-in. baking dish. Spread 2 rounded tablespoons filling over each eggplant slice. Carefully roll up and place seam side down in baking dish. Spoon remaining sauce over roll-ups. Sprinkle with remaining Parmesan cheese. Cover and bake at 375° for 30-35 minutes or until bubbly. **YIELD:** 5 servings.

frittelle di riso

(PICTURED AT FAR RIGHT)

*For this traditional Italian dinner, our Test Kitchen created these
rice fritters that serve as a sweet and satisfying dessert.*

7-1/2 cups water

2-1/2 cups uncooked arborio rice

1 cup sugar

1/2 cup milk

2 eggs

1 teaspoon baking powder

1/2 teaspoon salt

1/2 teaspoon vanilla extract

3/4 cup all-purpose flour

Oil for deep-fat frying

Confectioners' sugar and honey, optional

In a large saucepan, bring water and rice to a boil. Reduce heat; cover and simmer for 15-18 minutes or until liquid is absorbed and rice is tender. Stir in sugar and milk. Refrigerate until chilled. In a small bowl, whisk the eggs, baking powder, salt and vanilla; add to rice mixture. Stir in flour.

In an electric skillet or deep-fat fryer, heat oil to 375°. Shape tablespoonfuls of rice mixture into 2-in. ovals. Fry ovals, a few at a time, for 1 minute on each side or until golden brown. Drain on paper towels. Sprinkle with confectioners' sugar and drizzle with honey if desired. **YIELD:** 4 dozen.

zuppa di fagioli

(PICTURED ON PAGE 172)

*I like to welcome family home with steaming bowls of this hearty white bean soup.
It features plenty of vegetables as well as tender Italian meatballs.*

Mary Caron | *EDENTON, NC*

2 tablespoons dry bread crumbs

1 tablespoon grated Parmesan cheese

1/4 pound bulk Italian sausage

1 cup sliced leeks (white portion only)

1 medium carrot, chopped

1 celery rib, chopped

1 garlic clove, minced

1 tablespoon canola oil

2 cans (15-1/2 ounces each) great northern beans, rinsed and drained

2 cans (14-1/2 ounces each) reduced-sodium chicken broth

1 can (14-1/2 ounces) reduced-sodium beef broth

1 can (14-1/2 ounces) diced tomatoes in sauce

1 package (6 ounces) fresh baby spinach

3 tablespoons minced fresh basil

2 tablespoons minced fresh parsley

1/2 teaspoon salt

1/4 teaspoon pepper

In a large bowl, combine bread crumbs and cheese. Crumble sausage over mixture and mix well. Shape into 1/2-in. balls.

Place in a greased 15-in. x 10-in. x 1-in. baking pan. Bake at 350° for 8-10 minutes or until juices run clear; drain and set aside.

In a Dutch oven, saute leeks, carrot, celery and garlic in oil until tender. Stir in the beans, broths, tomatoes, spinach, basil, parsley, salt, pepper and reserved meatballs. Cook until spinach is tender and meatballs are heated through. **YIELD:** 10 servings (2-1/4 quarts).

chocolate cannoli

(PICTURED AT RIGHT)

Our Test Kitchen's version of a famous Italian dessert features a creamy filling dotted with chocolate chunks. The chopped pistachios are an attractive touch.

1 egg

1/4 cup sugar

1/4 cup butter, melted

1/2 teaspoon vanilla extract

1/4 teaspoon grated lemon peel

1/8 teaspoon almond extract

1/2 cup all-purpose flour

1/4 teaspoon baking powder

FILLING:

3/4 cup sugar

3 tablespoons cornstarch

1 cup milk

1-1/8 teaspoons vanilla extract

1 drop cinnamon oil, optional

1-3/4 cups ricotta cheese

1 milk chocolate candy bar with almonds (4-1/4 ounces), chopped

1/2 cup chopped pistachios

In a large bowl, beat the egg, sugar, butter, vanilla, lemon peel and almond extract until blended. Combine flour and baking powder; stir into egg mixture and mix well.

Bake in a preheated pizzelle iron according to manufacturer's directions until golden brown. Remove cookies and immediately shape into tubes. Place on wire racks to cool.

In a small saucepan, combine sugar and cornstarch. Stir in milk until smooth. Bring to a boil; cook and stir for 2 minutes or until thickened. Stir in vanilla and cinnamon oil if desired. Cool completely.

In a large bowl, beat ricotta cheese until smooth. Gradually beat in custard mixture. Fold in chocolate. Spoon or pipe into shells. Dip each side in pistachios. Serve immediately. Refrigerate leftovers. **YIELD:** 1 dozen.

osso buco

(PICTURED ON PAGE 173)

*My family has come to expect these tender veal shanks for every special occasion
we celebrate. Risotto and a green salad round out the meal nicely.*

Lorraine Caland | *THUNDER BAY, ON*

1/3 cup all-purpose flour

1/4 teaspoon salt

1/4 teaspoon pepper

6 to 7 pounds veal shanks, cut into
2-inch-thick slices

1/3 cup canola oil

1 medium onion, chopped

1 small carrot, chopped

1 celery rib, chopped

1 garlic clove, minced

2 tablespoons butter

1 can (14-1/2 ounces) diced tomatoes, undrained

1-3/4 cups chicken broth

1/2 teaspoon dried basil

1/2 teaspoon dried thyme

2 bay leaves

GARNISH (GREMOLATA):

1 tablespoon minced fresh parsley

1 tablespoon grated lemon peel

1 garlic clove, minced

In a large resealable plastic bag, combine the flour, salt and pepper. Add veal, a few pieces at a time, and shake to coat. In an oven-proof Dutch oven, brown meat in oil in batches on all sides; drain.

In a large skillet, saute the onion, carrot, celery and garlic in butter until tender. Return veal to the Dutch oven; top with vegetable mixture. Add the tomatoes, broth, basil, thyme and bay leaves.

Cover and bake at 325° for 2 to 2-1/4 hours or until the meat and vegetables are tender. Remove and discard the bay leaves. Just before serving, combine the garnish ingredients; sprinkle over the veal. **YIELD:** 10 servings.

almond peach gelato

This rich and delicious dessert is especially outstanding when served with warm peaches or peach pie.

Rita Kitsteiner | *TUCSON, AZ*

2 cups milk

1/2 cup confectioners' sugar

4 egg yolks, lightly beaten

2 to 3 teaspoons grated lemon peel

1 teaspoon almond extract

1 package (16 ounces) frozen unsweetened sliced peaches, thawed and chopped

1 cup half-and-half cream

1/2 cup slivered almonds

In a small heavy saucepan, heat milk to 175°; stir in confectioners' sugar until dissolved. Whisk a small amount of hot mixture into egg yolks. Return all to the pan, whisking constantly. Add lemon peel. Cook and stir over low heat until mixture reaches at least 160° and coats the back of a metal spoon.

Remove from the heat. Stir in extract. Cool quickly by placing pan in a bowl of ice water; stir for 2 minutes. Stir in the peaches, cream and almonds. Press waxed paper onto surface of custard. Refrigerate for several hours or overnight.

Fill cylinder of ice cream freezer two-thirds full; freeze according to manufacturer's directions. Refrigerate remaining mixture until ready to freeze. When ice cream is frozen, transfer to a freezer container; freeze for 2-4 hours before serving. **YIELD:** 1-1/2 quarts.

classic antipasto

(PICTURED AT RIGHT AND ON PAGE 173)

Antipasto means "before the pasta" and is the first course in a traditional Italian dinner.

Antipasto platters have a lively combination of flavors that tempt the taste buds for the fabulous foods to follow! They can consist of many items from the categories listed below. For the best flavor, be sure to use the highest-quality ingredients you can find and afford.

MEATS. Traditional types comprise of mortadella, smoked ham, prosciutto and varieties of salami (such as Genoa and Cotto).

CHEESES. Cubes or slices of hard, soft and semisoft cheeses in assorted flavors are a must. Fresh mozzarella, provolone, Asiago, Parmesan and fontina are natural choices.

OLIVES. Include an assortment of gourmet green and ripe olives such as kalamata and Manzanilla.

BEANS. Canned chickpeas and cannellini or fava beans make hearty additions.

MARINATED VEGETABLES. For even more selection, include marinated mushrooms, artichoke hearts, pepperoncinis and roasted red pepper strips. Store-bought giardiniera (pickled vegetables) is an easy choice.

BREADS. Rustic, fresh-baked Italian bread is a nice complement to an antipasto platter. Focaccia works well, too.

FISH. For an extremely authentic antipasto, you could feature some fish, such as sardines, anchovy fillets and smoked salmon.

OTHER OPTIONS. For a little more variety, you can include sliced, hard-cooked eggs and pine nuts or walnuts.

*B*irthdays and bridal showers, anniversaries and holiday parties...special events throughout the year call for extraordinary desserts.

Nothing pleases the eye—or the palate—quite like cake!

From light and fruity (such as luscious Lemon-Lime Meringue Cake at right) to rich and chocolaty (like Chocolate Turtle Cake on page 192), every creation in this chapter will take the cake at any gathering.

Your efforts in the kitchen will be well worth it...especially when you see the smiling faces of friends and family!

PIECE OF CAKE!
(PICTURED AT RIGHT)

Lemon-Lime Meringue Cake (p. 184)

cakes
FOR ANY OCCASION

lemon-lime meringue cake

(PICTURED ON PAGE 182)

Our home economists top a tender citrus curd-filled cake with lovely meringue for a mile-high masterpiece!

FILLING:

1-1/2 cups sugar

1/4 cup cornstarch

1/4 cup all-purpose flour

1-3/4 cups water

3 egg yolks, beaten

1/3 cup lemon juice

1/3 cup lime juice

2 tablespoons butter

2 teaspoons grated lemon peel

2 teaspoons grated lime peel

CAKE:

3/4 cup butter, softened

2 cups sugar

3 eggs

1-1/4 teaspoons vanilla extract

1/3 cup sour cream

1/3 cup lemon juice

1/3 cup lime juice

4 teaspoons grated lemon peel

2-2/3 cups all-purpose flour

2-1/2 teaspoons baking powder

1/2 teaspoon salt

1/4 teaspoon baking soda

1 cardboard cake circle (9 inches)

MERINGUE:

5 egg whites

1/4 teaspoon cream of tartar

2/3 cup sugar

In a small heavy saucepan, combine the sugar, cornstarch and flour. Stir in water until smooth. Cook and stir over medium-high heat until thickened and bubbly. Reduce the heat; cook and stir 2 minutes longer.

Remove from the heat. Stir a small amount of hot mixture into the egg yolks; return all to the pan, stirring constantly. Bring to a gentle boil; cook and stir 2 minutes longer. Remove from the heat. Gently stir in the juices, butter and peels.

Transfer filling to a small bowl; cool for 10 minutes. Refrigerate until chilled.

FOR CAKE: In a large bowl, cream butter and sugar until light and fluffy. Add eggs, one at a time, beating well after each addition. Beat in vanilla. Combine the sour cream, juices and lemon peel. Combine the flour, baking powder, salt and baking soda; add to the creamed mixture alternately with sour cream mixture, beating well after each addition.

Pour into three greased and floured 9-in. round baking pans. Bake at 350° for 18-22 minutes or until a toothpick inserted near the center comes out clean. Cool for 10 minutes before removing from pans to wire racks to cool completely.

Place the cake circle on a baking sheet; layer with one cake layer and half of filling. Repeat layers. Top with remaining cake layer.

FOR MERINGUE: In a large bowl, beat the egg whites and cream of tartar on medium speed until soft peaks form. Gradually beat in the sugar, 1 tablespoon at a time, on high until stiff glossy peaks form and sugar is dissolved. Spread the meringue over top and sides of cake. Bake at 350° for 28-32 minutes or until meringue is lightly browned. Carefully transfer to a cake plate. Refrigerate leftovers. **YIELD:** 12 servings.

EDITOR'S NOTE: To easily move the completed cake from the baking sheet to a platter, overlap three strips of parchment paper on the baking sheet. Top with cake circle; continue with recipe. After removing meringue-topped cake from oven, hold baking sheet near edge of platter. Have another person carefully slide parchment paper pieces off pan and onto platter. Remove paper from underneath cake.

angel food cake with berry sauce

(PICTURED AT RIGHT)

*Light and airy angel food cake from
our Test Kitchen is adorned with a lovely
berry sauce for a heavenly dessert.
The sauce can also be used to garnish
cake made from a mix.*

12 egg whites

1 cup confectioners' sugar

1 cup cake flour

1 teaspoon cream of tartar

1 teaspoon vanilla extract

1/4 teaspoon salt

1-1/4 cups sugar

1/3 cup blueberry vodka

SAUCE:

1 tablespoon cornstarch

1 tablespoon water

2-1/2 cups fresh raspberries, divided

2 cups fresh blueberries, divided

1/3 cup unsweetened pineapple juice

3 tablespoons raspberry liqueur

2 cups halved fresh strawberries

1 cup fresh blackberries

Place egg whites in a large bowl; let stand at room temperature for 30 minutes. Sift confectioners' sugar and flour together twice; set aside.

Add the cream of tartar, vanilla and salt to egg whites; beat on medium speed until soft peaks form. Gradually add the sugar, about 2 tablespoons at a time, beating on high until stiff glossy peaks form and the sugar is dissolved. Gradually fold in the flour mixture, about 1/2 cup at a time.

Gently spoon into an ungreased 10-in. tube pan. Cut through batter with a knife to remove air pockets. Bake on lowest oven rack at 325° for 50-60 minutes or until lightly browned and entire top appears dry. Immediately invert pan; cool completely, about 1 hour.

Run a knife around side and center tube of pan. Remove cake to a serving plate. Brush top and sides of cake with vodka.

FOR SAUCE: Combine cornstarch and water; set aside. In a small saucepan, combine 1-1/2 cups raspberries, 1 cup blueberries, pineapple juice and liqueur. Bring to a boil. Stir cornstarch mixture and add to the pan. Bring to a boil; cook and stir for 2 minutes or until thickened.

Remove from the heat; stir in the strawberries, blackberries and remaining raspberries and blueberries. Serve sauce with the cake. **YIELD:** 16 servings (6 cups sauce).

baby vanilla bean cake

(PICTURED AT FAR RIGHT)

Need an impressive dessert for a spring or summer celebration?
You'll fall for our Test Kitchen's moist cake with rich vanilla custard and cream cheese frosting.

FLOWERS:

1 teaspoon meringue powder

1 tablespoon water

Edible flowers of your choice

1/2 cup superfine sugar

CAKE:

1/2 cup butter, softened

1/2 cup shortening

2 cups sugar

5 eggs

1 vanilla bean

2 cups all-purpose flour

1 teaspoon baking soda

1/2 teaspoon salt

1 cup buttermilk

PASTRY CREAM:

1/4 cup sugar

2 tablespoons cornstarch

1/4 teaspoon salt

1 cup milk

1 vanilla bean

2 egg yolks, beaten

1 tablespoon butter

FROSTING & ASSEMBLY:

1 package (8 ounces) cream cheese, softened

1/2 cup butter, softened

4-1/2 cups confectioners' sugar

1 teaspoon vanilla extract

1 cardboard cake circle (5 inches)

4 wooden dowels (2 inches x 1/4 inch)

MAKING CANDIED FLOWERS

When using recipes that call for edible fresh flowers, make sure to properly identify the flowers before picking and use only the petals or blossoms (not the stems, leaves, pistil or stamen). Double-check that they're edible and have not been treated with chemicals. (If you're unsure if a flower is edible, check with your local poison control center.)

Edible flowers include calendula, chrysanthemum, common wild violet, dandelion, daylily, dianthus, edible orchid, fuchsia, impatiens, lilac, marigold, nasturtium, pansy, rose, snapdragon and scented geranium.

For candied flowers, select blossoms that are freshly cut and leave a long stem for easy handling. Inspect the flowers for insects or dirt before starting. Use as little sugar as possible to allow the beautiful color of the blossoms to show through. If you don't want to purchase superfine sugar, place granulated sugar in a blender or food processor; cover and pulse until fine.

Try to make candied flowers on a day with low humidity. Otherwise, they'll take longer to dry.

In a small bowl, dissolve meringue powder in water. Lightly brush over all sides of the flowers to coat completely; sprinkle with the sugar. Allow to dry on a waxed paper-lined tray for 4 hours or until firm and dry.

FOR CAKE: In a large bowl, cream the butter, shortening and sugar until light and fluffy. Add eggs, one at a time, beating well after each addition. Split vanilla bean in half lengthwise. With a sharp knife scrape the beans to remove the seeds; stir seeds into creamed mixture. Combine flour, baking soda and salt; add to the creamed mixture alternately with buttermilk, beating well after each addition.

Pour into a greased and floured 15-in. x 10-in. x 1-in. baking pan. Bake at 350° for 22-26 minutes or until a toothpick inserted near the center comes out clean. Cool for 15 minutes before removing from pan to a wire rack to cool completely.

FOR PASTRY CREAM: In a small saucepan, combine the sugar, cornstarch and salt. Stir in milk until smooth.

Split vanilla bean and scrape seeds; add bean and seeds to milk mixture. Cook and stir over medium-high heat until thickened and bubbly. Reduce heat to low; cook and stir 2 minutes longer.

Stir a small amount of hot mixture into egg yolks; return all to the pan, stirring constantly. Bring to a gentle boil; cook and stir for 2 minutes. Transfer to a small bowl; discard vanilla bean. Stir in butter. Cool for 15 minutes, stirring occasionally. Refrigerate until chilled.

TO FROST AND ASSEMBLE: For frosting, in a small bowl, beat cream cheese and butter until fluffy. Add confectioners' sugar and vanilla; beat until smooth.

Cut cake into two 6-in. squares, two 4-in. squares and one 2-inch square. Place a 6-in. cake on a cake plate; top with 2/3 cup pastry cream and remaining 6-in. cake. Cut the

cardboard circle into a 3-1/2-in. square; top with one 4-in. cake. Layer with remaining pastry cream and 4-in. cake.

Frost tops and sides of 6-in. layer cake; insert dowels 1 to 2 in. apart into center of cake to support the next layers. Top with 4-in. layer cake; frost top and sides. Top with the 2-in. cake; frost top and sides. Decorate with candied flowers as desired. **YIELD:** 10 servings.

EDITOR'S NOTE: Meringue powder is available from Wilton Industries. Call 1-800/794-5866 or visit www.wilton.com. Verify that flowers are edible and have not been treated with chemicals.

snowflake cake

(PICTURED AT FAR RIGHT)

There will be a flurry of fuss when our home economists' eye-catching cake appears on your holiday table.
Have fun fashioning snowflakes from fondant.

CAKE BATTER:

3-1/2 cups shortening

7-1/2 cups sugar

30 egg whites

4 cups milk

3 tablespoons plus 1 teaspoon clear vanilla extract

10 cups all-purpose flour

3 tablespoons plus 1 teaspoon baking powder

1 teaspoon salt

COCONUT FILLING:

1 cup sugar

1/3 cup cornstarch

1/4 teaspoon salt

2 cans (14 ounces each) coconut milk

1 cup half-and-half cream

8 egg yolks, beaten

2 tablespoons butter

1 teaspoon clear vanilla extract

1 cup flaked coconut

FROSTING:

1 cup shortening

1 cup butter, softened

8 cups confectioners' sugar

6 tablespoons milk

2 teaspoons clear vanilla extract

DECORATIONS & ASSEMBLY:

11 wooden dowels (eight 2-3/4 inches x 1/4 inch, three 3 inches x 1/4 inch)

3 cardboard cake circles (one 8 inch, two 5 inch)

3 packages (1-1/2 pounds each) ready-to-use rolled white fondant

Assorted snowflake cookie cutters

White edible glitter

1 small new paintbrush

Additional clear vanilla extract

2 to 3 drops blue food coloring

Pastry bag and round pastry tip #4

Rock candy

In a large bowl, cream shortening and sugar until light and fluffy. In another bowl, combine the egg whites, milk and vanilla. Combine the flour, baking powder and salt; add to creamed mixture alternately with egg white mixture, beating well after each addition.

Pour 2 cups batter into each of four greased and floured 6-in. round baking pans. Pour 3 cups batter into each of four greased and floured 9-in. round baking pans. For the 6-in. pans, bake at 350° for 35-40 minutes or until a toothpick inserted near center comes out clean. For 9-in. pans, bake at 350° for 27-33 minutes or until a toothpick inserted near the center comes out clean. (Smaller cake pans have a deeper fill and need to bake longer.) Cool the cakes for 10 minutes before removing from pans to wire racks to cool completely.

FOR FILLING: In a large heavy saucepan, combine the sugar, cornstarch and salt. Gradually whisk in coconut milk and cream until smooth. Cook and stir over medium-high heat until thickened and bubbly. Reduce heat; cook and stir 2 minutes longer. Remove from the heat. Stir a small amount of hot filling into egg yolks; return all to pan, stirring constantly. Bring to a gentle boil; cook and stir 2 minutes longer. Remove from the heat; stir in butter and vanilla.

Transfer to a large bowl. Cool to room temperature. Cover surface of filling with waxed paper; refrigerate until cooled. Stir in coconut.

FOR FROSTING: In a large bowl, beat shortening and butter until light and fluffy. Add the confectioners' sugar, milk and vanilla; beat until smooth.

TO ASSEMBLE CAKE: Level cake tops if necessary. Place a 9-in. cake on a serving plate; spread with 1-1/4 cups filling. Top with second 9-in. cake; spread top with 3/4 cup frosting. Insert the four 2-3/4-in. wooden dowels 1 to 2 in. apart into center of cake to support the next layers.

Place third 9-in. cake on an 8-in. cardboard circle; place over cake on platter. Spread with 1-1/4 cups filling. Top with remaining 9-in. cake. Frost top and sides of cake with about 2 cups frosting, forming a crumb coating. Roll out 1-1/4 pounds of fondant into a 21-in. circle. Drape over cake and gently smooth, working from the center. Trim ends. Insert four 2-3/4-in. dowels 1 to 2 in. apart into center of cake. Set aside.

On a work surface, place a 6-in. cake on a 5-in. cardboard circle. Spread with 1 cup filling; top with second 6-in. cake. Spread top with 1/2 cup frosting. Insert remaining dowels 1 to 2 in. apart into center of cake. Place third 6-in. cake on remaining cardboard circle and position on dowels; spread with 1 cup filling. Top with remaining cake. Frost top and sides of cake with about 1-1/4 cups frosting. Roll out 1-1/4 pounds of fondant into an 18-in. circle. Drape over cake and gently smooth, working from the center. Trim ends. Gently place 6-in. layer cake on 9-in. layer cake.

Roll out remaining fondant to an 1/8-in. thickness. Cut with snowflake cookie cutters. Reroll scraps if desired. Place glitter in a small bowl. Press one side of each snowflake into glitter. With a paintbrush, brush vanilla over plain sides of snowflakes; secure onto cake.

In a small bowl, beat food coloring and remaining frosting until smooth. Cut a small hole in the corner of a pastry bag; insert pastry tip. Fill with blue frosting; pipe desired design over cake. Decorate with rock candy. Refrigerate leftovers. **YIELD:** 40 servings.

EDITOR'S NOTE: Cake batter may need to be mixed in batches, depending on the size of your mixing bowl. The edible glitter is available from Wilton Industries. Call 1-800/794-5866 or visit www.wilton.com.

chocolate mousse cheesecake

(PICTURED AT FAR RIGHT)

As if cheesecake wasn't enough of an indulgence, this version also features irresistible chocolate mousse. It's a delightful, do-ahead dessert for special occasions.

Julie Dunsworth | OVIEDO, FL

1-1/4 cups graham cracker crumbs

3 tablespoons sugar

3 tablespoons baking cocoa

1/3 cup butter, melted

CHEESECAKE LAYER:

12 ounces cream cheese, softened

3/4 cup sugar

2 eggs, lightly beaten

1 cup (8 ounces) sour cream

3 teaspoons vanilla extract

3 teaspoons Kahlua

MOUSSE & TOPPING LAYERS:

1 envelope unflavored gelatin

1/4 cup cold water

4 egg yolks

3/4 cup milk

1/3 cup sugar

1-1/2 teaspoons instant coffee granules

4 squares (1 ounce each) semisweet chocolate, chopped

1 tablespoon light rum

1-1/2 teaspoons vanilla extract, divided

2 cups heavy whipping cream

1/4 cup confectioners' sugar

GARNISH:

5 ounces dark chocolate candy coating, chopped

5 ounces white candy coating, chopped

In a small bowl, combine the cracker crumbs, sugar, cocoa and butter; press onto the bottom of a greased 9-in. springform pan. Bake at 350° for 10 minutes. Cool on a wire rack.

FOR CHEESECAKE: In a large bowl, beat cream cheese and sugar until smooth. Add eggs; beat on low speed just until combined. Add the sour cream, vanilla and Kahlua; beat just until combined. Pour over crust. Place pan on a baking sheet.

Bake for 30-35 minutes or until center is almost set. Cool on a wire rack for 10 minutes. Carefully run a knife around edge of pan

DOUBLE CHOCOLATE CURLS

White chocolate spirals add interest to the large chocolate curls that decorate Chocolate Mousse Cheesecake (pictured at far right). Here's how to make them.

1. Spread a thin layer of melted dark chocolate candy coating on a baking sheet. Immediately drag a fork through the chocolate on a diagonal. Let stand until set.

2. Carefully spread melted white candy coating over the dark candy coating, filling the gaps in the chocolate. Let stand until set.

3. Holding a dough scraper or sturdy metal spatula at a 45° angle; scrape over the top of chocolate, being careful not to press too hard. The strips will curl as they come away.

to loosen; cool 1 hour longer. Refrigerate until completely cooled.

FOR MOUSSE AND TOPPING: In a small bowl, sprinkle gelatin over water; let stand for 1 minute or until softened. In a small saucepan, combine the egg yolks, milk, sugar and coffee granules. Cook and stir over medium heat until mixture reaches 160° or is thick enough to coat the back of a metal spoon.

Remove from the heat; whisk in gelatin until dissolved. Stir in the chocolate, rum and 1/2 teaspoon vanilla. Pour into a small bowl. Set bowl in a larger bowl of ice water; stir occasionally until thickened.

Meanwhile, in a large bowl, beat cream until it begins to thicken. Add confectioners' sugar and remaining vanilla; beat until stiff peaks form. Fold half of the cream into the mousse mixture; spread over the cheesecake. Top with the remaining cream. Cover and refrigerate overnight.

FOR CHOCOLATE CURL GARNISH: Melt the dark chocolate candy coating. Spread a thin layer of over baking sheet; drag a fork through the chocolate. Let stand at room temperature until set.

Melt white candy coating; carefully spread over dark candy coating. Let stand at room temperature just until set. Holding a dough scraper or sturdy metal spatula at a 45° angle, scrape over the top of the chocolate to form striped curls. Decorate cake with the curls. **YIELD:** 12 servings.

chocolate turtle cake

(PICTURED AT FAR RIGHT AND ON FRONT COVER)

Our home economists developed this decadent chocolate cake showcasing a creamy caramel layer and rich ganache. They even decorated it in two different ways (see the cover and photo at far right) to help spark your own creativity!

1 cup dark baking cocoa

1 cup boiling water

1 cup butter, softened

2-1/4 cups sugar

4 eggs

1-1/2 teaspoons vanilla extract

2-3/4 cups all-purpose flour

2 teaspoons baking soda

1/2 teaspoon baking powder

1/2 teaspoon salt

1 cup buttermilk

CARAMEL LAYER:

1 teaspoon butter

1 cup chopped pecans

1/2 cup plus 1 tablespoon sugar

1/2 cup plus 1 tablespoon packed brown sugar

1 cup heavy whipping cream, divided

1/2 cup dark corn syrup

6 tablespoons butter, cubed

GANACHE LAYER:

1 teaspoon butter

1 cup chopped pecans

1 cup dark chocolate chips

2/3 cup heavy whipping cream

FROSTING:

2 squares (1 ounce each) unsweetened chocolate, chopped

1/3 cup dark chocolate chips

4 cups confectioners' sugar

3/4 cup butter, softened

1/4 cup milk

1 tablespoon dark baking cocoa

1 teaspoon vanilla extract

GARNISHES:

Chocolate curls or other decorations

Dissolve the cocoa in boiling water; cool. In a large bowl, cream the butter and sugar until light and fluffy. Add eggs, one at a time, beating well after each addition. Beat in the vanilla. Combine the flour, baking soda, baking powder and salt; add to the creamed mixture alternately with the buttermilk and cocoa mixture, beating well after each addition.

Pour into three greased and floured 9-in. round baking pans. Bake at 350° for 20-25 minutes or until a toothpick inserted near the center comes out clean. Cool for 10 minutes before removing from pans to wire racks to cool completely.

FOR CARAMEL LAYER: Line a 9-in. round pan with foil and grease the foil with butter. Sprinkle with pecans; set aside.

In a large heavy saucepan, combine the sugars, 1/2 cup cream, corn syrup and butter. Bring to a boil over medium heat. Cook and stir until smooth and blended, about 5 minutes. Gradually stir in remaining cream. Bring to a boil over medium-low heat, stirring constantly. Cook and stir until a candy thermometer reads 238° (soft-ball stage), about 10 minutes.

Remove from the heat. Quickly pour mixture into the prepared pan (do not scrape saucepan). Cool.

FOR GANACHE LAYER: Line a 9-in. round pan with foil; grease foil with 1 teaspoon butter. Sprinkle with pecans; set aside. Place chocolate chips in a small bowl. In a small saucepan, bring cream just to a boil. Pour over chocolate; whisk until smooth. Pour over pecans. Cool to room temperature; chill until set.

FOR FROSTING: In a microwave, melt the unsweetened chocolate and chocolate chips; stir until smooth. Cool slightly. In a large bowl, beat the confectioners' sugar, butter, milk, cocoa and vanilla until smooth; beat in melted chocolate.

TO ASSEMBLE CAKE: Place one cake layer on a serving plate; remove foil from caramel and place on top. Top with another cake layer; remove foil from ganache and place on top. Top with remaining cake layer. Frost top and sides of cake. Garnish as desired.
YIELD: 16 servings.

$\mathcal{W}$ith its alluring aroma, rich flavor and eye-opening quality, there's nothing quite like a steaming cup of coffee.

Whether it's the center of a casual chat between friends or a way to draw out an enjoyable evening with company, the coveted beverage has a way of bringing people together.

Connoisseurs will delight in the selection of coffee-infused sippers, treats and even entrees featured here.

Linger over soothing cups of Creamy Vanilla Coffee and cream-topped mugs of Honey Spiced Latte. Or perk up a dinner party with an upscale Orange & Coffee Martini or French Iced Coffee.

VERSATILE BEVERAGE
(PICTURED AT RIGHT)

crazy
FOR COFFEE!

french iced coffee

(PICTURED ON PAGE 194)

This creamy, frozen treat has the perfect balance of sweetness and coffee flavor. It is wonderfully refreshing on a hot summer day. Freezing it in batches helps the beverage thaw evenly and gives it a nice, slushy texture.

Simone Nichols | *DILLON, MT*

5 cups hot brewed coffee

1-1/2 cups sugar

6 cups milk

3 cups heavy whipping cream

1/2 cup chocolate syrup

In a large bowl, whisk coffee and sugar until sugar is dissolved. Stir in the remaining ingredients. Freeze in 1-1/2-quart portions in freezer containers overnight.

Place in refrigerator 2-3 hours before serving or until slushy. Serve immediately. **YIELD:** 15 servings (3-3/4 quarts).

chocolate cappuccino mousse cake

Layers of coffee-flavored angel food cake and decadent chocolate mousse are covered with a to-die-for buttercream frosting. Each slice of this dessert is like a piece of heaven. It takes some time to prepare, but the compliments that follow make the effort worth it.

Jane Woods | *FORT WORTH, TX*

1 package (16 ounces) angel food cake mix

1 cup plus 2 tablespoons cold water

2 tablespoons brewed coffee

FILLING:

4 squares (1 ounce each) bittersweet chocolate, chopped

1 teaspoon instant coffee granules

1 teaspoon ground cinnamon

1-3/4 cups heavy whipping cream

FROSTING:

2/3 cup butter, softened

5-1/2 cups confectioners' sugar

6 tablespoons coffee liqueur

2-1/2 teaspoons vanilla extract

Line the bottoms of three 9-in. round baking pans with waxed paper; set aside. In a large bowl, beat the cake mix, water and coffee on low speed for 30 seconds. Beat on medium for 1 minute. Gently spoon batter into prepared pans. Bake at 350° for 20-25 minutes or until tops are golden brown and dry. Cool in pans on wire racks.

Meanwhile, in a large bowl, combine the chocolate, coffee granules and cinnamon. In a small saucepan, cook and stir cream over medium heat until hot (do not boil). Pour over chocolate mixture; stir until smooth. Refrigerate for about 1 hour or until chilled and slightly thickened, stirring occasionally. Beat on medium speed just until stiff peaks form.

In a large bowl, beat the frosting ingredients until light and fluffy. Place one cake layer on a serving plate; spread with half of the filling. Repeat layers. Top with remaining cake layer. Spread frosting over the top and sides of cake. Refrigerate leftovers. **YIELD:** 16 servings.

jumpin' espresso bean chili

(PICTURED AT RIGHT)

Chili is a hearty dish I love experimenting with. This meatless version I created is low in fat, but high in flavor. Everyone tries to guess the secret ingredient...no one ever thinks it's coffee!

Jessie Apfel | *BERKELEY, CA*

3 medium onions, chopped

2 tablespoons olive oil

2 tablespoons brown sugar

2 tablespoons chili powder

2 tablespoons ground cumin

1 tablespoon instant coffee granules

1 tablespoon baking cocoa

3/4 teaspoon salt

2 cans (14-1/2 ounces each) no-salt-added diced tomatoes

1 can (15 ounces) black beans, rinsed and drained

1 can (15 ounces) kidney beans, rinsed and drained

1 can (15 ounces) garbanzo beans or chickpeas, rinsed and drained

Sour cream, thinly sliced green onions, shredded cheddar cheese and pickled jalapeno slices, optional

In a Dutch oven, saute the onions in oil until tender. Add the brown sugar, chili powder, cumin, coffee granules, cocoa and salt; cook and stir for 1 minute.

Stir in the tomatoes and beans. Bring to a boil. Reduce heat; cover and simmer for 30 minutes. Serve with sour cream, onions, cheese and jalapeno slices if desired. **YIELD:** 7 servings.

STORING AND MAKING COFFEE

Ground coffee loses its flavor quickly so it's best to buy it in small quantities. (If you purchase beans, only grind as much as you need immediately.)

Keep coffee in an airtight container in a cool, dark place. It can absorb other flavors in the refrigerator or freezer.

Chlorinated water can affect the taste of brewed coffee. Filtered water is ideal. Coffee manufacturers generally recommend between 1 and 2 tablespoons ground coffee for every 3/4 cup (6 ounces) water.

honey spiced latte

(PICTURED ON PAGE 194)

*Our home economists combine rich molasses, golden honey and
a host of spices to create this warm and comforting drink.*

1/2 cup ground coffee

1-1/2 cups cold water

1-1/3 cups milk

2 tablespoons honey

2 tablespoons molasses

4 teaspoons sugar

1/4 teaspoon ground ginger

1/4 teaspoon ground cinnamon

1/8 teaspoon ground nutmeg

1/8 teaspoon ground cloves

Whipped cream, optional

Place ground coffee in the filter of a drip coffeemaker. Add water; brew according to manufacturer's instructions.

In a small saucepan, combine the milk, honey, molasses, sugar and spices. Cook and stir over medium heat until steaming. Remove from the heat. Transfer to a blender; cover and process for 15 seconds or until foamy.

Divide among four mugs; add the coffee. Garnish with whipped cream if desired. **YIELD:** 4 servings.

creamy vanilla coffee

(PICTURED ON PAGE 195)

*My husband and his friends would often buy a similar version of this creamy,
vanilla-flavored beverage at a nearby coffeehouse. Because daily stops got to be expensive,
I decided to try and make my own. This smooth sensation was the result.*

Heather Kunkel | *WELLSVILLE, NY*

1/3 cup ground coffee

1 cup water

1/4 cup sugar

2 tablespoons instant vanilla pudding mix

2-1/2 cups milk

Place ground coffee in the coffee filter of a drip coffeemaker. Add water; brew according to manufacturer's directions.

In a small bowl, combine sugar and pudding mix. Stir in milk and coffee. Chill until serving. **YIELD:** 3 servings.

CINNAMON STICK STIRRERS

When it's time for a coffee break, stir things up...deliciously. Replace spoons with hand-dipped cinnamon sticks that serve as flavorful stirrers.

Dip each cinnamon stick in melted chocolate, then coat in your choice of sweet indulgences such as raw sugar, crushed peppermint, and melted caramel or white candy coating.

pepper-crusted beef tenderloin

(PICTURED AT RIGHT)

A coffee-enhanced rub lends robust taste to juicy beef tenderloin. I often prepare this recipe for my family around the holidays instead of the traditional turkey or ham. The rich mashed potato stuffing adds an extra-special touch.

Rebecca Anderson | AUSTIN, TX

1 cup plus 2 tablespoons dry red wine
or beef broth, divided

1 beef tenderloin (2 pounds)

1 large potato, quartered

1/2 cup grated Parmesan cheese

3 tablespoons milk

4 tablespoons butter, divided

2 bacon strips, cooked and crumbled

1 tablespoon horseradish sauce

5 garlic cloves, minced, divided

1/2 teaspoon garlic salt

1 tablespoon minced chives, optional

3 tablespoons ground coffee

1 tablespoon brown sugar

1 tablespoon coarsely ground pepper

1-1/4 teaspoons salt, divided

1 medium onion, halved and sliced

1 tablespoon olive oil

1 teaspoon lemon juice

Pour 1 cup wine into a large resealable plastic bag; add the beef. Seal bag and turn to coat; refrigerate at least 1 hour.

Place potato in a small saucepan and cover with water. Bring to a boil. Reduce heat; cover and cook for 15-20 minutes or until tender. Drain; mash with cheese, milk, 2 tablespoons butter, bacon, horseradish sauce, 2 garlic cloves, garlic salt and chives if desired; set aside.

Drain and discard marinade. In a small bowl, combine the coffee, brown sugar, pepper and 1 teaspoon salt; rub over beef. Cut a lengthwise slit down the center of the tenderloin to within 3/4 in. of bottom. Open tenderloin so it lies flat; cover with plastic wrap. Flatten to 3/4-in. thickness. Remove plastic wrap; mound potato mixture over the center. Close tenderloin; tie at 2-in. intervals with kitchen string. Place on a rack in a shallow roasting pan.

Bake, uncovered, at 425° for 40-45 minutes or until meat reaches desired doneness (for medium-rare, a meat thermometer should read 145°; medium, 160°; well-done, 170°). Remove the meat to a serving platter. Cover and let stand for 10 minutes.

Meanwhile, in a small skillet, cook onion and remaining garlic in oil and remaining butter over medium heat for 15-20 minutes or until onion is golden brown, stirring frequently. Stir in the lemon juice, remaining wine and salt. Slice tenderloin; serve with sauce.
YIELD: 8 servings.

orange & coffee martini

(PICTURED ON PAGE 195)

With its pretty jeweled color and complementary orange-coffee flavor, this impressive martini from our Test Kitchen lends an elegant, upscale feel to any party.

Ice cubes

1/4 cup strong brewed coffee, chilled

1 ounce vodka

1/2 ounce orange liqueur

1/2 ounce hazelnut liqueur

Fill a mixing glass or tumbler three-fourths full with ice cubes. Add the remaining ingredients; stir until condensation forms on the outside of the glass. Strain into a chilled cocktail glass. Serve immediately. **YIELD:** 1 serving.

mocha nut roll

A tender, eye-catching cake is the perfect indulgence for coffee- and chocolate-lovers alike!

Susan Bettinger | *BATTLE CREEK, MI*

4 eggs, separated

1/3 cup plus 1/2 cup sugar

1/2 teaspoon vanilla extract

1/2 cup all-purpose flour

1 teaspoon baking powder

1/4 teaspoon salt

1/4 cup finely chopped walnuts

MOCHA FILLING:

1/2 cup sugar

3 tablespoons all-purpose flour

2 teaspoons instant coffee granules

1/4 teaspoon salt

1-1/4 cups milk

1 square (1 ounce) unsweetened chocolate, chopped

1 egg, lightly beaten

1 tablespoon butter

1 teaspoon vanilla extract

Confectioners' sugar and chocolate curls, optional

Line a greased 15-in. x 10-in. baking pan with waxed paper; grease the paper and set aside.

In a large bowl, beat egg yolks on high speed for 5 minutes or until thick and lemon-colored. Gradually beat in 1/3 cup sugar. Stir in vanilla. Combine the flour, baking powder and salt; gradually add to yolk mixture and mix well (batter will be very thick).

In a small bowl with clean beaters, beat egg whites on medium speed until soft peaks form. Gradually beat in remaining sugar 1 tablespoon at a time, on high until stiff peaks form. Gradually fold into batter. Spread evenly into prepared pan.

Bake at 375° for 10-15 minutes or until cake springs back when lightly touched. Cool in pan for 5 minutes. Invert onto a kitchen towel dusted with confectioners' sugar. Gently peel off waxed paper. Roll up cake in the towel jelly-roll style, starting with a short side. Cool completely on a wire rack.

Meanwhile, in a small saucepan, combine the sugar, flour, coffee granules and salt. Stir in milk and chocolate. Bring to a boil. Cook and stir for 2 minutes. Remove from the heat. Stir a small amount of hot filling into egg; return all to the pan, stirring constantly. Bring to a gentle boil. Cook and stir for 2-3 minutes or until mixture reaches 160°. Remove from the heat; gently stir in butter and vanilla. Cool to room temperature.

Unroll cake; spread filling evenly over cake to within 1/2 in. of edges. Roll up again. Place seam side down on a serving platter. Just before serving, sprinkle with confectioners' sugar and garnish with chocolate curls if desired. **YIELD:** 12 servings.

java crunch ice cream

(PICTURED AT RIGHT)

My daughter loves this decadent ice cream and begs me to make it often. Robust instant coffee pairs well with chocolate-covered pecans and buttery toffee chips.

Jamie Parker | LUBBOCK, TX

4 cups heavy whipping cream

4 cups half-and-half cream

1 can (14 ounces) sweetened condensed milk

2 cans (5 ounces each) evaporated milk

3 tablespoons instant coffee granules

1 teaspoon vanilla extract

2 cups pecan halves

1 cup almond brickle chips or English toffee bits

8 ounces dark chocolate candy coating, chopped

In a large bowl, combine the first six ingredients. Refrigerate until chilled.

In a small bowl, combine pecans and brickle chips. In a microwave, melt candy coating; stir until smooth. Pour over pecan mixture. Transfer to a 15-in. x 10-in. pan. Refrigerate until chocolate is firm; chop and set aside.

Fill cylinder of ice cream freezer two-thirds full; freeze according to the manufacturer's directions. Refrigerate remaining mixture until ready to freeze. When ice cream is frozen, transfer to a freezer container and stir in reserved pecan mixture; freeze for 2-4 hours before serving. **YIELD:** 2-3/4 quarts.

coffee bean bark

Chocolate-coated coffee beans add a yummy crunch to this pretty two-toned bark. Our home economists assure that coffee-lovers won't be able to resist pieces of the tasty treat.

1 teaspoon plus 2 tablespoons butter, divided

2 cups (12 ounces) semisweet chocolate chips

2 teaspoons instant coffee granules

2/3 cup coarsely chopped coffee beans, divided

1 package (10 to 12 ounces) vanilla or white chips

Line a 15-in. x 10-in. pan with foil and grease foil with 1 teaspoon butter; set aside. In a large microwave-safe bowl, combine the chocolate chips, coffee granules and remaining butter. Microwave on high for 1-2 minutes or until melted; stir until smooth. Stir in 1/3 cup coffee beans. Pour into prepared pan. Chill until firm.

In a microwave, melt vanilla chips; stir until smooth. Stir in remaining coffee beans. Spread over chocolate layer. Chill until firm. Break into pieces. YIELD: 1-1/2 pounds.

glazed gingerbread cake

This is a favorite dessert during the holidays and at special occasions. I've tried creating various glazes to drizzle over the moist, flavorful cake but have found that it's delicious as is as well. A tall glass of cold milk is the only addition I'd suggest.

Edith Ekstedt | PASO ROBLES, CA

1 cup raisins

1 cup molasses

1/2 cup packed brown sugar

1/3 cup canola oil

1/3 cup strong brewed coffee

1/3 cup orange juice

3 eggs

3 cups whole wheat flour

1/4 cup nonfat dry milk powder

1 tablespoon ground ginger

1 teaspoon cream of tartar

1 teaspoon baking soda

1/2 teaspoon each ground cinnamon, mace and nutmeg

1 tablespoon grated orange peel

GLAZE:

1 cup confectioners' sugar

4 tablespoons milk

2 tablespoons butter, melted

1/4 teaspoon vanilla extract

Place the raisins in a bowl. Cover with boiling water; let stand for 5 minutes. Drain and set aside.

In a large bowl, combine the molasses, brown sugar, oil, coffee and juice. In a small bowl, beat eggs on high speed for 3-4 minutes or until thick and lemon-colored. Combine the flour, milk powder, ginger, cream of tartar, baking soda, cinnamon, mace and nutmeg. Add to the creamed mixture alternately with the egg mixture; beat just until combined. Fold in orange peel and reserved raisins.

Transfer to a greased and floured 9-in. fluted tube pan. Bake at 350° for 55-60 minutes or until toothpick inserted near the center comes out clean. Cool for 10 minutes before removing from pan to a wire rack to cool completely.

In a small bowl, combine glaze ingredients. Pour over the cake. YIELD: 10-12 servings.

espresso
panna cotta

(PICTURED AT RIGHT)

I got this idea after seeing different dessert presentations at various restaurants. The martini glasses make an elegant impression for such a luscious dessert.

Nicole Clayton | *PRESCOTT, AZ*

1 envelope unflavored gelatin

1 cup milk

3 cups heavy whipping cream

1/2 cup sugar

2 tablespoons instant espresso powder or instant coffee granules

1/8 teaspoon salt

Dark and white chocolate curls

In a small saucepan, sprinkle gelatin over milk; let stand for 1 minute. Heat milk over low heat, stirring until gelatin is completely dissolved. Stir in the cream, sugar, espresso powder and salt. Cook and stir until sugar is dissolved. Remove from the heat.

Pour into six dessert dishes. Cover and refrigerate for 1 hour, stirring every 20 minutes. Refrigerate for at least 5 hours longer or until set. Just before serving, garnish with chocolate curls. **YIELD:** 6 servings.

Wouldn't it be great to open your freezer and see a selection of homemade main dishes, soups and breads waiting for you and your family to enjoy? It doesn't have to be a dream!

All of the recipes in this chapter yield big batches. So you can enjoy some now and put the remainder in the freezer for fast meals in the future.

Broccoli Beer Cheese Soup and Cider Turkey Soup will warmly welcome your family to the dinner table, especially when paired with slices of Onion-Dill Batter Bread.

FRESH FROM THE FREEZER
(PICTURED AT RIGHT)

stocking
YOUR FREEZER

broccoli beer cheese soup

(PICTURED ON PAGE 204)

This soup tastes just as wonderful without the beer, making a great broccoli cheese soup.
I always make extra and pop individual servings in the freezer.

Lori Lee | *BROOKSVILLE, FL*

5 celery ribs, finely chopped

3 medium carrots, finely chopped

1 small onion, finely chopped

3 tablespoons butter

4 cans (14-1/2 ounces each) chicken broth

4 cups fresh broccoli florets, chopped

1/4 cup chopped sweet red pepper

1 teaspoon salt

1/2 teaspoon pepper

1/2 cup all-purpose flour

1/2 cup water

3 cups (12 ounces) shredded cheddar cheese

1 package (8 ounces) cream cheese, cubed

1 bottle (12 ounces) beer or nonalcoholic beer

Optional toppings: cooked and crumbled bacon, chopped green onions, shredded cheddar cheese, sour cream and salad croutons

In a soup kettle, saute the celery, carrots and onion in butter until almost tender; add broth, broccoli, red pepper, salt and pepper. Combine flour and water until smooth; stir into kettle. Bring to a boil. Reduce the heat; simmer, uncovered, for 30-40 minutes or until thickened and vegetables are tender.

Stir in the cheeses and beer; cook until heated through and cheese is melted, stirring occasionally (do not boil). Serve desired amount with toppings of your choice. Cool remaining soup; transfer to freezer containers. Freeze for up to 3 months.

TO USE FROZEN SOUP: Thaw in the refrigerator overnight. Transfer to a saucepan. Cover and cook over medium-low heat until heated through, stirring occasionally (do not boil). **YIELD:** 12 servings (3 quarts).

FREEZING FACTS

There are some simple tips to follow for successfully freezing foods. Here are the cold, hard facts. Most importantly, be sure to wrap the foods well and then keep track of what dishes are in your freezer so that you use them within the proper amount of time.

BREADS AND MUFFINS. Cool completely after baking. Wrap tightly in a freezer-safe resealable plastic bag, heavy-duty aluminum foil, airtight container or freezer paper. Freeze for up to 1 month. To thaw, slightly unwrap and defrost at room temperature for 2 to 3 hours. Serve at room temperature. Or to reheat, wrap in foil; bake at 350° for 15-20 minutes.

CASSEROLES. Line casserole dishes with heavy-duty foil before assembling. Fill the casserole; wrap the dish in heavy-duty aluminum foil and freeze. When frozen, remove foil-wrapped food from the dish and place in a freezer-safe resealable bag. Freeze for up to 3 months. To use, place the food in the original container; defrost in the refrigerator. Bake as directed.

SOUPS. Cool completely. Place in sturdy plastic containers, leaving 1/2-in. head space for expansion. Thaw in the refrigerator; remove from the plastic container. Reheat in a saucepan on the stovetop or in a microwave-safe bowl.

vegetarian lasagna alfredo

(PICTURED AT RIGHT)

A dry Alfredo mix is what hurries along the preparation of this tasty pasta casserole. It's family pleasing with lots of sauce and veggies.

JamieLynn Griffith | BUFFALO, NY

18 lasagna noodles

7 cups fresh broccoli florets

2 eggs, beaten

2 cartons (15 ounces each) ricotta cheese

4 teaspoons Italian seasoning

8 medium fresh tomatoes, chopped

4 envelopes Alfredo sauce mix, divided

6 cups (24 ounces) shredded part-skim mozzarella cheese

Cook noodles according to package directions. Meanwhile, place broccoli in a steamer basket. Place in a large saucepan over 1 in. of water; bring to a boil. Cover and steam for 5-7 minutes or until crisp-tender.

In a large bowl, combine eggs, ricotta cheese and Italian seasoning; gently stir in tomatoes and broccoli. Set aside.

Drain noodles. Prepare two envelopes of Alfredo sauce mix according to package directions. Spread 1/4 cup sauce in each of two greased 13-in. x 9-in. baking dishes. Top each with three noodles, 1 cup ricotta mixture, 1 cup mozzarella cheese and 1/4 cup sauce. Repeat layers. Top with remaining noodles, sauce and mozzarella cheese.

Cover and freeze one lasagna for up to 3 months. Bake remaining lasagna, uncovered, at 350° for 35-40 minutes or until bubbly and edges are lightly browned. Let stand for 15 minutes before cutting. Prepare one envelope of sauce mix according to package directions; serve with lasagna.

TO USE FROZEN LASAGNA: Thaw in the refrigerator overnight. Remove from the refrigerator 30 minutes before baking. Bake, uncovered, at 350° for 50-60 minutes or until bubbly and edges are lightly browned. Let stand for 15 minutes before cutting. Prepare remaining envelope of sauce mix according to package directions; serve with lasagna. **YIELD:** 2 lasagnas (12 servings each).

cider turkey soup

(PICTURED ON PAGE 205)

Our home economists stir in apple cider to give this soup a bit of sweetness.

1 leftover turkey carcass (from a 12-pound turkey)

3-1/2 quarts water

1 quart apple cider

2 celery ribs, cut into 2-inch pieces

1 large onion, cut into wedges

1 large apple, cut into wedges

1 large carrot, cut into 2-inch pieces

8 sprigs fresh thyme

2 sprigs fresh sage

SOUP:

3 cups shredded cooked turkey breast

2 cups cooked long grain and wild rice

2 large carrots, shredded

1 large onion, chopped

1 cup chopped celery

1 teaspoon salt

1/2 teaspoon dried thyme

1/4 teaspoon pepper

Place the first nine ingredients in a stockpot. Slowly bring to a boil over low heat; cover and simmer for 1-1/2 hours.

Discard carcass. Strain broth through a cheesecloth-lined colander; discard vegetables and herbs. If using immediately, skim fat. Or cool, then refrigerate for 8 hours or overnight. Remove fat from surface before using. Broth may be refrigerated for 3 days or frozen for 4-6 months.

Place the soup ingredients in a stockpot; add the broth. Bring to a boil. Reduce heat; cover and simmer for 30 minutes or until vegetables are tender. Serve immediately or cool and transfer to freezer containers. May be frozen for up to 3 months.

TO USE FROZEN SOUP: Thaw soup in the refrigerator overnight. Transfer to a saucepan. Cover and cook over medium heat until heated through. **YIELD:** 15 servings (3-3/4 quarts).

moist bran muffins

My family can get tired of the same old breakfasts. That's why I keep a batch of these tender muffins in the freezer.
Nancy Kearney | MASSILLON, OH

2 cups bran flakes

1 cup All-Bran

1 cup boiling water

1/2 cup butter, softened

3/4 cup sugar

3/4 cup packed brown sugar

2 eggs

2 cups buttermilk

2 tablespoons molasses

2-1/2 cups all-purpose flour

3 teaspoons baking soda

1-1/2 teaspoons baking powder

1 teaspoon ground cinnamon

1/2 teaspoon salt

1 cup raisins

In a large bowl, combine cereals and boiling water; let stand for 5 minutes. Meanwhile, in a large bowl, cream butter and sugars until light and fluffy. Add eggs, one at a time, beating well after each addition.

Stir in the buttermilk, molasses and cereal mixture. Combine the flour, baking soda, baking powder, cinnamon and salt; add to creamed mixture just until moistened. Fold in raisins.

Fill greased or paper-lined muffin cups three-fourths full. Bake at 375° for 18-20 minutes or until a toothpick comes out clean. Cool for 5 minutes before removing from pans to wire racks. Serve warm. Wrap remaining muffins in foil and freeze for up to 3 months.

TO USE FROZEN MUFFINS: Thaw the muffins at room temperature. **YIELD:** 2-1/2 dozen.

jalapeno chicken enchiladas

(PICTURED AT RIGHT)

With tomatillos and jalapenos, these chicken enchiladas have authentic Mexican flavor. Serve them with sour cream to cut some of the heat.

Jolie Stinson | LEBANON, OR

2 pounds tomatillos, husks removed and rinsed

2 medium onions, quartered

4 jalapeno peppers, halved lengthwise and seeded

8 garlic cloves, peeled

2 tablespoons olive oil

1 cup chopped fresh cilantro

2 tablespoons lime juice

4 teaspoons ground cumin

2 teaspoons salt

FILLING:

1 medium onion, chopped

1/4 cup olive oil

6 garlic cloves, minced

3 teaspoons ground cumin

1/2 cup all-purpose flour

4 cups chicken broth

1/4 cup minced fresh cilantro

6 cups shredded cooked rotisserie chicken

ASSEMBLY:

20 flour tortillas (8 inches), warmed

4 cups (16 ounces) shredded Monterey Jack cheese

Sour cream, chopped tomatoes and fresh cilantro leaves, optional

Place the tomatillos, onions, jalapenos and garlic in two 15-in. x 10-in. x 1-in. baking pans. Drizzle with oil. Bake at 425° for 20-25 minutes or until tender and browned.

Cool slightly. Transfer vegetables and cooking liquid to a food processor. Add the cilantro, lime juice, cumin and salt. Cover and pulse until chunky; set aside.

For filling, in a large skillet, saute onion in oil until tender. Add garlic and cumin; cook and stir 1 minute longer. Stir in flour until blended; gradually add broth. Bring to a boil; cook and stir for 2 minutes or until thickened. Remove from the heat. Stir in cilantro and 1 cup of the tomatillo mixture. Stir in chicken.

To assemble, spread 1/4 cup tomatillo mixture into two greased 13-in. x 9-in. baking dishes. Spread 1 tablespoon tomatillo mixture and 1/2 cup chicken mixture down the center of each tortilla; sprinkle each with 2 tablespoons cheese. Roll up and place seam side down into baking dishes. Spoon remaining tomatillo mixture over enchiladas; sprinkle with cheese.

Cover and freeze one dish for up to 3 months. Bake the second dish, uncovered, at 350° for 30-35 minutes or until bubbly. Garnish with sour cream, tomatoes and cilantro if desired.

TO USE FROZEN ENCHILADAS: Thaw in the refrigerator overnight. Remove from refrigerator 30 minutes before baking. Cover and bake at 350° for 40-45 minutes or until bubbly. **YIELD:** 2 dishes (10 servings each).

EDITOR'S NOTE: When cutting hot peppers, disposable gloves are recommended. Avoid touching your face.

moist meat loaves

When a lady from our church served this at her son's birthday party, I just had to have the recipe! Now it's the only meat loaf I make. It's great for potlucks.

Jenny Ingraham | KARLSTAD, MN

8 eggs, lightly beaten

2-2/3 cups milk

6 cups (24 ounces) shredded cheddar cheese

12 slices white bread, cubed

2 large onions, finely chopped

2 cups shredded carrots

7-1/2 teaspoons salt

1 teaspoon pepper

8 pounds lean ground beef

ADDITIONAL INGREDIENTS
(for each meat loaf):

1/4 cup packed brown sugar

1/4 cup ketchup

1 tablespoon prepared mustard

In two very large bowls, combine the eggs, milk, cheese, bread, onions, carrots, salt and pepper. Crumble beef over mixture and mix well. Pat into four ungreased 9-in. x 5-in. loaf pans.

Cover and freeze three meat loaves for up to 3 months. Bake the remaining loaf, uncovered, at 350° for 1 hour. Combine the brown sugar, ketchup and mustard; spread over loaf. Bake 15-20 minutes longer or until no pink remains and a meat thermometer reads 160°.

TO USE FROZEN MEAT LOAF: Thaw in the refrigerator overnight. Remove from the refrigerator 30 minutes before baking. Bake, uncovered, at 350° for 1 hour. Combine brown sugar, ketchup and mustard; spread over loaf. Bake 30-35 minutes longer or until no pink remains and a meat thermometer reads 160°. **YIELD:** 4 loaves (6 servings each).

onion-dill batter bread

(PICTURED ON PAGE 204)

My mother used to bake terrific rye batter bread. I've experimented with the recipe through the years and have come up with many versions, including this one.

Wayne Krumel | PENSACOLA, FL

4-1/4 to 4-1/2 cups all-purpose flour

1/4 cup toasted wheat germ

1/4 cup wheat bran

3 tablespoons sugar

2 packages (1/4 ounce each) active dry yeast

3 teaspoons salt

1 cup milk

1 cup water

1 egg

2 tablespoons canola oil

2 tablespoons dried minced onion

1 tablespoon dill weed

1 teaspoon sesame seeds

In a large bowl, combine 2 cups flour, wheat germ, wheat bran, sugar, yeast and salt. In a small saucepan, heat milk and water to 120°-130°. Add to dry ingredients; beat until moistened. Add the egg, oil, onion and dill; beat on low speed for 30 seconds. Beat on high for 2-1/2 minutes.

Stir in remaining flour; beat until smooth. Do not knead. Cover and let rise in a warm place until doubled, about 50 minutes.

Stir dough down. Transfer to two greased 1-1/2-qt. round baking dishes. Moisten fingers with water; pat dough evenly. Sprinkle with sesame seeds. Cover and let rise until doubled, about 20 minutes.

Bake at 350° for 50-60 minutes or until golden brown. (Cover loosely with foil if top browns too quickly.) Remove from baking dishes to wire racks to cool. Wrap in foil and freeze for up to 3 months.

TO USE FROZEN BREAD: Thaw at room temperature. **YIELD:** 2 loaves.

stuffed banana peppers

(PICTURED AT RIGHT)

The combination of meats gives these stuffed peppers their distinctively different flavor.

Thomas Kendzlic | *PITTSBURGH, PA*

6 cups tomato sauce, divided

24 banana peppers

4 eggs, beaten

1 cup seasoned bread crumbs

1-1/3 cups grated Parmesan cheese, divided

1/4 cup minced fresh basil or 4 teaspoons dried basil

6 garlic cloves, minced

1/2 teaspoon salt

1/2 teaspoon pepper

1/2 pound ground beef

1/2 pound bulk hot Italian sausage

1/2 pound ground veal

1/4 cup olive oil

Grease two 13-in. x 9-in. baking dishes. Spread 1/2 cup tomato sauce in each dish; set aside.

Cut tops off peppers and remove seeds. In a large bowl, combine the eggs, bread crumbs, 2/3 cup Parmesan cheese, basil, garlic, salt and pepper. Crumble the beef, sausage and veal over mixture; mix well. Spoon into peppers.

In a large skillet, cook peppers in oil in batches over medium heat for 1-2 minutes on each side or until lightly browned. Arrange 12 peppers in each prepared dish. Top with remaining sauce; sprinkle with remaining cheese.

Cover and freeze one dish for up to 3 months. Cover and bake the remaining dish at 350° for 35-40 minutes or until meat is no longer pink and peppers are tender.

TO USE FROZEN STUFFED PEPPERS: Thaw in the refrigerator overnight. Remove from the refrigerator 30 minutes before baking. Cover and bake at 350° for 45-50 minutes or until meat is no longer pink and peppers are tender. **YIELD:** 2 dishes (6 servings each).

EDITOR'S NOTE: When cutting hot peppers, disposable gloves are recommended. Avoid touching your face.

*N*othing beats cheering on your favorite team to the Final Four with friends and some tasty game-watching grub. So gather all the basketball fanatics on your roster for a March Madness party.

With the perfect game plan of savory bites and sweet snacks, your party is guaranteed to score points. Hearty fan fare such as Spicy Chicken Wings, Mini Phyllo Tacos and Bacon Cheese Poppers satisfy the biggest appetites. Slam dunk hot soft pretzels into thick and creamy Horseradish Cheese Spread or munch on zesty Ranch Snack Mix.

When the final buzzer sounds, enjoy decadent, caramel-covered Favorite Dipped Pretzel Rods. Victory never tasted so sweet!

GAME FOOD ROSTER
(PICTURED AT RIGHT)

Bacon Cheese Poppers (p. 214)
Spicy Chicken Wings (p. 216)
Horseradish Cheese Spread (p. 218)
Favorite Dipped Pretzel Rods (p. 218)
Ranch Snack Mix (p. 214)
Mini Phyllo Tacos (p. 216)

march madness
MANIA

bacon cheese poppers

(PICTURED ON PAGE 212)

Guests who head straight for a tray of jalapeno poppers will devour this crowd pleaser. The blue cheese filling is wonderful, but it's the slight crunch from bread crumbs and crumbled bacon that sets the bites apart from any other version.

Charlene Chambers | ORMOND BEACH, FL

16 jalapeno peppers

1 package (8 ounces) cream cheese, softened

1-1/2 cups (6 ounces) shredded Monterey Jack cheese

1 cup (4 ounces) sharp shredded cheddar cheese

1/2 cup crumbled blue cheese

6 bacon strips, cooked and crumbled

1/4 teaspoon salt

1/4 teaspoon onion powder

1/4 teaspoon garlic powder

1/4 teaspoon grated lemon peel

1/4 teaspoon chili powder

1/2 cup panko (Japanese) bread crumbs

Sour cream or ranch salad dressing

Cut jalapenos in half lengthwise and remove seeds; set aside. In a small bowl, beat the cheeses, bacon, salt, onion powder, garlic powder, lemon peel and chili powder. Spoon into pepper halves. Dip tops of stuffed peppers into bread crumbs.

Transfer to two greased 15-in. x 10-in. baking pans. Bake at 350° for 20-25 minutes or until heated through. Serve with sour cream or ranch dressing. **YIELD:** about 2-1/2 dozen.

EDITOR'S NOTE: When cutting hot peppers, disposable gloves are recommended. Avoid touching your face.

ranch snack mix

(PICTURED ON PAGE 213)

I first tasted this snack mix when a co-worker shared it. Because of its simple preparation and popular cheese flavor, it's a staple for game-day gatherings at our place.

Linda Doescher | WESTON, WI

1 package (16 ounces) pretzel sticks

1 package (13 ounces) crisp cheese puff snacks

1 can (11-1/2 ounces) mixed nuts

1 package (7-1/2 ounces) Bugles

1 package (7-1/2 ounces) miniature cheese filled butter-flavored crackers

1 package (7 ounces) cheddar cheese-filled pretzel snacks

1 bottle (12 ounces) butter-flavored popcorn oil

2 envelopes ranch salad dressing mix

In a large bowl, combine the first six ingredients. In a small bowl, combine oil and dressing mix. Pour over snack mixture; toss to coat.

Transfer to a large ungreased roasting pan. Bake, uncovered, at 250° for 50 minutes, stirring every 10 minutes. Cool completely. Store in airtight containers. **YIELD:** 10 quarts.

crowd-pleasing ravioli nachos

(PICTURED AT RIGHT)

Lightly breaded and deep-fried, ravioli goes to a new level in this nacho-like appetizer. Kids and grown-ups can't get enough of the crispy, cheesy appetizer.

Robert Doornbos | JENISON, MI

1 package (25 ounces) frozen cheese ravioli

1 package (25 ounces) frozen sausage ravioli

3 eggs, beaten

2 cups seasoned bread crumbs

2 tablespoons grated Parmesan cheese

1/4 teaspoon crushed red pepper flakes

1/4 teaspoon pepper

1/8 teaspoon garlic salt

Oil for frying

3/4 cup Alfredo sauce

3/4 cup spaghetti sauce

2 cups (8 ounces) shredded cheddar cheese

5 green onions, sliced

1 can (3.8 ounces) sliced ripe olives, drained

Additional spaghetti sauce, optional

Cook ravioli according to package directions. Drain and pat dry. Place eggs in a shallow bowl. In another shallow bowl, combine the bread crumbs, Parmesan cheese, pepper flakes, pepper and garlic salt. Dip ravioli in the eggs, then bread crumb mixture.

In an electric skillet or deep-fat fryer, heat oil to 375°. Fry ravioli, a few at a time, for 1-2 minutes on each side or until golden brown. Drain on paper towels.

Arrange ravioli in an ungreased 15-in. x 10-in. baking pan. Spoon sauces over ravioli; sprinkle with cheddar cheese. Bake at 350° for 3-5 minutes or until cheese is melted. Sprinkle with onions and olives. Serve immediately with additional spaghetti sauce if desired. **YIELD:** 6-1/2 dozen.

mini phyllo tacos

(PICTURED ON PAGE 213)

For a winning appetizer, serve crispy phyllo cups filled with taco-seasoned ground beef and zesty shredded cheese. The handheld munchies are sure to be named MVP of the menu.

Roseann Weston | PHILIPSBURG, PA

1 pound lean ground beef

1/2 cup finely chopped onion

1 envelope taco seasoning

3/4 cup water

1-1/4 cups shredded taco cheese, divided

2 packages (1.9 ounces each) frozen miniature phyllo tart shells

In a small skillet, cook beef and onion over medium heat until meat is no longer pink; drain. Stir in taco seasoning and water. Bring to a boil. Reduce heat; simmer, uncovered, for 5 minutes. Remove from the heat; stir in 1/2 cup cheese.

Place tart shells in an ungreased 15-in. x 10-in. baking pan. Fill with the taco mixture. Bake at 350° for 6 minutes. Sprinkle with the remaining cheese; bake 2-3 minutes longer or until heated through. Serve warm. **YIELD:** 2-1/2 dozen.

spicy chicken wings

(PICTURED ON PAGE 212)

These fall-off-the-bone-tender wings have just the right amount of heat. The creamy, blue cheese dressing has a slight tartness that creates the perfect flavor combination for dipping.

Kevalyn Henderson | HAYWARD, WI

1/2 cup soy sauce

1/3 cup sugar

1 teaspoon salt

1 teaspoon grated orange peel

1 garlic clove, minced

1/4 teaspoon pepper

3 pounds frozen chicken wingettes and drumettes, thawed

3 teaspoons chili powder

3/4 teaspoon cayenne pepper

3/4 teaspoon hot pepper sauce

BLUE CHEESE DIP:

1 cup mayonnaise

1/2 cup blue cheese salad dressing

1/3 cup buttermilk

2 teaspoons Italian salad dressing mix

In a small bowl, combine the soy sauce, sugar, salt, orange peel, garlic and pepper; set aside 1/4 cup. Pour remaining marinade into a large resealable plastic bag; add chicken. Seal bag and turn to coat; refrigerate for 1 hour.

Transfer chicken and marinade to a greased 13-in. x 9-in. baking dish. Cover and bake at 325° for 1-1/2 hours or until chicken juices run clear.

Using tongs, transfer chicken to a greased 15-in. x 10-in. baking pan. In a small bowl, combine the chili powder, cayenne, pepper sauce and reserved marinade. Drizzle over chicken.

Bake, uncovered, for 30 minutes, turning once. In a small bowl, whisk the dip ingredients. Serve with the wings. **YIELD:** 2 dozen (1-3/4 cups dip).

buffalo chicken-topped potatoes

(PICTURED AT RIGHT)

If your favorite appetizers are cheesy potato skins and buffalo chicken wings, you'll find this recipe one to cheer about. Loaded with cheese, sour cream and onion, stuffed potatoes get a sassy bite from mild wing sauce.

Michelle Gauer | SPICER, MN

4 medium potatoes (about 1-1/2 pounds)

3/4 cup shredded cheddar cheese, divided

1/2 cup sour cream

2 tablespoons buffalo wing sauce, divided

1 pound boneless skinless chicken breasts, cubed

1/4 teaspoon salt

1/4 teaspoon chili powder

1 tablespoon canola oil

2 tablespoons white vinegar

2 tablespoons butter

Additional sour cream and chopped green onions

Scrub and pierce potatoes. Bake at 375° for 1 hour or until tender. When cool enough to handle, cut each potato in half lengthwise. Scoop out the pulp, leaving thin shells.

In a large bowl, mash pulp with 1/2 cup cheese, sour cream and 1 tablespoon buffalo wing sauce. Spoon into potato shells. Sprinkle with remaining cheese. Place the filled shells on a baking sheet. Bake 8-12 minutes longer or until heated through.

Meanwhile, sprinkle chicken with salt and chili powder. In a large skillet, cook chicken in oil over medium heat for 6-8 minutes or until juices run clear. Stir in vinegar, butter and remaining buffalo wing sauce; cook and stir 2-3 minutes longer. Spoon the chicken mixture over potatoes. Serve with the additional sour cream and onions. **YIELD:** 8 servings.

horseradish cheese spread

(PICTURED ON PAGE 213)

*Cheesy, thick and rich, this flavorful dip stays put on freshly baked soft pretzels.
It's also delicious spread on slices of crusty French bread.*

Cathy Bodell | *FRANKFORT, MI*

1 package (16 ounces) process cheese (Velveeta), cubed

3/4 cup mayonnaise

1/3 cup prepared horseradish

1/4 cup milk

1/8 teaspoon hot pepper sauce

Baked soft pretzels, optional

In a heavy saucepan over low heat, combine the cheese, mayonnaise, horseradish, milk and pepper sauce. Cook and stir until cheese is melted and mixture is blended. Serve with the pretzels if desired. **YIELD:** 2-1/2 cups.

favorite dipped pretzel rods

(PICTURED ON PAGE 213)

*Coated in gooey caramel, then covered with chocolate and peanut butter chips, these decadent dipped pretzels
are a delicious way to celebrate. For added variety, make some using butterscotch chips.*

Connie Banner | *CASTLEWOOD, VA*

1 package (14 ounces) caramels

3 to 4 tablespoons water

1-1/3 cups miniature semisweet chocolate chips

1 package (10 ounces) peanut butter chips

1 cup chopped pecans

1 package (12 ounces) pretzel rods

In a heavy saucepan over low heat, melt caramels with water. In a large shallow bowl, combine chips and pecans.

Pour caramel mixture into a 2-cup glass measuring cup. Dip each pretzel about one-third of the way into the caramel mixture (reheat in microwave if mixture becomes too thick for dipping). Allow excess caramel to drip off, then roll pretzels in the chip mixture. Place on waxed paper until set. Store the pretzels in airtight containers. **YIELD:** 2-1/2 dozen.

LEFTOVER MELTED CHOCOLATE

When you have leftover melted chocolate from making candies or desserts, pour it into a small nonstick cake pan, smooth it into an even layer and refrigerate until hardened. Then "pop" it out onto a cutting board, chop into small chunks and store in the fridge to be used in any recipe that calls for chocolate chips.

mini-burger potato bites

(PICTURED AT RIGHT)

The caramelized onions and creamy sauce make these yummy bites a huge hit at parties. People say they're even better than the mini burger appetizers that are so popular at restaurants.

Maribeth Condo | *LINDENHURST, IL*

16 frozen waffle-cut fries

2 medium onions, cut into 1/8-inch slices

1 tablespoon butter

1 tablespoon olive oil

1 teaspoon sugar

1/2 teaspoon salt

1/8 teaspoon pepper

1 pound ground beef

2 teaspoons steak seasoning

3 egg yolks

4-1/2 teaspoons lemon juice

1-1/2 teaspoons water

1/2 cup butter, melted

4 slices cheddar cheese, quartered

Bake the waffle fries according to package directions.

In a large skillet, cook onions in butter and oil over medium heat for 10 minutes. Add the sugar, salt and pepper; cook for 3-5 minutes more or until the onions are golden brown, stirring frequently.

Meanwhile, in a large bowl, combine beef and steak seasoning. Shape into 16 patties. Cook in a large skillet until a meat thermometer reads 160° and juices run clear, turning once.

For sauce, in a double boiler or metal bowl over simmering water, constantly whisk the egg yolks, lemon juice and water until mixture reaches 160° or is thick enough to coat the back of a metal spoon. Reduce heat to low. Slowly drizzle in warm melted butter, whisking constantly.

Top each waffle fry with a burger and cheese. Broil 4-5 in. from the heat for 1-2 minutes or until cheese is melted. Top with onions and sauce. **YIELD:** 16 appetizers.

EDITOR'S NOTE: This recipe was tested with McCormick's Montreal Steak Seasoning. Look for it in the spice aisle.

spicy zucchini relish

(PICTURED AT FAR RIGHT)

I can't seem to make enough of this zippy, chunky relish. Zucchini creates a nice change of pace from the usual pickle relish, and the assortment of peppers adds a tongue-tingling bite.

Amy Martin | *BELLEFONTAINE, OH*

5 cups shredded zucchini

1 cup grated onion

4-1/2 teaspoons salt

1-1/2 teaspoons cornstarch

1-1/2 teaspoons ground mustard

1-1/2 teaspoons ground turmeric

1 teaspoon celery seed

3/4 teaspoon pepper

3/4 cup white vinegar

1/2 cup finely chopped sweet red pepper

4-1/2 teaspoons chopped seeded jalapeno pepper

1-1/4 teaspoons chopped seeded habanero pepper

In a large resealable plastic bag, combine the zucchini, onion and salt. Seal bag and turn to coat: refrigerate for 8 hours or overnight. Rinse with water; drain.

In a large saucepan, combine the cornstarch, mustard, turmeric, celery seed and pepper. Gradually whisk in vinegar until blended. Stir in peppers and zucchini mixture. Bring to a boil. Reduce heat; simmer, uncovered, for 30 minutes. Cool. Cover and refrigerate for at least 4 hours before serving. **YIELD:** 3 cups.

EDITOR'S NOTE: When cutting hot peppers, disposable gloves are recommended. Avoid touching your face.

coney island hot dog sauce

(PICTURED AT FAR RIGHT)

Put a spin on a stadium favorite with this hearty, chili-like topping featuring ground beef smothered in a sweet-and-sassy sauce. The blend of flavors has mass appeal that makes it a winner for any large-group gathering.

Carole Bull | *TRAVERSE CITY, MI*

1/4 pound ground beef

1 medium onion, finely chopped

1 cup water

1 can (8 ounces) tomato sauce

1/4 cup sweet pickle relish

3 tablespoons cider vinegar

1 tablespoon chili powder

1 tablespoon prepared mustard

1/2 teaspoon salt

1/4 teaspoon pepper

Dash cayenne pepper, optional

In a small skillet, cook the beef and onion over medium heat until meat is no longer pink; drain. Stir in the water, tomato sauce, relish, vinegar, chili powder, mustard, salt, pepper and cayenne pepper if desired. Bring to a boil. Reduce the heat; simmer, uncovered, for 40-50 minutes or until desired thickness, stirring occasionally. **YIELD:** 1-1/4 cups.

curry ketchup with a kick

(PICTURED AT RIGHT)

Turn up the heat on ordinary ketchup with this spicy version that stars curry. Delicious on brats and grilled sausages, it can be served warm or cold.

Alexandra Williams | PFOFELD, GERMANY

1 bottle (20 ounces) ketchup

1 cup water

1/2 cup curry powder

1-1/2 teaspoons paprika

1-1/2 teaspoons Worcestershire sauce

In a large saucepan, combine all ingredients. Bring to a boil. Reduce heat; cover and simmer for 20-25 minutes or until thickened, stirring occasionally. Cover and refrigerate for at least 8 hours. **YIELD:** 2 cups.

MARCH MADNESS PARTY GAME PLAN

It's easy to get into the spirit of the college basketball tournament season. Start by wearing your favorite team's colors, or flavor the party with a little humor by donning black-and-white stripes.

You might even host your own competition by telling guests that the most spirited fan will receive a prize, such as a basketball, gift basket or gift card.

Carry the team spirit over into the other aspects of your party, too, by using plates, napkins, tablecloths and decorations that sport team colors. Decorations can be as simple as balloons and streamers in team colors or as elaborate as passing out foam basketballs, pompoms and team penants.

And for easy cleanup at the end of the night, place basketball hoops over the trashcans. Your guests won't be able to resist making slam dunks!

If you're heading out on July Fourth to a patriotic parade, a picnic in the park or a festive fireworks display, remember to take along tried-and-true treats.

No matter where you're headed, foods that travel well lend to the success of the day.

Start things off on a sweet note with Fruit & Cereal Snack Mix. Feel free to vary the flavor by substituting your family's favorite dried fruit.

If you pledged not to fuss on this national holiday, Puff Pastry Stars are for you. The recipe calls for a mere four ingredients!

Family and friends will salute you for making an All-American dessert like Patriotic Cupcake Cones.

PATRIOTIC PICNIC
(PICTURED AT RIGHT)

fourth of july
FESTIVITIES

patriotic cupcake cones

(PICTURED ON PAGE 223)

Young and old alike will get a kick out of our home economists' cute cupcakes prepared in crunchy ice cream cones. The red colored cake and white frosting make them a perfect patriotic treat.

1/2 cup shortening

1-1/2 cups sugar

2 eggs

1 bottle (1 ounce) red food coloring

3 teaspoons white vinegar

1 teaspoon butter flavoring

1 teaspoon vanilla extract

2-1/2 cups cake flour

1/4 cup baking cocoa

1 teaspoon baking soda

1 teaspoon salt

1 cup buttermilk

24 ice cream cake cones (about 3 inches tall)

FROSTING:

1-1/2 cups shortening

1-1/2 teaspoons vanilla extract

6 cups confectioners' sugar

4 to 5 tablespoons milk

Blue jimmies

In a large bowl, cream shortening and sugar until light and fluffy. Add eggs, one at a time, beating well after each addition. Stir in the food coloring, vinegar, butter flavoring and vanilla. Combine the flour, cocoa, baking soda and salt; add to the creamed mixture alternately with buttermilk, beating well after each addition. Pour the batter into each cake cone to within 3/4 in. of the top. Place in ungreased muffin cups.

Bake at 350° for 20-25 minutes or until a toothpick inserted near the center comes clean. Cool completely.

In a large bowl, beat the shortening, vanilla and confectioners' sugar. Add enough milk to achieve spreading consistency. Cut a small hole in the corner of pastry or plastic bag; insert a large star tip. Fill the bag with frosting. Pipe onto cupcakes. Sprinkle with the jimmies. **YIELD:** 2 dozen.

CLEVER CUPCAKE CARRIER

Unlike traditional cupcakes, Patriotic Cupcake Cones are top-heavy, making it a bit challenging to transport them to picnics. But you can create your own convenient carriers.

First search for some sturdy cardboard boxes. If they're flimsy, they won't hold the heavy cupcake cones.

Measure the diameter of the bottom of a cupcake cone. Draw the same size circles on top of the box, allowing enough room between each. Turn the top over and cut out the circles with a sharp utility knife. Put the top back on the bottom piece. To keep the carrier more secure, you may want to tape the top and bottom pieces together. Set a cupcake cone in each hole.

red and blue berry lemonade slush

(PICTURED AT RIGHT)

This refreshing fruity beverage from our Test Kitchen showcases fresh raspberries and blueberries. Remove it from the freezer before heading out to your event.

2 cups lemon juice

1-1/2 cups fresh raspberries

1-1/2 cups fresh blueberries

1 to 1-1/4 cups sugar

3 cups cold water

In a blender, combine the lemon juice, raspberries, blueberries and sugar. Cover and process until blended. Strain and discard seeds. In a 2-1/2 qt. pitcher, combine berry mixture and water. Pour into a freezer container. Cover and freeze for 8 hours or overnight.

Just before serving, remove from the freezer and let stand for 45 minutes or until slushy. YIELD: 2 quarts.

fruit & cereal snack mix

(PICTURED ON PAGE 222)

Tart dried cranberries and cherries are a nice contrast to the sweet cereal in this kid-friendly snack.
John Lancaster | UNION GROVE, WI

8 cups Cinnamon Toast Crunch cereal

1-1/4 cups chopped dried apples

3/4 cup dried cranberries

3/4 cup raisins

1/2 cup dried cherries

In a large bowl, combine all the ingredients. Store in an airtight container. YIELD: 2-1/2 quarts.

puff pastry stars

(PICTURED ON PAGE 222)

Our home economists fashion festive star treats from convenient frozen puff pastry. Feel free to experiment with different seasonings, such as taco seasoning mix, garlic salt or Cajun seasoning. For a sweet snack, sprinkle on cinnamon-sugar.

1 frozen puff pastry, thawed

2 tablespoons canola oil

1 tablespoon ranch salad dressing mix

3 tablespoons shredded Parmesan cheese

Unfold puff pastry. In a small bowl, combine oil and dressing mix; brush over pastry. Using a floured 3-in. star-shaped cookie cutter, cut out 10 stars. Place on a greased baking sheet. Sprinkle with the cheese.

Bake at 400° for 7-9 minutes or until puffy and golden brown. Serve warm. **YIELD:** 10 appetizers.

grape leather

Instead of giving your kids packaged fruit snacks, offer them fruit leather! This nutritious treat from our Test Kitchen keeps in a sealed bag at room temperature for one month.

1-1/2 pounds seedless red grapes

2 tablespoons sugar

1 tablespoon lemon juice

Sort and wash the grapes; remove stems. Place the grapes in a steamer basket; place in a large saucepan over 1 in. of water. Bring to a boil; cover and steam for 15 minutes or until soft.

Transfer grapes to a blender or food processor; cover and puree. Strain grapes through a food mill into a small bowl; discard skin. Stir in sugar and lemon juice.

Line a 15-in. x 10-in. x 1-in. baking pan with parchment paper. Spread fruit mixture evenly onto parchment paper. Bake at 200° for 2-1/2 to 3-1/2 hours or until fruit leather feels slightly sticky. Cool completely.

Transfer the fruit leather to a new 15-in. x 10-in. sheet of parchment paper. Roll up the leather in parchment paper jelly-roll style, starting with a short side (do not unroll). Cut into six 1-1/2-in. pieces. Store in an airtight container in a cool dry place for up to 1 month. **YIELD:** 6 servings.

EDITOR'S NOTE: Drying time will vary depending on temperature and humidity.

strawberry salsa

(PICTURED AT RIGHT)

Sweet and savory flavors combine in this summertime salsa. I like to serve it with tortilla chips as an appetizer or on top of grilled chicken and pork as a condiment.

Amy Hinkle | TOPEKA, KS

2 pints cherry tomatoes, quartered

1 pint fresh strawberries, chopped

8 green onions, chopped

1/2 cup minced fresh cilantro

6 tablespoons olive oil

2 tablespoons balsamic vinegar

1/2 teaspoon salt

Tortilla chips

In a large bowl, combine the tomatoes, strawberries, onions and cilantro. In a small bowl, combine the oil, vinegar and salt; gently stir into the tomato mixture. Chill until serving. Serve with the tortilla chips. **YIELD:** 6 cups.

STRAWBERRY BASICS

Strawberries are available year-round, although the peak season is April through June. The sweet fruit does not continue to ripen after picking, so purchase berries that are bright red and that have little green or white color.

Refrigerate strawberries in a paper towel-lined, moisture-proof container for 2 to 3 days. They can also be frozen for up to 1 year.

Use a strawberry huller or the tip of a serrated grapefruit spoon to easily remove the stem-hull. Just insert the tip of the spoon into the strawberry next to the stem and cut around the stem.

easy refrigerator pickles

(PICTURED AT FAR RIGHT)

*My husband grows cucumbers, garlic and dill in the garden and eagerly waits for
me to make these pickles. The recipe comes from my grandmother.
It has stood the test of time after all these years!*

Angela Lienhard | *BLOSSBURG, PA*

14 pickling cucumbers

40 fresh dill sprigs

4 garlic cloves, sliced

2 quarts water

1 cup cider vinegar

1/2 cup sugar

1/3 cup salt

1 teaspoon mixed pickling spices

Cut each cucumber lengthwise into six spears. In a large bowl,
combine the cucumbers, dill and garlic; set aside. In a Dutch oven,
combine the remaining ingredients. Bring to a boil; cook and stir just
until sugar is dissolved. Pour over cucumber mixture; cool. Cover
tightly; refrigerate at least 24 hours. YIELD: 4-1/2 quarts.

lemon potato salad

(PICTURED AT FAR RIGHT)

*Of all the dishes served at my wedding, this fresh-tasting salad was the favorite among guests.
Because it doesn't have mayonnaise, it's great warm-weather fare. Using
Yukon Gold potatoes instead of russets is deliciously different.*

Nicole Evans Groth | *BLOOMINGTON, IN*

2 pounds Yukon Gold potatoes, cut into
1/2-inch cubes

4 green onions, sliced

1/3 cup olive oil

1/4 cup lemon juice

4 teaspoons snipped fresh dill or 1 teaspoon
dill weed

1 teaspoon sugar

3/4 teaspoon salt

1/2 teaspoon pepper

Place potatoes in a large saucepan; cover with water. Bring to a boil.
Reduce heat; cover and simmer for 8-10 minutes or until tender.

Drain potatoes and place in a large bowl; add green onions. In a small
bowl, whisk the remaining ingredients. Pour over potato mixture;
toss to coat. Serve warm or at room temperature. Refrigerate leftovers.
YIELD: 7 servings.

peachy pork ribs

(PICTURED AT RIGHT)

Ribs are a wonderful main course to take to picnics because they can be baked in the oven ahead of time. At your event, simply finish them off on the grill with a fruity basting sauce.

Tom Arnold | MILWAUKEE, WI

2 racks pork baby back ribs (4 pounds), cut into serving-size pieces

1/2 cup water

3 medium ripe peaches, peeled and cubed

2 tablespoons chopped onion

2 tablespoons butter

1 garlic clove, minced

3 tablespoons lemon juice

2 tablespoons orange juice concentrate

1 tablespoon brown sugar

2 teaspoons soy sauce

1/2 teaspoon ground mustard

1/4 teaspoon salt

1/4 teaspoon pepper

Place ribs in a shallow roasting pan; add water. Cover and bake at 325° for 2 hours.

Meanwhile, for sauce, place peaches in a blender; cover and process until blended. In a small saucepan, saute onion in butter until tender. Add garlic; saute 1 minute longer. Stir in the lemon juice, orange juice concentrate, brown sugar, soy sauce, mustard, salt, pepper and peach puree; heat through.

Coat grill rack with cooking spray before starting the grill. Drain ribs. Spoon some of the sauce over ribs. Grill, covered, over medium heat for 8-10 minutes or until browned, turning occasionally and brushing with sauce. **YIELD:** 4 servings.

When a heat wave hits during the dog days of summer, you can keep your cool by hosting a fun-filled pool-side party.

Guests will declare your bash the hottest in town when they dive into refreshing sides such as Marinated Cucumber Pasta Salad and Pasta with Mozzarella, Tomatoes and Fresh Basil.

For main dishes that make a splash—while keeping the kitchen cool—Apricot Chicken Drumsticks and Couscous Tuna Towers are a stroke of genius.

AL FRESCO FARE
(PICTURED AT RIGHT)

Apricot Chicken Drumsticks (p. 232)
Couscous Tuna Towers (p. 234)
Marinated Cucumber Pasta Salad (p. 232)
Pasta with Mozzarella,
Tomatoes and Fresh Basil (p. 236)

keeping cool
BY THE POOL

apricot chicken drumsticks

(PICTURED ON PAGE 231)

During the summer months, you can find my family gathered around the grill enjoying delicious dishes like this. You can serve the drumsticks chilled or hot off the grill.

Mary Ann Sklanka | BLAKELY, PA

12 chicken drumsticks (3 pounds)

1 teaspoon salt

1/4 teaspoon pepper

1/4 cup canola oil

1/4 cup apricot jam, warmed

1/4 cup prepared mustard

1 tablespoon brown sugar

Sprinkle chicken with salt and pepper. For sauce, in a small bowl, combine the remaining ingredients.

Coat grill rack with cooking spray before starting the grill. Grill the chicken, covered, over medium heat for 15-20 minutes or until a meat thermometer reads 180°, turning and basting occasionally with the sauce. Cool for 5 minutes. Cover and refrigerate until chilled. **YIELD:** 6 servings.

marinated cucumber pasta salad

(PICTURED ON PAGE 231)

The sweet-and-sour dressing in this recipe is a nice change of pace from more traditional varieties. My nursing supervisor shared the recipe with me...and I'm glad she did!

Sue Dorrance | WEST BEND, WI

1 package (16 ounces) mostaccioli

1 medium cucumber, thinly sliced

6 green onions, chopped

MARINADE:

1 cup sugar

1 cup white vinegar

1/4 cup canola oil

1 jar (2 ounces) diced pimientos, drained

1 tablespoon minced fresh parsley

2 teaspoons Dijon mustard

1 teaspoon salt

1 teaspoon garlic powder

1/2 teaspoon pepper

Cook mostaccioli according to package directions; drain and rinse in cold water. In a large bowl, combine the mostaccioli, cucumber and onions.

In a jar with a tight-fitting lid, combine the marinade ingredients; shake well. Pour over pasta mixture; toss to coat. Cover and refrigerate overnight, stirring occasionally. Serve with a slotted spoon. **YIELD:** 16 servings.

caribbean fruit soup

(PICTURED AT RIGHT)

This fruit soup is a delicious, refreshing way to begin a summer meal. Jerk seasoning gives each spoonful a little kick.

Cheryl Perry | *ELIZABETH CITY, NC*

1 cup each chopped peeled fresh peaches, nectarines, papaya and mango

1 cup chopped fresh pineapple

1 cup diced cantaloupe

1 cup chopped seeded peeled cucumber

1 cup chopped sweet red pepper

1/4 cup thinly sliced green onions

2 cups frozen non-alcoholic pina colada mix, thawed

1 cup passion fruit or mango nectar

1/4 cup minced fresh cilantro

2 tablespoons plus 2 teaspoons lime juice, divided

1 tablespoon sugar

1 tablespoon Caribbean jerk seasoning

1 teaspoon salt

1 teaspoon grated fresh gingerroot

1 teaspoon minced seeded jalapeno pepper

2 medium bananas, sliced

1 cup flaked coconut

In a large bowl, combine the peaches, nectarines, papaya, mango, pineapple, cantaloupe, cucumber, red pepper and onions. In a blender or food processor, place half the fruit mixture; cover and process until smooth.

Transfer to a large bowl; stir in the remaining fruit mixture, pina colada mix, nectar, cilantro, 2 tablespoons lime juice, sugar, jerk seasoning, salt, ginger and jalapeno. Cover and refrigerate for 3 hours or until chilled.

Toss bananas with remaining lime juice. Garnish the soup with bananas and coconut. **YIELD:** 12 servings (2 quarts).

couscous tuna towers

(PICTURED ON PAGE 231)

These attractive tuna towers will impress your dinner guests. Plus, the cost of ingredients is easy on the wallet.

Jennifer Honeycutt | SOUTH NASHVILLE, TN

1 small onion, chopped

1 tablespoon canola oil

2/3 cup uncooked couscous

1-1/4 cups water

2 cans (6 ounces each) light water-packed tuna, drained and flaked

1/3 cup minced fresh parsley

2 tablespoons capers, drained

2 tablespoons sliced ripe olives, drained

1 tablespoon grated lemon peel

1 tablespoon lemon juice

Dash salt and pepper

1 tablespoon red wine vinaigrette

2 cups torn curly endive

8 thick slices red tomatoes

8 thick slices yellow tomatoes

In a small skillet, saute onion in oil until tender. Add couscous; saute 1-2 minutes longer or until couscous is lightly browned. Add water; bring to a boil. Reduce heat; cover and simmer for 8 minutes. Cool slightly.

In a large bowl, combine the couscous mixture, tuna, parsley, capers, olives, lemon peel, lemon juice, salt and pepper; set aside.

Pour vinaigrette over endive; toss to coat. On each of eight serving plates, layer a red tomato slice, a yellow tomato slice, 1/2 cup couscous mixture and 1/4 cup endive leaves. **YIELD:** 8 servings.

POOL-PARTY PROVISIONS

To make guests comfortable at your pool-side party, set out a basket of sunny-day supplies, such as fluffy beach towels, sunscreen, spray bottles filled with water and bottled water for drinking.

grilled halibut tacos with salsa verde

(PICTURED AT RIGHT)

Roasting the vegetables for the salsa in these fish tacos intensifies the flavors and provides such a wonderful, smoky taste.

Michelle Anderson | *EAGLE, ID*

1 pound tomatillos, husks removed and rinsed

1 small sweet onion, cut into 1/2-inch slices

4 garlic cloves, unpeeled

1/2 cup fresh cilantro leaves

1 serrano pepper, seeded

1 tablespoon lime juice

Dash salt and pepper

TACOS:

1/4 cup lime juice

1/4 cup olive oil

1 tablespoon salt

1 tablespoon garlic powder

1 tablespoon ground coriander

2 teaspoons ground cumin

1/2 teaspoon cayenne pepper

2 pounds halibut steaks

8 corn tortillas (6 inches)

2-1/2 cups shredded cabbage

Coat grill rack with cooking spray before starting the grill. For salsa, place tomatillos, onion and garlic on a grilling grid; transfer to grill rack. Grill, covered, over medium heat until tender and browned, turning frequently. Cool to room temperature.

Remove skin from garlic. Transfer grilled vegetables to a food processor. Add cilantro, serrano pepper, lime juice, salt and pepper. Cover and pulse until chunky. Refrigerate until serving.

In a large resealable plastic bag, combine the lime juice, oil, salt, garlic powder, coriander, cumin and cayenne; add halibut. Seal bag and turn to coat; refrigerate for up to 1 hour.

Drain and discard marinade. Grill halibut, covered, over medium heat for 4-6 minutes on each side or until fish flakes easily with a fork. Flake fish into 1-1/2 in. pieces; cool to room temperature.

To serve, top tortillas with fish, cabbage and salsa. **YIELD:** 8 servings.

EDITOR'S NOTE: When cutting hot peppers, disposable gloves are recommended. Avoid touching your face.

strawberry-mango daiquiri pops

*When hosting a summer party for adults, offer them a treat that takes them back to their childhood!
Our home economists developed these refreshing pops that are infused with rum and fruity flavor.*

1 cup water

1/2 cup mango nectar

1/4 cup light rum

3 tablespoons lime juice

1 pound halved fresh strawberries

1 cup coarsely chopped peeled mango

1/3 cup sugar

Place half of the water, mango nectar, rum, lime juice, strawberries, mango and sugar in a blender. Cover; process until blended. Fill each mold or cup with 1/4 cup of the mixture; top with holders or insert sticks into cups. Freeze. Repeat with the remaining ingredients. **YIELD:** 20 servings.

pasta with mozzarella, tomatoes and fresh basil

(PICTURED ON PAGE 230)

*During the summer season, I like to prepare this pasta salad featuring garden-ripe tomatoes and basil.
Fresh mozzarella adds a tasty touch. The dish can be prepared in advance so it's easy on the host.*

Ken Churches | *SAN ANDREAS, CA*

12 ounces fresh mozzarella cheese, cubed

6 tablespoons olive oil

4 teaspoons minced garlic

1 teaspoon salt

1 teaspoon pepper

1 package (16 ounces) uncooked linguine

1 cup chopped fresh basil leaves

3 medium tomatoes, chopped

In a large bowl, combine the cheese, oil, garlic, salt and pepper; let stand at room temperature for 1 hour.

Meanwhile, cook linguine according to package directions; drain and rinse in cold water. Add to the cheese mixture. Stir in basil and tomatoes. Serve at room temperature or chilled. **YIELD:** 6 servings.

fruit kabobs with margarita dip

(PICTURED AT RIGHT)

Older guests will love the margarita flavor of this cool and creamy dip. Serve the kabobs either as a snack or dessert.

Michelle Zapf | KINGSLAND, GA

1 package (3 ounces) cream cheese, softened

1/2 cup sour cream

1/4 cup confectioners' sugar

1 tablespoon lime juice

1 tablespoon frozen orange juice concentrate

1 tablespoon tequila

1/2 cup heavy whipping cream

12 fresh strawberries

6 pineapple chunks

1 medium mango, peeled and cubed

6 seedless red grapes

2 slices pound cake, cubed

In a large bowl, combine the first six ingredients. Beat in whipping cream until fluffy. Alternately, thread fruits and cake on metal or wooden skewers. Serve with dip. YIELD: 6 kabobs (1-1/2 cups dip).

lemon raspberry smoothies

(PICTURED ABOVE)

Summers get pretty hot here in Arizona, so we're always looking for a cool treat while hanging out around the pool. My love of raspberry lemonade inspired me to create this recipe.

Linda Nelson | PHOENIX, AZ

2 cups frozen unsweetened raspberries

2 cups lemonade

1 cup raspberry yogurt

Place half the raspberries, lemonade and yogurt in a blender; cover and process until blended. Pour into chilled glasses; repeat with remaining ingredients. Serve immediately. YIELD: 4 servings.

bracadabra! Work your magic this Halloween by hosting a bewitching bash and serving a slew of enchanting treats.

To spellbind family and friends as soon as they enter your hallowed haunt, offer them hurricane glasses filled with lovely layered Hocus-Pocus Sherbet Potion.

You're sure to charm even wicked souls with Witch's Crispy Hat and Yogurt-Filled Chocolate Cauldrons.

MESMERIZING MENU
(PICTURED AT RIGHT)

bewitching
HALLOWEEN

yogurt-filled chocolate cauldrons

(PICTURED ON PAGE 239)

Cute chocolate "cauldrons" hold a cool, creamy, orange-flavored yogurt in this recipe from our home economists.
The unfilled cups can be made days in advance and stored at room temperature.

6 squares (1 ounce each) semisweet chocolate

1 tablespoon shortening

1-1/2 cups vanilla yogurt

2 tablespoons orange juice concentrate

1/4 teaspoon grated orange peel

1 drop green paste food coloring

1 drop orange paste food coloring

6 orange or green candy sticks

In a microwave-safe bowl, melt chocolate and shortening; stir until smooth. Using a pastry brush, brush the inside of six paper or foil muffin cup liners with melted chocolate mixture. Chill until set, about 25 minutes. Add a second coat of chocolate; chill until set. Carefully remove and discard paper liners.

In a small bowl, combine the yogurt, orange juice concentrate and peel. Combine 1 tablespoon yogurt mixture and green food coloring. Mix remaining yogurt mixture and orange coloring; spoon into the cauldrons. Drop 1/2 teaspoon green yogurt onto each; swirl with a candy stick. **YIELD:** 6 servings.

spell-binding stew

Alongside a green salad and crusty bread, this stew is a hot and hearty meal.
My dad wasn't fond of stews, but he loved this version.

Marilyn Love | *CALGARY, AB*

2 tablespoons lemon juice

4 tablespoons Worcestershire sauce, divided

1/4 teaspoon seasoned salt

2 pounds beef stew meat, cut into 1-inch cubes

3 garlic cloves, minced

2 tablespoons olive oil

4 medium parsnips, peeled and sliced

4 medium carrots, sliced

3 medium potatoes, peeled and cubed

1 medium onion, cut into wedges

2 cups canned stewed tomatoes

1-1/2 cups beef broth, divided

1/2 cup ketchup

1/2 teaspoon dried chervil

1/4 teaspoon dried basil

1/4 teaspoon dried thyme

3 tablespoons all-purpose flour

1/2 cup frozen corn

1/2 cup frozen peas

In a large resealable plastic bag, combine the lemon juice, 2 tablespoons Worcestershire sauce and seasoned salt; add the beef. Seal bag and turn to coat; refrigerate for at least 4 hours.

Drain and discard marinade. In an ovenproof Dutch oven, brown beef and garlic in oil. Add the parsnips, carrots, potatoes, onion, tomatoes, 1 cup broth, ketchup, herbs and remaining Worcestershire sauce.

In a small bowl, combine flour and remaining broth until smooth. Gradually stir into the stew. Bring to a boil; cook and stir for 2 minutes or until thickened.

Cover and bake at 325° for 1-1/2 hours. Add the corn and peas. Cover and bake 30-45 minutes longer or until meat and vegetables are tender. **YIELD:** 6 servings (2-1/2 quarts).

black cat dippers with pumpkin pie dip

(PICTURED AT RIGHT)

Here's an easy recipe sure to impress party guests. The black cat dippers accompanying the in-a-dash dip are prepared with convenient refrigerated pie pastry.

Diane Turner | *BRUNSWICK, OH*

1 package (8 ounces) cream cheese, softened

1 can (15 ounces) solid-pack pumpkin

1 cup confectioners' sugar

1 tablespoon pumpkin pie spice

1 tablespoon honey

1 package (15 ounces) refrigerated pie pastry

1 egg

1 tablespoon milk

Black paste food coloring

1/4 cup sugar

1/2 teaspoon ground cinnamon

In a large bowl, beat cream cheese until fluffy. Add pumpkin, confectioners' sugar, pie spice and honey; beat until smooth. Cover and refrigerate until serving.

Roll out each pie pastry directly on an ungreased baking sheet to 1/8-in. thickness. Cut with a floured 2-in. cat-shaped cookie cutter, leaving at least 1 in. between cutouts. Remove excess dough and reroll scraps if desired. Beat the egg, milk and food coloring; brush over cutouts. Combine sugar and cinnamon; sprinkle over cutouts.

Bake at 400° for 6-7 minutes or until the edges begin to brown. Remove to wire racks to cool. Serve with the pumpkin dip. **YIELD:** 2-1/2 dozen black cats (3 cups dip).

witch's crispy hat

(PICTURED ON PAGE 238)

You won't want to keep this clever recipe from our Test Kitchen under your hat!
The chocolate-covered rice cereal treat will appeal to kids of all ages.

8 cups miniature marshmallows

1/2 cup butter, cubed

12 cups crisp rice cereal

3-1/3 cups confectioners' sugar

1-1/2 cups heavy whipping cream

8 squares (1 ounce each) unsweetened chocolate, chopped

4 teaspoons vanilla extract

3/4 cup butter, softened

1 ice cream sugar cone

4 sour apple Laffy Taffy candies

4 grape Laffy Taffy candies

In a Dutch oven, combine marshmallows and butter. Cook and stir over medium-low heat until melted and blended. Remove from the heat; stir in cereal. Press 4 cups into a greased 9-in. round pan and remaining mixture into a greased 15-in. x 10-in. x 1-in. pan; cool.

In a large saucepan, combine confectioners' sugar and cream. Bring to a boil, stirring constantly. Remove from the heat; stir in chocolate until melted and smooth. Stir in vanilla. Cool until the mixture is thickened, about 25 minutes, stirring occasionally.

In a large bowl, cream the butter. Gradually beat in chocolate mixture until blended. Cover and refrigerate up to 30 minutes.

To assemble hat, cut out six circles from the cereal mixture in the 15-in. x 10-in. pan by using 5-1/2-in., 5-in., 4-1/2-in., 4-in., 3-in. and 2-in. round cookie cutters (save remaining mixture for another use). Remove cereal mixture from the 9-in. pan and place onto a serving platter. Top with remaining circles, stacking from large to small. Top with sugar cone. Spread with frosting.

Unwrap and microwave apple candies on high for 10-20 seconds or until softened. Roll out to 1/8-in. thickness. Cut with 3-in. moon and 1-1/2-in. star-shaped cookie cutters. Repeat with the grape candies. Press the moons and stars onto the hat. Refrigerate leftovers. **YIELD:** 1 witch's hat (30 servings).

CUTTING THE WITCH'S CRISPY HAT

To easily slice and serve the Witch's Crispy Hat, carefully remove the hat from the base; set on a cutting board. Cut the base into wedges. With a chef's knife, cut the hat in half from the top down; place the two halves cut side down on the cutting board. Cut each piece in half lengthwise. Cut each portion into slices.

witch's broomstick bread

(PICTURED AT RIGHT)

No one can resist the aroma or flavor of homemade bread. Our home economists fashioned the dough into a witch's broomstick to accompany this Halloween meal.

2 teaspoons active dry yeast

1-1/2 cups warm water (110° to 115°)

2 tablespoons olive oil

2 teaspoons sugar

2 teaspoons salt

4 to 4-1/2 cups all-purpose flour

2 tablespoons butter, melted, divided

1/2 cup shredded Italian cheese blend

1/2 cup shredded Parmesan cheese, divided

1/2 teaspoon poppy seeds

1/4 teaspoon garlic powder

1/4 teaspoon dried oregano

1/8 teaspoon crushed red pepper flakes

1 jar (26 ounces) meatless spaghetti sauce, warmed, optional

In a large bowl, dissolve yeast in warm water. Add the olive oil, sugar, salt and 2-1/2 cups flour. Beat until smooth. Stir in enough remaining flour to form a soft dough (dough will be sticky).

Turn onto a floured surface; knead until smooth and elastic, about 6-8 minutes. Place in a greased bowl, turning once to grease the top. Cover and let rise in a warm place until doubled, about 1 hour.

Punch dough down. Turn onto a lightly floured surface. Remove a third of dough; cover and set aside. Roll remaining dough into a 10-in. circle. Transfer to a parchment paper-lined baking sheet.

Brush 1 tablespoon butter over bottom half of circle to within 1/4 in. of edges. Sprinkle with the Italian cheese blend, 1/4 cup Parmesan cheese, poppy seeds, garlic powder, oregano and pepper flakes. Fold dough over filling. Using scissors or a pizza cutter, cut dough into 1/2-in.-wide strips to within 1/2 in. of fold; twist and curl strips into a brush.

Shape remaining dough into an 12-in. rope. Twist dough and place above brush for a handle. Brush the remaining butter over dough. Sprinkle with remaining Parmesan cheese.

Bake at 350° for 30-35 minutes or until golden brown. Serve with spaghetti sauce if desired. YIELD: 16 servings.

goblin bean burritos

These burritos are packed with beans, peppers and rice, making them great tasting and good for you at the same time.

Judy Parker | *MOORE, OK*

1 medium onion, chopped

1/2 cup chopped green pepper

1/2 cup chopped sweet yellow pepper

3 garlic cloves, minced

1 jalapeno pepper, seeded and chopped

1 tablespoon canola oil

2 cups cooked brown rice

1 can (15 ounces) black beans, rinsed and drained

1 can (15 ounces) pinto beans, rinsed and drained

1 can (14-1/2 ounces) petite diced tomatoes, drained

1 teaspoon ground cumin

1/2 teaspoon chili powder

1/2 teaspoon salt

1/2 teaspoon pepper

1/2 cup minced fresh cilantro, divided

8 whole wheat tortillas (8 inches), warmed

1/2 cup sour cream

1/2 cup chopped tomatoes

1/2 cup thinly sliced green onions

1/2 cup shredded cheddar cheese

In a large skillet, saute the onion, peppers, garlic and jalapeno in oil until tender. Stir in rice, beans, tomatoes, cumin, chili powder, salt and pepper; heat through. Stir in 1/4 cup cilantro.

Spoon 3/4 cupful filling off center on each tortilla. Fold sides and ends over filling and roll up. Top with sour cream, tomatoes, green onions, cheese and remaining cilantro. **YIELD:** 8 servings.

hocus-pocus sherbet potion

(PICTURED ON PAGE 238)

Our home economists worked their magic in the kitchen and whipped up this clever beverage. Sherbet and ice cream combine with orange juice and berries to create the playful layers.

2 pints orange sherbet, softened

1/2 cup orange juice

1 pint vanilla ice cream, softened

1/2 cup fresh or frozen unsweetened blueberries

1/2 cup fresh or frozen unsweetened blackberries

In a small bowl, combine sherbet and orange juice. In a blender, combine the ice cream, blueberries and blackberries. Cover and process until blended. Layer sherbet and berry mixtures into each of four chilled glasses. Serve immediately. **YIELD:** 4 servings.

witch's broom party favors

(PICTURED AT RIGHT)

Have guests fly off after your party with these candy-filled broomsticks!

11-inch length of 1/4-inch wooden dowel

Acrylic craft paints—orange, green, purple and white

Small flat paintbrush

Wrapped candy

Small orange and green paper bags (ours measured 3-1/2 inches wide x 6-1/2 inches high)

4-inch length of 3-1/2-inch-wide purple or black fringe for each

Craft glue

18-inch length of orange, purple and yellow rattail cord

Paint colored stripes around wooden dowel for broom handle.

Let dry. Place wrapped candy inside paper bags. Place painted dowel inside bag; twist top of bags tightly around dowel. Wrap fringe piece around twisted area and glue to hold. Wrap rattail cord around top of fringe and tie ends in a small bow.

EDITOR'S NOTE: A Halloween pencil could be used in place of the painted dowel.

WICKED WITCH PUMPKIN

Jolly jack-o'-lanterns are just dandy. But how about adding a touch of terror to your Halloween celebration by crafting a wicked witch pumpkin?

In the photo at left, we painted a fresh pumpkin with green acrylic paint. When dry, we turned the pumpkin on its side so that the stem became the nose. After carving eyes and a mouth, we topped the pumpkin with a witch's wig and hat. Place a candle inside for an even more eerie glow.

reference index

Use this index as a guide to the many helpful hints, food facts, decorating ideas and step-by-step instructions throughout the book.

general recipe index

This handy index lists every recipe by food category, major ingredient and/or cooking method.

alphabetical index

Refer to this index for a complete alphabetical listing of all recipes in this book.

Here's Your Chance to Be Published!

Send us your special-occasion recipes, and you could have them featured in a future edition of this classic cookbook.

Year after year, the recipe for success at every holiday party or special-occasion celebration is an attractive assortment of flavorful food. So we're always on the lookout for mouthwatering appetizers, entrees, side dishes, breads, desserts and more...all geared toward the gatherings you attend or host throughout the year.

Here's how you can enter your family-favorite holiday fare for possible publication in a future *Holiday & Celebrations Cookbook*:

- Print or type each recipe on one sheet of 8-1/2" x 11" paper. Please include your name, address and daytime phone number on each page. Be specific with directions, measurements and the sizes of cans, packages and pans.
- Please include a few words about yourself, when you serve your dish, reactions it has received from family and friends and the origin of the recipe.
- Send to "Celebrations Cookbook," 5400 S. 60th Street, Greendale WI 53129 or E-mail to recipes@reimanpub.com. Write "Celebrations Cookbook" on the subject line of all E-mail entries and include your full name, postal address and phone number on each entry.

Contributors whose recipes are printed will receive a complimentary copy of the book...so the more recipes you send, the better your chances of "being published!"